The Arrival of the King

"Scholars have long noted the chiastic grouping of Psalms 15–24, but Carissa Quinn here provides a deeper dive into the structure and message of this grouping, placing it on a more empirical footing. Her attention not only to the structures of the grouping but also to its narrative story-line advances our understanding of the Psalter's overall message: the duality of Yahweh's eternal kingship and that of his faithful human king/messiah. Highly recommended."

DAVID M. HOWARD JR., professor of Old Testament and Hebrew, Bethel Seminary

"Carissa Quinn has ventured into exciting new territory in studying the compositional design of the Psalms. She has sharpened a number of methodological tools and then put them to fruitful use in analyzing Psalms 15–24. This book is packed with insight and represents an important step forward in Psalms studies."

TIM MACKIE, cofounder of BibleProject

"Considering the importance of Psalms 16 and 22 for the apostolic witness concerning Jesus, the pride of place that Psalm 19 occupies in discussions about revelation, and the widespread familiarity of Psalm 23 throughout the world, Dr. Quinn's book comes as a breath of fresh air filled with invaluable insights about the need to interpret these beloved psalms within their carefully and strategically designed literary context. For anyone who wants to better understand the book of Psalms, Dr. Quinn's book is a must."

SETH D. POSTELL, academic dean, Israel College of the Bible

"The arrival of this book is a fitting way to herald the arrival of the King. Carissa has provided a compelling and stimulating look at this subsection of the Psalms, which provides not only insight into these important psalms, but also maps a way for reading the entire Psalter. This book is a difference-maker for all who cherish the Psalms!"

RAY LUBECK, professor of Bible and theology, Multnomah University

"The value of Quinn's volume is her method of measuring the strength/rarity of correspondences between texts, which has often been subjected to criticisms of arbitrariness. In my view, Quinn has successfully demonstrated that the correspondences within Psalms 15–24 are quantifiable. With the rapid rise and use of Artificial Intelligence that employs Large Language Processing Models, Quinn's contribution is incredibly timely and will inspire new possibilities of biblical scholarship with machine learning."

PETER C. W. HO, associate professor of Old Testament, Singapore Bible College

The Arrival
of the King

———

The Shape

and Story of

Psalms 15–24

CARISSA QUINN

STUDIES IN
SCRIPTURE
& BIBLICAL
THEOLOGY

LEXHAM
ACADEMIC

The Arrival of the King: The Shape and Story of Psalms 15–24
Studies in Scripture & Biblical Theology

Lexham Academic, an imprint of Lexham Press
1313 Commercial St., Bellingham, WA 98225
LexhamPress.com

Unless otherwise noted, Scripture quotations are the author's own translation.

Print ISBN 9781683597148
Digital ISBN 9781683597155
Library of Congress Control Number 9781683597148

Lexham Editorial: Derek Brown, John Barach, Mandi Newell
Cover Design: Christine Christophersen
Typesetting: Justin Marr

For Mom,
who has taught me about hope and joy within suffering,
and whose life exemplifies the praise of the king:

"Yhwh is my rock, my fortress, and my deliverer;
my God is my rock, in whom I take refuge,
my shield and the horn of my salvation, my stronghold."
—Psalm 18:3

Contents

Acknowledgments

This book began its journey as my doctoral dissertation at Gateway Seminary. Its publication is possible due to the guidance and generosity of various people.

I am indebted to my doctoral supervisor, David Howard, whose class on the Psalms first captivated my interest in the literary artistry of the poems and the links between them. I feel incredibly fortunate to have received his guidance, encouragement, and thorough and thoughtful responses throughout the dissertation process. I would also like to thank the other members of my dissertation committee, Paul Wegner and Clint McCann, for participating as wise and helpful interlocutors and supporters. A warm thank you to Derek Brown and the editorial team at Lexham Press for bringing this project to completion.

Special thanks are due to the BibleProject Scholar Team—Tim Mackie, Renjy Abraham, Ben Tertin, Hakeem Bradley, and Aaron Shaw, whose enthusiasm for analysis of the structures and story of Scripture is contagious, and each of whom contributes an essential role in creating an environment of curiosity, camaraderie, and lively discussion. I am deeply grateful for the ways the broader BibleProject team has encouraged and supported me in finding ways that my work and research can be mutually supportive.

I am grateful for Steve Moore and the network of my associate John Wesley Fellows at A Foundation for Theological Education, for their belief in me, participation as thought partners, friendship, and passionate commitment to the thriving of both the academy and the church.

Finally, I cannot overstate the value of the support and love from my family, friends, and personal mentors, who have been with me through thick and thin these past years. Thank you for lifting me up, cheering me on, and celebrating with me. It's my sincere desire that this book will spark interest in and curiosity about the story that the Psalter tells, and hope in the king about whom that story speaks.

List of Abbreviations

AIL	Ancient Israel and Its Literature
ANET	*Ancient Near Eastern Texts Relating to the Old Testament*
ATANT	Abhandlungen zur Theologie des Alten und Neuen Testaments
Bar.	Baraita
BBR	*Bulletin for Biblical Research*
BCOT	Baker Commentary on the Old Testament
BDB	*The Brown-Driver-Briggs Hebrew and English Lexicon*
Ber.	Berakot
BETL	Bibliotheca Ephemeridum Theologicarum Lovaniensium
BK	*Biblischer Kommentar*
CahRB	Cahiers de la Revue biblique
CBQ	*Catholic Biblical Quarterly*
CCEL	Christian Classics Ethereal Library
CCSL	Corpus Christianorum: Series Latina
EBTC	Evangelical Biblical Theology Commentary
ETL	*Ephemerides Theologicae Lovanienses*
FAT	Forschungen zum Alten Testament
FOTL	Forms of the Old Testament Literature
HAR	*Hebrew Annual Review*
HAT	Handbuch zum Alten Testament
HBS	Herders biblische Studien
IBT	Interpreting Biblical Texts
JBL	*Journal of Biblical Literature*
JETS	*Journal of the Evangelical Theological Society*
JSOT	*Journal for the Study of the Old Testament*
JSOTSup	Journal for the Study of the Old Testament Supplement Series
Kid.	Kiddushim

LHB/OTS	Library of Hebrew Bible/Old Testament Studies
LXX	Septuagint
Midr. Psalms	Midrash on Psalms
MT	Masoretic Text
NCBC	New Century Bible Commentary
NEchtB	Die Neue Echter Bibel
NIB	*The New Interpreter's Bible*
NICOT	New International Commentary on the Old Testament
NIV	New International Version
NIVAC	New International Version Application Commentary
OBO	Orbis Biblicus et Orientalis
RB	*Revue biblique*
SBL	Society of Biblical Literature
SJOT	*Scandinavian Journal of the Old Testament*
SSN	Studia Semitica Neerlandica
TOTC	Tyndale Old Testament Commentaries
UCSD	The University of California San Diego
VT	*Vetus Testamentum*
WBC	Word Biblical Commentary
ZAW	*Zeitschrift für die alttestamentliche Wissenschaft*

Abstract

This book contributes to understanding the design of the Psalter through an editorial-critical exploration of the collection of Psalms 15–24. The exploration builds on the methods developed by D. M. Howard Jr. and M. K. Snearly to analyze the rarity of shared linking elements between psalms—lexemes, forms of lexemes, phrases, themes, structures, and superscripts. The more numerous and rare these connecting elements are, the stronger the relationship between two psalms. This study also relies on the work of J. Kugel, R. Alter, and A. Berlin on Hebrew parallelism—that it involves not only repetition, but dynamic movement—and applies this principle to the level of entire psalms.

By using a methodology that identifies links between psalms, this study confirms that Psalms 15–24 form a chiastic collection of the following parallel psalms: 15 and 24; 16 and 23; 17 and 22; and 18, 20, and 21. Psalm 19 stands at the center of the collection and is found to be closely linked with Psalms 15 and 24 as the frame, as well as with Psalms 18, 20, and 21 as the hinge of the collection. An assessment of the development between these sets of parallel psalms shows that there are consistent differences from the psalms in the first half of the chiasm to their parallel psalms in the second half, including spatial and communal expansion, intensifications in the theme of Yhwh's presence, and the identification of Yhwh as king. Together, these differences show a progression in the storyline of the collection toward the fullness of Yhwh's kingdom and his arrival as king. Psalms 18–21 at the center of the collection depict a central figure—the Torah-obedient king—through whose deliverance by Yhwh the kingdom comes about.

In addition to progression toward the kingdom, this collection also exhibits an alternation between the ideal vision of the kingdom presented in the frame of the collection (Pss 15, 19, and 24) and the realities of human experience and suffering presented in the intervening psalms. In other words, until the arrival of Yhwh as king, life is depicted as a journey involving suffering, yet confidence, in his kingship and his deliverance of his faithful king.

1

Introduction

The book of Psalms has been a treasured collection by various groups for many centuries. Early and abundant use of the Psalter attests to its value: the New Testament quotes from the Psalms more than any other book of the Hebrew Bible, and of the manuscripts found at Qumran, those of the Psalms outnumber any other. To the present day, the Psalms play a consistent role in liturgy and worship for those who regard the Hebrew Bible as holy Scripture, and for good reason. The Psalms are accessible and resonate with the full scope of human experience; within the Psalter, one can find expressions of joy, pain, anger, confusion, and hope. Whereas some emotions might be considered uncomfortable or even inappropriate, the Psalms invite the reader into an experience of every emotion and expression of that emotion to the divine and within the communal setting. This is both the challenge and the beauty of the Psalter. It is an invitation into the depth of human experience—both suffering and the new hope that can follow it. For those who consider the book of Psalms to be sacred text, these poems uniquely express the words of humans to God and simultaneously the words of God to humans. Perhaps even more profound is that they are generally associated with the Davidic king, both in the stories that they tell as well in the superscripts that title many of them. As such, the psalms are central for understanding the role of the Davidic king in the overarching story of Scripture.

In both the academy and the church, it is common to treat each psalm as a discrete unit, entirely unrelated to its literary context; this is true whether a reader's goal is reconstruction of the original setting (*Sitz im Leben*), exploration of the design or form of a psalm, or theological or devotional relevance. But the message of the Psalms need not be limited to reading each psalm in isolation. An examination of Psalms 15–24 challenges the tendency to read psalms as isolated units by raising various questions. For example, is it a coincidence that the only two entrance liturgies in the entire Psalter, Psalms 15 and 24, exist in close proximity? Likewise, four of the five occurrences of the phrase "I/he will not be shaken" in Book I of the Psalter exist within Psalms 15–24; could this perhaps be a linking device?[1] The correspondence between Psalms 20 and 21 is striking: in the former, the community petitions Yhwh to give the king his heart's desire, and in the latter, the community rejoices that Yhwh has given the king his heart's desire. Could the authors be nudging the audience to read these psalms together?[2] And if these psalms, then what about the entirety of the Psalter?

THE DESIGN OF THE PSALTER

The inquiry into the design and story of the Psalter relies on whether the individual psalms it contains reveal a coherent arrangement on both the micro-level (between individual psalms and within psalm-groups) and the macro-level (the entire Psalter). With regard to the macro-level, various scholars and readers of the Psalter have observed that the Psalms are intentionally arranged to tell a story.

One of the literary features of the Psalter that attests to its intentional design is the cohesion between Psalms 1 and 2 and their function as an introduction to the whole of the storyline. These two psalms are the only untitled psalms in the LXX, suggesting that they were recognized by translators as serving a special purpose. In the MT, in addition to Psalms 1–2, only Psalms 10 and 33 are untitled in Book I, and a strong case has been made that the reason is that each of these psalms is to be read in combination with its immediate predecessor.[3] Psalms 1 and 2 are closely joined by their lack of superscript, various corresponding lexemes, and the אשרי (blessed)-clause inclusio (Pss 1:1; 2:12).[4] In

---

1. Pss 10:6; 15:5; 16:8; 17:5; 21:8 (all chapter and verse numbers here and following refer to the Masoretic Text unless otherwise indicated).
2. I will use the terms "author" and "editor" loosely to refer to a person or group who either composed, arranged, and/or recomposed (edited) psalms into their present synchronic arrangement. I will not distinguish between an editor and an author for primarily two reasons: first, it is nearly impossible to distinguish between these differing hands; and, second, it is possible that editors authored new material and that authors composed new psalms in relation to others. Rather than distinguishing between an original author and subsequent editors, I will refer to the group responsible for the present composition as either author(s) or editor(s).
3. G. H. Wilson, "The Use of 'Untitled' Psalms in the Hebrew Psalter," ZAW 97, no. 3 (1985): 404–13.
4. For a thorough study of Pss 1 and 2 as an introduction, see R. L. Cole, Psalms 1–2: Gateway to the Psalter (Sheffield: Sheffield Phoenix, 2012).

content, Psalm 1 encourages meditation on Yhwh's Torah and contrasts
Yhwh's way with the way of the wicked. Psalm 1 describes the blessing
that those who follow Yhwh will experience; they'll live at peace and
flourish, just like in the garden story of Genesis 1-2. Psalm 2 reveals how
this ideal will come about—through God raising up his messianic king.
This king will follow God as a son, and though he will suffer by the hand
of powerful rulers, Yhwh will make him and those who take refuge in
him victorious. This description refers back to the promise God made to
King David, that through his line, God's kingdom would be established
(2 Sam 7). Together, Psalms 1 and 2 anticipate a storyline focused on the
Torah-obedient king who will suffer, yet prevail.

The placement of a psalm about Torah next to a psalm about the human king in significant positions is a second structural device found
throughout the Psalter. The combination of Torah/wisdom and royal psalms occurs not only in the introduction (Pss 1-2), but also at the
seams of each book of the Psalter, demarcating and framing them. The
books are as follows: Book I includes Psalms 1-41; Book II: Psalms 42-72;
Book III: Psalms 73-89; Book IV: Psalms 90-106; Book V: Psalms 107-150.
Royal and Torah psalms, often in combination, occur at Psalms 72-73;
89-90; 107; 144-145.[5] These psalms also occur in structurally significant
positions within collections, as we will see later in the collection of
Psalms 15-24, where they stand at the center as the hinge of the plotline
(Pss 18-21).[6]

A third type of structural device used to demarcate the different
books in the Psalter is the doxology. Doxologies divide the Psalter into
five discrete books—a practice attested in other Ancient Near Eastern
hymnic collections.[7] Doxologies with strikingly similar content occur
at the ends of Books I through IV: each uses the phrase *blessed be Yhwh*

---

5. Wilson, "Shaping the Psalter: A Consideration of Editorial Linkage in the Book
of Psalms," in *The Shape and Shaping of the Psalter*, ed. J. C. McCann Jr., JSOTSup
159 (Sheffield: JSOT, 1993), 72-82. Wilson follows B. Childs and C. Westermann on
this point.
6. See also Pss 118-119, the middle of Book V.
7. Doxologies occur at Pss 41:14; 72:18-19; 89:53; 106:48. The Sumerian Temple
Hymns and the zà-mí collection from Abu Salabikh also evidence the closing function of doxologies. See Wilson, *The Editing of the Hebrew Psalter*, Society of Biblical
Literature Dissertation Series 76 (Chico, CA: Scholars, 1985), 16-18, 23; J. A. Black,
"Some Structural Features of Sumerian Narrative Poetry," in *Mesopotamian Epic
Literature: Oral or Aural?*, ed. M. E. Vogelzang and H. L. J. Vanstiphout (Lampeter,
Wales: Edwin Mellen, 1992), 71-101.

(ברוך יהוה) and the lexemes *forever* (עולם) and *amen* (אמן; often *amen and amen* [אמן ואמן]), and three also contain the phrase *the God of Israel* (אלהי ישראל; Pss 41:14; 72:18–19; 89:53; 106:48). The doxological language at the end of Book V is climactic: The last line of Psalm 145 contains the same significant lexemes from Books I–IV, *Yhwh*, *bless*, and *forever* (v. 21). The context is that all creatures would offer *praise* (תהלה) and *bless Yhwh forever*. Psalms 146–150, which follow and close Book V, seem to function as a final doxology to the entire Psalter, with each psalm beginning and ending with the call to *praise Yah* (הללו־יה)—short for Yhwh—a phrase that also closed out the doxology of Book IV (Ps 106:48).

This five-psalm group at the end of the Psalter is the fourth major structuring device—the final *hallel* (praise) and conclusion of the Psalter.[8] The five-part structure reflects the five books of the Psalter (and the Torah) and concludes the overarching story in a crescendo of praise. Right in the middle, at the apex of the final *hallel* is Psalm 148, which is a call for all creation to praise Yhwh because he raises up a horn of salvation—in other words, brings victory for the afflicted. The five-part conclusion ends with Yhwh as the reigning king, surrounded by the praise of his people.

In addition to an introduction (Pss 1–2), a conclusion (Pss 146–150), and a five-book structure, the general movement from lament to praise in the psalms is a fifth literary device that indicates intentional arrangement of the whole.[9] The lament psalm is most prominent in Books I and II of the Psalter, and praise psalms in Books IV and V. This movement indicates a storyline that shifts in content from beginning to end, building to the final crescendo of praise (Pss 146–150).

The content of the Psalter also forms a coherent story: After the introduction of a future Torah-obedient king through whom God will establish his kingdom, Book I traces the affliction of David and God's establishment of him as his king. But in Books II–III, the kingdom falls to enemy nations and the people are left without a king and without a home. There's a sharp contrast between the ideal depicted in the introduction

---

8. On this point, I follow Wilson and E. Zenger, who argue that Ps 145:21, "Let every creature praise his holy name for ever and ever," precipitates the crescendo or praise that follows. Wilson, "The Shape of the Book of Psalms," *Interpretation* 46 (1992): 132–33; Zenger, "'Daß alles Fleisch den Namen seiner Heiligung segne' (Ps 145,21): Die Komposition Ps 145–150 als Anstoß zu einer christlich-jüdischen Psalmenhermeneutik," *Biblische Zeitschrift* 41 (1997): 1–27.
9. See Westermann, "The Formation of the Psalter," in *Praise and Lament in the Psalms*, trans. K. R. Crim and R. N. Soulen (Atlanta: John Knox, 1981), 250–58.

of the Psalms and the reality of human suffering and oppression. This is why the lament song is so prominent in these early books. The people cry out for God to rescue them. They also sing songs of hope, asking God to fulfill his promises to David and send his Messiah to establish his kingdom. Books IV and V capitalize on that hope. Book IV begins with a Psalm of Moses—the only one titled as such in the Psalter—and the book is full of songs about Yhwh the king. The message is that just as Yhwh was Israel's king during the time of Moses—long before the establishment of the Davidic monarchy —so Yhwh remains Israel's faithful king when there is no Davidic king on the throne. But Book V of the Psalter features a return of the Davidic king: whereas Books III–IV (Pss 73-106) contain only three psalms titled *of David* (לדוד; Pss 86; 101; 103), Book V contains fifteen (Pss 108-110; 122; 124; 131; 133; 138-145), and consists of renewed hope that God will continue to be faithful to his promise to bring about his kingdom through his anointed king. The center of the final *hallel*, Psalm 148, confirms that God will bring victory to his people (raising up a horn).[10] In light of the storyline, this likely refers to his anointed king from Psalm 2; he will bring victory to his people through his king. The culminating praise is highly appropriate in light of this renewed hope.

Understanding the shape and storyline of the Psalter relies not only on macro-level structural devices and shifts in content from beginning to end, but also on the cohesion and coherence between neighboring psalms and within collections. The study of lower-level structures and features can both fill in the gaps of the story and also shed light on the kinds of structural devices we might expect at the macro-level. With regard to lower-level arrangement, the presence of smaller groupings by genre, superscript, author, and theme within the Psalter is evidence of an editorial hand at work, as it is in other Mesopotamian psalm collections.[11]

---

10. The most proximate use of the phrase "exalt the horn" to Ps 148 is Ps 89. There, the horn of the people is exalted in victory, just as in Ps 148, but the reason is because the king's horn is exalted in victory. There is a close relationship between the victory of the king and the victory of the people. The same is true in 1 Sam 2, where the king's horn is exalted (v. 10), meaning that God gives him victory over his enemies, and in turn, this benefits the godly, afflicted ones.

11. In his Yale dissertation published in 1985, Wilson identifies these same editorial markers in Mesopotamian psalm collections, which supports the validity of their function in the biblical Psalter. Wilson, *Editing*, 121-98. See also J. A. Grant, who argues that the presence of intact groupings is one of three key evidences for the

Finally, and as an introduction to the focus of this study, links or concatenation between neighboring psalms and among psalm groups can indicate intentional arrangement.[12] Concatenation is defined by U. Cassuto as "association of ideas, but also, and primarily, association of words and expressions, a technique whose initial purpose was possibly to aid the memory."[13] C. Barth lists seventeen principles of concatenation, including things like exact repetition of forms, roots word-pairs, and word sequences.[14] The phrase in Psalms 15, 16, and 17 mentioned above, "I/he will not be shaken," is an excellent example of concatenation.

The study of the shape and message of smaller collections or groups of psalms within the Psalter can shed light on the shape and message of the whole. In this book, I explore the significant connections, shape, and message of Psalms 15–24 as a collection. If there is evidence of design, then individual psalms may be interpreted within their literary context, rather than solely as isolated units or set primarily within the setting in which they originated and were used. The field of study which recognizes an overarching shape to the Psalter and/or intentional links between neighboring psalms can be termed "editorial criticism," since it seeks to detect evidence of an editorial hand at work in the shaping of the Psalter. It can also be referred to as "shape of the Psalter" studies. With the paradigm shift in biblical studies in recent decades whereby texts are read as literary wholes, scholarship on the Psalter as a coherent book has become more prevalent.[15]

---

shape of the Psalter. Grant, "Editorial Criticism," in *Dictionary of the Old Testament: Wisdom, Poetry, and Writings*, ed. T. Longman III and P. Enns (Downers Grove, IL: IVP Academic, 2008), 150–51.

12. Two of the more in-depth studies involving concatenation between neighboring psalms are those of W. Zimmerli and D. M. Howard Jr. Zimmerli identifies what he calls "twin psalms" (*Zwillingspsalmen*) throughout the Psalter based primarily on key word links (*Stichwörter*) and themes. Howard and several of his students systematically analyze key-word and thematic links among groups of psalms to understand the literary shape of (a) collection(s). Zimmerli, "Zwillingspsalmen," in *Wort, Lied, und Gottesspruch: Beiträge zu Psalmen und Propheten*, ed. J. Schreiner (Würzburg: Echter, 1972), 105–13; Howard, *The Structure of Psalms 93–100*, UCSD Biblical and Judaic Studies 5 (Winona Lake, IN: Eisenbrauns, 1997).

13. U. Cassuto, "The Sequence and Arrangement of the Biblical Sections," in *Biblical and Oriental Studies*, vol. 1 (Jerusalem: Magnes, 1973), 1–2.

14. C. Barth, "Concatenatio im ersten Buch des Psalters," in *Wort and Wirklichkeit: Studien zur Afrikanistik und Orientalistik*, ed. B. Benzing, O. Böcher, and G. Mayer (Meisenheim am Glan: Hain, 1976), 30–40.

15. The emergence of this interpretive method is represented by the following: Childs, *Introduction to the Old Testament as Scripture* (Philadelphia: Fortress, 1979); Zimmerli,

A BRIEF HISTORY OF PSALMS STUDY

I mentioned previously that it is common to treat the psalms as isolated units for analysis or meditation. But this has not always been the case. The more recent focus on the design of the Psalter is in fact a re-emergence of an ancient method. A brief history of the reception of the Psalter reveals that early Jewish and Christian interpreters have observed evidence of design within the Book of Psalms, whether arrangement of individual psalms, collections, or entire books. For example, the authors of the New Testament viewed the Psalter as a definitive *book* (Acts 1:20 and Luke 20:42); the church fathers regarded the order and number as significant[16]; rabbinic interpreters were attentive to concatenation between neighboring psalms, literary context, and the *Torah*-like shape created by the five doxologies[17]; and the Reformers gave attention to arrangement and distinct collections.[18]

The rise of historical criticism in the seventeenth century shifted the focus in biblical studies to a reconstruction both of hypothetical source texts and of the history of Israel and its religion. Studies on the text of the Psalms were overshadowed by interest in the reconstruction of other texts and the events behind them. In the 1920s, a branch of historical criticism was developed that would put the Psalms center stage: form criticism. The father of form criticism, H. Gunkel, explored the literary forms of psalms and identified the categories of psalms that we are familiar with today, like laments, hymns, royal psalms, and wisdom psalms.[19] His focus as such was partially literary—identifying typical, overarching structures of psalms—and partially historical—reconstructing the life situation (*Sitz im Leben*) that presumably gave rise to

---

"Zwillingspsalmen"; Westermann, *Praise and Lament*; and Barth, "Concatenatio."

16. E.g., Origen, *Origenis Opera Omnia*, ed. C. H. E. Lommatzsch, 25 vols. (Berlin: Haude et Spener, 1831-1838), XI: 352-54, 370-71; Augustine, *Enarrationes in Psalmos I-L*, ed. E. Dekkers and J. Fraipont, CCSL 38 (Steenbrugge: Brepols, 1990), §3; Jerome, *Commentarioli in Psalmos*, ed. G. Morin, CCSL 72 (Turnhout: Brepols, 1959), Ps 1.

17. For early contextual interpretation and concatenation, see *Bar. Ber.* 10a, *Midr. Psalms* 3:2, and *Midr. Psalms* 111:1. For a later example, see D. Kimḥi, *The First Book of Psalms according to the Text of the Cambridge MS Bible with the Longer Commentary of R. David Qimchi*, ed. S. M. Schiller-Szinessy (Cambridge: Deighton, Bell, 1883), 53. On the fivefold division, see *Midr. Psalms* 1:2 and *Kid.* 33a.

18. E.g., J. Calvin regarded Ps 1 as the preface, and M. Luther identified distinct collections. Calvin, *Commentary on the Book of Psalms*, trans. J. Anderson (repr., Grand Rapids: Eerdmans, 1949), 1; Luther, *Luthers Werke*, 63 vols. (Weimar: Böhlau, 1883-1987), 4:3-4.

19. H. Gunkel, *Die Psalmen*, 4th ed. (Gottingen: Vandenhoeck und Ruprecht, 1926).

each form. While his work opened new doors for study for the Psalms, historical and cultic reconstruction of individual psalms further eclipsed attention to the shape of the Psalter as a whole. Nonetheless, I rely on the insights of Gunkel into the recurring structures and patterns of certain psalms. His work also demonstrates that the composition of psalms was an endeavor that gave much attention to literary design, and that the departure from typical patterns and conventions itself can convey meaning. Further advance in the study of the Psalms was made by Gunkel's student, S. Mowinckel.[20] Mowinckel hypothesized that the psalms were used and performed at major festivals, giving special focus to an annual enthronement festival. While I find reconstruction of an annual enthronement festival both too tenuous and too comprehensive, I agree from a literary perspective that the psalms are often focused on Yhwh as the king and the human king as his representative. These are themes to pay close attention to if we are to understand the message of the psalms and the Psalter.[21]

The methods and goals of historical criticism are still prevalent in biblical scholarship today, and yet the close of the twentieth century brought with it a focus of literary approaches to biblical texts, for example, rhetorical criticism, structural analysis, narrative criticism, and canonical criticism. In particular, B. Childs's *Introduction to the Old Testament as Scripture*, where he argues for a holistic and canonical reading, paved the way for a return to literary approaches to the Psalter. C. Westermann and W. Brueggemann are two scholars whose work also represents the early shift to focus on literary structures and use, but within the context of neighboring psalms.[22] Westermann notes the

---

20. S. Mowinckel, *The Psalms in Israel's Worship* (New York: Abingdon, 1967). Mowinckel's original work is his *Psalmenstudien I–VI* (Kristiania: Skrifter utgitt av Det Norske Videnskaps-Akademi i Oslo, 1921–1924) and *Psalmenstudien: Das Thronbesteigungsfest Jahwäs and der Ursprung der Eschatologie* (1920).

21. While both historical-critical and literary approaches are useful, it is important to recognize they have different goals. The former seeks to reconstruct original backgrounds and texts, while the latter aims to understand the text in its present shape. This inevitably leads to different methods and resulting observations. See S. E. Gillingham, who advocates for a plurality approach to the Psalter in her *One Bible, Many Voices: Different Approaches to Biblical Studies* (Trowbridge, Wilts: Redwood, 1998).

22. Westermann, *The Psalms: Structure, Content and Message*, 7th ed. (Minneapolis: Augsburg Fortress, 1980); Westermann, *Praise and Lament*; W. Brueggemann, *The Message of the Psalms: A Theological Commentary*, Augsburg Old Testament Studies (Minneapolis: Fortress, 1984).

movement in the Psalter from lament to praise, and Brueggemann observes patterns where neighboring psalms progress from what he calls psalms of orientation, disorientation, and reorientation. Both scholars build on the work of form criticism in their attention to the structures of psalms, but push Psalms scholarship forward to see psalms within their broader literary context.

The Yale dissertation of Childs's student G. H. Wilson in 1985 provided a definitive framework for a holistic reading of the Psalter and initiated a revival of interest in the shape of the Psalter. Through comparative study with other ancient Mesopotamian psalms scrolls, Wilson found that the Masoretic Psalter contains various tacit editorial markers that evidence intentional arrangement.[23] Studies on the design of the Psalter have proliferated following Wilson's study, for example, in the works of J. L. Mays (1987, 1994), Brueggemann (1991), J. Walton (1991), F.-L. Hossfeld and E. Zenger (1993), J. C. McCann Jr. (1993, 1996), P. D. Miller Jr. (1994), M. Millard (1994), J. F. D. Creach (1996), B. C. Davis (1996), D. M. Howard Jr. (1997), D. C. Mitchell (1997, 2006), N. deClaissé-Walford (1997, 2014), Zenger (1998), R. L. Cole (2000), F. X. Kimmitt (2000), J.-M. Auwers (2000), J.-L. Vesco (2006), W. P. Brown (2010), P. E. Sumpter (2013), M. K. Snearly (2015), O. P. Robertson (2015), P. C. W. Ho (2019).[24]

---

23. Wilson compares the Mesopotamian Hymnic Incipits, the Sumerian Temple Hymns, and the Qumran Psalms scrolls with the Masoretic Psalter and finds the following tacit editorial groupings in the latter: genre, deity addressed, concatenation, lack of superscription, and thematic correspondence. Wilson, *Editing*, 121–98.

24. J. L. Mays, "The Place of the Torah-Psalms in the Psalter," *JBL* 106 (1987): 3–12; W. Brueggemann, "Bounded by Obedience and Praise: The Psalms as Canon," *JSOT* 50 (1991): 63–92; J. Walton, "Psalms: A Cantata about the Davidic Covenant," *JETS* 34 (1991): 24; F.-L. Hossfeld and Zenger, *Die Psalmen I: Psalmen 1–50*, NEchtB 29 (Würzburg: Echter, 1993); Hossfeld and Zenger, "'Wer darf hinaufziehn zum Berg JHWHs?' Zur Redaktionsgeschichte und Theologie der Psalmengruppe 15–24," in *Biblische Theologie und gesellschaftlicher Wandel: für Norbert Lohfink*, ed. G. Braulik, W. Gross, and S. McEvenue (Freiburg: Herder, 1993), 166–82; McCann, "Books I–III and the Editorial Purpose," in McCann, *Shape and Shaping*, 93–107; Mays, *Psalms*, Interpretation (Louisville: John Knox, 1994); M. Millard, *Die Komposition des Psalters: Ein formgeschichtlicher Ansatz*, FAT 9 (Tübingen: J. C. B. Mohr, 1994); P. D. Miller Jr., "Kingship, Torah Obedience, and Prayer: The Theology of Psalms 15–24," in *Neue Wege der Psalmenforschung*, ed. K. Seybold and Zenger, HBS 1 (Freiburg: Herder, 1994), 127–42; McCann, "The Book of Psalms: Introduction, Commentary, and Reflections," in *NIB*, vol. 4 (Nashville: Abingdon, 1996), 639–1280; J. F. D. Creach, *Yahweh as Refuge and the Editing of the Hebrew Psalter*, JSOTSup 217 (Sheffield: Sheffield Academic, 1996); B. C. Davis, "A Contextual Analysis of Psalms 107–118," PhD diss., Trinity Evangelical Divinity School, 1996; Howard, *Structure*; D. C. Mitchell, *The Message of the Psalter: An Eschatological Programme in the Book of Psalms*, JSOTSup 252 (Sheffield: JSOT,

My investigation of Psalms 15-24 as a collection is situated within this field of the shape of the Psalter and also is built on the foundation of the earliest interpreters. If I successfully demonstrate that the correspondences among Psalms 15-24 are not likely coincidental but indicate that each psalm is a component of a larger narrative, a new set of questions is raised related to the nature of that narrative strand. For example, why does the lament of Psalm 22 follow on the heels of the royal victory of Psalms 20-21? What does the song of trust in Psalm 23 have to do with the lament of Psalm 22? What role is played by the creation hymn of Psalm 19, which seems to interrupt the narrative flow of the psalm group? These are the sorts of questions that drive me to discover whether this psalm group exists as a unified collection and what the resulting shape and storyline of that collection is.

PSALMS 15-24 AS A COLLECTION: A REVIEW OF SCHOLARLY WORKS

I have chosen Psalms 15-24 as the subject of this study for a variety of reasons—a crucial reason being that it has been recognized as a discrete collection by various scholars. Many have observed that Psalms 15 and 24, as the only two entrance liturgies in the Psalter, are strikingly

---

1997); N. L. deClaissé-Walford, *Reading from the Beginning: The Shaping of the Hebrew Psalter* (Macon, GA: Mercer University Press, 1997); Zenger, "The Composition and Theology of the Fifth Book of Psalms," *JSOT* 23 (1998): 77-102; Cole, *The Shape and Message of Book III: Psalms 73-89*, JSOTSup 307 (Sheffield: Sheffield Academic, 2000); F. X. Kimmitt, "The Shape of Psalms 42-49," PhD diss., New Orleans Baptist Theological Seminary, 2000; J.-M. Auwers, *La composition littéraire du Psautier: un état de la question*, CahRB (Paris: Gabalda, 2000); Mitchell, "Lord, Remember David: G. H. Wilson and the Message of the Psalter" *VT* 56 (2006): 526-48; J.-L. Vesco, *Le Psautier de David traduit et commenté*, 2 vols. (Paris: Cerf, 2006); W. P. Brown, "Psalms as Collections and Clusters," in *Psalms*, IBT (Nashville, TN: Abingdon, 2010), 85-107; Brown, "'Here Comes the Sun!': The Metaphorical Theology of Psalms 15-24," in *The Composition of the Book of Psalms*, ed. Zenger, BETL 238 (Leuven: Peeters, 2010), 259-77; P. E. Sumpter, "The Coherence of Psalms 15-24," *Biblica* 94 (2013): 186-209; deClaissé-Walford, "The Canonical Approach to Scripture and the Editing of the Hebrew Psalter," in *The Shape and Shaping of the Book of Psalms: The Current State of Scholarship*, ed. deClaissé-Walford, AIL 20 (Atlanta: SBL Press, 2014), 1-11; deClaissé-Walford, "The Meta-Narrative of the Psalter," in *Oxford Handbook of the Psalms*, ed. Brown (Oxford: Oxford University Press, 2000), 363-75; M. K. Snearly, *The Return of the King: Messianic Expectation in Book V of the Psalter*, LHB/OTS 624 (London: Bloomsbury T&T Clark, 2015); O. P. Robertson, *The Flow of the Psalms: Discovering Their Structure and Theology* (Phillipsburg, NJ: P&R, 2015); P. C. W. Ho, *The Design of the Psalter: A Macrostructural Analysis* (Eugene, OR: Pickwick, 2019).

similar, so that these two psalms frame and demarcate the collection.[25] A variety of scholars have identified thematic or lexical links among some of the individual psalms within the group of Psalms 15–24.[26] A handful of scholars have also explored Psalms 15–24 as a unified collection, namely, P. Auffret (1982), Hossfeld and Zenger (1993), Miller (1994), Brown

25. According to form-critical categories, various commentators classify Pss 15 and 24 as the only temple liturgies in the Psalter, recognizing their unique similarities. See S. Spiegel, *A Prophetic Attestation of the Decalogue: Hosea 6:5, with Some Observations on Psalms 15 and 24* (Cambridge, MA: Harvard University Press, 1934); Gunkel, *Die Psalmen*, 102; M. Mannati and E. de Solms, *Les Psaumes: Traduction des Psaumes 1* (Paris: Desclée de Brouwer, 1966), 52–53, 244; F. Delitzsch, *The Psalms, Commentary on the Old Testament*, vol. 1 (repr., Grand Rapids: Eerdmans, 1982); C. A. Briggs and E. G. Briggs, *A Critical and Exegetical Commentary on the Book of Psalms*, vol. 1 (Edinburgh: T&T Clark, 1906); D. Kidner, *Psalms 1–72: An Introduction and Commentary on Books I–II of the Psalms*, TOTC (London: InterVarsity, 1973); E. Beaucamp, "L'unité du recueil des montées, Psaumes 120–134," *Liber Annuus Studii Biblici Franciscani* 29 (1979): 73–90; A. A. Anderson, *Psalms 1–72*, NCBC (Grand Rapids: Eerdmans, 1972); P. Auffret, "Les Psaumes 15 à 24," in *La sagesse a bâti sa maison, Études de structures littéraires dans l'Ancien Testament et spécialement dans les psaumes*, OBO 49 (Göttingen: Vandenhoeck & Ruprecht, 1982), 407–38; P. C. Craigie, *Psalms 1–50*, 2nd ed., WBC 19 (Nashville: Thomas Nelson, 2004); E. S. Gerstenberger, *Psalms: Part 1*, FOTL (Grand Rapids: Eerdmans, 1988); H.-J. Kraus, *Psalms*, trans. H. C. Oswald, vol. 1 (Minneapolis: Augsburg, 1988); Hossfeld and Zenger, "'Wer darf hinaufziehn zum Berg JHWHs?'"; Mays, *Psalms*; Miller, "Kingship, Torah Obedience, and Prayer: the Theology of Psalms 15–24," in *Neue Wege der Psalmenforschung*, ed. Seybold and Zenger, HBS 1 (Freiburg: Herder, 1994), 127–42; McCann, "The Book of Psalms"; T. Podella, "Transformationen kultischer darstellungen: Toraliturgien in Ps 15 und 24," *SJOT* 13, no. 1 (1999): 95–130; K. Schaefer, *Psalms*, Berit Olam (Collegeville, MN: Liturgical Press, 2001); Wilson, *Psalms*, vol. 1, NIVAC (Grand Rapids: Zondervan, 2002); R. J. Clifford, *Psalms 1–72*, Abingdon Old Testament Commentaries (Nashville: Abingdon, 2002); M. D. Futato, *The Book of Psalms*, Cornerstone Biblical Commentary (Carol Stream, IL: Tyndale House, 2005); J. Goldingay, *Psalms*, vol. 1, BCOT (Grand Rapids: Baker Academic, 2006); B. K. Waltke and J. M. Houston, *The Psalms as Christian Worship: A Historical Commentary* (Grand Rapids: Eerdmans, 2010); Brown, "Psalms as Collections"; Brown, "'Here Comes the Sun!'"; A. P. Ross, *A Commentary on the Psalms*, vol. 1, Kregel Exegetical Library (Grand Rapids: Kregel, 2011); Sumpter, "Coherence"; deClaissé-Walford, R. A. Jacobson, and B. L. Tanner, *The Book of Psalms*, NICOT (Grand Rapids: Eerdmans, 2014).

26. E.g., Zimmerli, "Zwillingspsalmen"; Delitzsch, *Psalms*; Kidner, *Psalms 1–72*; Anderson, *Psalms 1–72*; Auffret, "Les Psaumes 15 à 24"; Hossfeld and Zenger, "'Wer darf hinaufziehn zum Berg JHWHs?'"; Mays, *Psalms*; Miller, "Kingship"; McCann, "The Book of Psalms"; Schaefer, *Psalms*; Gillingham, *The Image, the Depths and the Surface: Multivalent Approaches to Biblical Study*, JSOTSup 354 (Sheffield: Sheffield Academic, 2002); Wilson, *Psalms*; Clifford, *Psalms 1–72*; Futato, *The Book of Psalms*; Waltke and Houston, *Psalms as Christian Worship*; Brown, "Psalms as Collections"; Brown, "'Here Comes the Sun!'"; Ross, *Commentary on the Psalms*; Sumpter, "Coherence"; Ho, *Design*; J. M. Hamilton Jr., *Psalms*, 2 vols, EBTC (Bellingham, WA: Lexham, 2021).

(2010), and Sumpter (2013). The majority of commentators follow their conclusions that Psalms 15–24 form a unified group.[27] To date, there do not exist any book-length treatments of Psalms 15–24 as a collection, nor a defined methodology applied to the collection. In this book, I stand on the shoulders of the scholars who have produced shorter studies on the collection and investigate the shape and message further by using in-depth analysis of repeated elements.

Each of the aforementioned scholars who has produced arti-cle-length studies on the collection has observed a variety of correspondences within the psalm group. Auffret, a French, structuralist, argued that these psalms form a chiastic structure with Psalm 19 at the center, and those who come after him follow suit.[28] Auffret's work is highly significant in that it initiates the study of Psalms 15–24 as a collection and draws out significant structural and lexical connections between paired psalms. Auffret not only observes correspondences between psalms, but also intensification and fulfillment.[29] Although Auffret does not categorize different types of correspondences, I adopt many of those types as criteria in this study, including structural correspondences, phrases, lexemes, and themes. In addition, the pattern of intensification and fulfillment between psalm pairs is something I will take further.

Those who come after Auffret assume the existence of the chiastic structure that he identified and take his work further by interpreting the structures he had observed. Two studies on the structure of this collection simultaneously appear in the mid-1990s. The first is by Hossfeld and Zenger in 1993, and the second by Miller in 1994. Hossfeld and Zenger are leaders in the diachronic reconstruction of the Psalter and have performed extensive work on the composition and theology of the Psalms.[30] In their 1993 article, "Wer darf hinaufziehn zum Berg JHWHs? [Who is allowed to access the mountain of Yhwh?]", Hossfeld

27. Auffret, "Les Psaumes 15 à 24", 407–38; Hossfeld and Zenger, "'Wer darf hi-naufziehn zum Berg JHWHs?'" 166–82; Miller, "Kingship," 127–42; Brown, "Psalms as Collections," 85–107; Brown, "'Here Comes the Sun!'"; Sumpter, "Coherence," 186–209.
28. Auffret, "Les Psaumes 15 à 24."
29. Auffret notes intensification of structures from Ps 17 to 22, and fulfillment in Pss 20 and 21 when compared with 19. Auffret, "Les Psaumes 15 à 24," 411–14, 421, 423, 425–28.
30. Hossfeld and Zenger, *Die Psalmen I*; Hossfeld and Zenger, *Psalms 2: A Commentary on Psalms 51–100*, trans. L. M. Maloney, Hermeneia (Minneapolis: Fortress, 2005); Hossfeld and Zenger, *Psalms 3: A Commentary on Psalms 101–150*, trans. Maloney, Hermeneia (Minneapolis: Fortress, 2011).

and Zenger continue the work of Auffret on Psalms 15–24 as a collection but move beyond identifying the structure to address the function of the collection from a diachronic perspective. They rely on identifying redactional insertions and argue that these redactions serve broadly to connect the psalms together and also draw out the redactors' theology. Using this method, they distinguish between pre-exilic, exilic, and post-exilic texts. They conclude that as a whole, Psalms 15–24 reflect an Israelite minority-group's search for a collective identity during the tumultuous exilic and post-exilic periods and are the first to suggest that the royal (Davidic) identity is "democratized" or extended to the community in this group.[31] In the present book, I depart from Hossfeld and Zenger's approach in that I do not postulate which sections of text were added by whom and when. Rather, I focus on a different stage in the process of textual shaping, that of the final editor(s) or redactor(s). Yet synchronic and diachronic study share many of the same literary processes for identifying connections between texts, so I rely on the insight of Hossfeld and Zenger into (especially thematic) links between psalms.

Miller's "Kingship, Torah Obedience, and Prayer," which originated around the same time as Hossfeld and Zenger's study, represents such a synchronic study.[32] Miller focuses on the theology of this psalm group, particularly expressed in the twin themes of kingship and Torah obedience, and the theme of prayer as exemplified by the king. Miller's study advances the interplay between themes of kingship and Torah based on the introduction to the Psalter, and he is sensitive to the function of the collection's placement within the whole Psalter. His work is particularly helpful for understanding the relationship and placement of the royal and Torah psalms at the center of the collection.[33] Like Hossfeld and Zenger, Miller suggests that the kingship is democratized to the people, but he adds that the people are also required to trust in Yhwh, just as the king is.[34] Following Miller, I will further investigate the connections between the themes of Torah and kingship, when correspondences link psalms together with these major themes.

More than a decade passes, and two more studies emerge on this collection. The first is Brown's chapter titled "Psalms as Collections

---

31. Hossfeld and Zenger, "Wer darf hinaufziehn zum Berg JHWHs?," 167.
32. Miller, "Kingship."
33. Miller, "Kingship," 127–28; see also Miller, "The Beginning of the Psalter," in McCann, *Shape and Shaping*, 83–92.
34. Miller, "Kingship," 127–31.

and Clusters," which first appears in his book on Psalms and later as "'Here Comes the Sun!': The Metaphorical Theology of Psalms 15-24," in Zenger's 2010 volume on the composition of the Psalter.[35] Brown's unique contributions include his attention to poetic imagery and metaphor and to the relationship between Psalm 19 and the rest of the collection. Brown calls Psalm 19 the metaphorical "summit" of the collection, which governs interpretation of the rest.[36] I will also explore the function of Psalm 19 in light of its connections to other psalms, but will investigate those links in light of the question of what role Psalm 19 plays in the storyline. Brown sees the psalms building inward toward the summit, but what changes when we read the collection linearly? Like Auffret, Brown also gives attention to how elements develop between psalm pairs. Brown moves study of this collection forward through investigation of how metaphors link parallel psalms and create dynamic movement between them. Because Brown's claims regarding the meaning created by metaphorical links in the collection are unique, it is all the more important to develop criteria for discerning links between psalms and assessing the strengths of cohesion between those psalms. Like Auffret, Brown also notices similarities between Psalms 19 and 24, but he also includes Psalm 15 in this relationship.[37] I further analyze the correspondences between these three psalms as well. Like those who have gone before him, Brown contends that the Davidic identity is democratized, though he does so through observation of the link of the word *servant* (עבד), wherein David's voice is heard in Psalm 19 and democratized to anyone who would walk in Yhwh's way.[38]

Sumpter's "The Coherence of Psalms 15-24" emerges three years after Brown's, in 2013.[39] The article is inspired by his dissertation on Psalm 24[40] and contributes to the study of the collection in some key ways. First, following Auffret and Brown, he further examines the connections between Psalms 15, 19, and 24, calls these the frame of the collection, and notices differences between these psalms and the intervening psalms, which depict the struggle of faith.[41] Somewhat in line with Brown's

---

35. Brown, "Psalms as Collections"; Brown, "'Here Comes the Sun!'"
36. Brown, "Psalms as Collections," 99.
37. Brown, "Psalms as Collections," 98-99.
38. Brown, "Psalms as Collections," 102-05; Brown, "'Here Comes the Sun!'," 270-75.
39. Sumpter, "Coherence," 191-92.
40. Sumpter, "The Substance of Psalm 24: An Attempt to Read the Bible after Brevard Childs," PhD diss., University of Gloucestershire, 2011.
41. Sumpter, "Coherence," 191-92.

reading, Sumpter also advocates for a concentric reading of the chiastic collection for understanding its narrative strand. He also more systematically attends to the development of content from each psalm to its chiastic parallel, noticing certain consistent developments from the first half to the second, which include intensifications and eschatological movement. Regarding democratization, Sumpter challenges the idea with what he observes to be a more redemptive function of the king on behalf of the people.[42]

Each of the works on Psalms 15–24 as a collection to date is sensitive to links between psalms and offers a major contribution to understanding this psalm group. In my study, I build on and extend these previous works in various ways. These previous works on Psalms 15–24 are relatively brief, and none constitutes a book-length treatment of the collection. For example, while Auffret is sensitive to many lexical links between psalms, less than a page of his study is devoted to the chiastic psalm pairs 15 and 24 and 16 and 23 together. Each article-length work assumes a chiastic form and identifies what the author sees as some of the most significant links between psalms. In this book, I perform a thorough analysis of the shape and message of each individual psalm. I also develop a thorough method with criteria for identifying the most significant links between psalms, so that I can identify which psalms are most closely connected to which others. As a result, I identify whether these psalms form a chiasm, as well as other structures that emerge. I also clarify the connections between and role of Psalms 15, 19, and 24. Auffret had identified connections between Psalms 19 and 24, and Brown and Sumpter have included in this analysis Psalm 15. In this study, I further examine the relationships between these three psalms, the developments from one to the next, and their role in the storyline of the collection.

I also develop criteria for identifying consistent developments between parallel psalms. Various scholars have made mention of development between parallel psalms in the chiasm they detect. For example, Auffret and Brown observe an intensifying movement between the structures of Psalms 17 and 22; Hossfeld and Zenger, Miller, Brown, and Sumpter see extensions from the individual to the community; Brown notes metaphorical development and especially how Psalms 20 and 21 reflect back on the deliverance of Psalm 18; Sumpter observes

---

42. Sumpter, "Coherence," 191, 195, 197, 201, 209.

an overarching eschatological movement. While these observations of development are insightful, further rationale for development between parallel psalms is needed, as well as specific criteria for identifying development. In this book, I develop a method based on principles of Hebrew parallelism for discerning movement between parallel texts.

Finally, I seek to explore the storyline of this collection in light of the structure and developments that take place within. I explore both a chiastic and linear reading and consider how the story develops. As part of this analysis, I give attention to the relationship between the themes of kingship and Torah, and also seek to clarify the relationship between the king and the community in this collection. Hossfeld and Zenger, Miller, and Brown each demonstrate aspects of democratization in this psalm group, wherein the royal identity is extended to the community. Sumpter challenges this idea by emphasizing a cause-and-effect redemptive role of the king. In this book, I give attention to how the significant links between psalms, the expansions from the individual to the community, and the overarching storyline portray the role of the king—whether as redeemer or one to be identified with, or something else.

My hope is that this present study will function as a new piece of the puzzle toward better understanding the overarching shape and message of the Psalter. In it, I approach the coherence and cohesion of the Psalter from the micro-level upward by evaluating links between and among individual psalms, and I develop a new methodology for doing so. As additional studies such as this continue, I am convinced that the overall shape and message of the Psalter will emerge all the more clearly.

2

Methodology: Identifying Relationships between Psalms

Although inquiry into the Psalter's design has increased following G. H. Wilson's study in 1985, the method is not accepted by all. The primary objection leveled against such studies is that they are impressionistic and tend to draw unsupported conclusions from the arrangement of psalms.[1] The concern is the neglect of in-depth analysis, resulting in cursory observations about a few psalms being presented as evidence of overarching literary arrangement. Wilson himself expresses his concern that "too often the necessary in-depth analysis has not been done."[2] Although investigation into the shape of the Psalter has a long and validating history, these cautionary voices must be met with a methodology that guards against these pitfalls.

What are the ways that authors link psalms together? And how can we know whether perceived links are intended or coincidental? These two questions deserve thoughtful answers, since such links can influence what we understand a psalm to mean. While there are links where the intentionality of the link is highly plausible (e.g., direct quotations or unique superscripts), others are not so easy to discern. What can keep interpreters from either missing intentional links or seeing more than is there?

Simply put, when we compare two psalms, we can observe repeated elements (lexemes, themes, structures, etc.), determine the rarity of these links, and notice how many rare links occur between the psalms. This process can be carried out in various legitimate ways. A

---

1. R. E. Murphy, "Reflections on Contextual Interpretation of the Psalms," in McCann, *Shape and Shaping*, 21-28; Goldingay, *Psalms*, 36; N. Whybray, *Reading the Psalms as a Book*, JSOTSup 222 (Sheffield: Sheffield Academic, 1996), 119.
2. Wilson, "Understanding the Purposeful Arrangement of the Psalms in the Psalter: Promises and Pitfalls," in McCann, *Shape and Shaping*, 48.

person may choose to read closely and make note of what seems like an abundance of unique repetitions. This is perhaps the most accessible practice of noticing links between psalms, yet the danger here is impressionistic findings. For more precision, one may use Bible software or a concordance to identify whether a repetition is rare—in other words, whether it occurs within the psalm-pair at a higher rate than its average within the broader literary context (i.e., the collection, book-level, or entire Psalter). This can be taken even a step further by using a mathematical formula to calculate the plausibility of intentionality (i.e., whether a repetition is statistically significant). To my mind, each of these practices has its place, and I myself have performed this study in all three of these ways.[3] In this book, I develop a methodology for analyzing rarity, rather than statistical significance, because it seems more at home within the field of literary studies. This method is still thorough and precise, yet accessible, and has yielded the same overall structure for the collection of Psalms 15–24 as an analysis of statistically significant repetitions.

My hope in this book is to advance the study of the shape of the Psalter by putting forth a thorough methodology for discerning the shape and message of collections. In this study, I identify which psalms within Psalms 15–24 are most closely connected to one other through the analysis of repeated elements. To my mind, my methodology can advance the field in primarily three ways. First, it is common to think of repetition in terms of lexemes, or words. In this study, I expand the criteria beyond lexical repetition to include other Ancient Near Eastern editorial strategies. Second, rather than simply noting how many repetitions occur, I analyze the *strength* of each repeated element between psalms. Third, I propose a method for interpreting those psalms that are most closely connected, which involves discovering not only the cohesion but also the differences between psalms in a psalm pair.

PARALLELISM BETWEEN DISTANT TEXTS

Within an individual psalm, it is not far-fetched to think that repeated elements contribute to the psalm's structure and inner-cohesion. But what about repetitions between two discrete psalms, especially when they are

---

3. See C. Quinn, "A Methodology for the Cohesion of Psalms: Psalms 15, 19, and 24 as a Test Case," in *Holistic Readings on the Psalms and the Twelve*, ed. M. Ayars and Ho, forthcoming.

not side by side? I propose that the concept of Hebrew parallelism can be our guide for understanding relationships between texts.

My own close study of the Hebrew Scriptures has convinced me that many of the literary devices and structures that exist on the micro-level also often find expression on the macro-level, so that micro-level analysis can shape our expectations about what kinds of poetic devices will unfold at higher levels. Hebrew parallelism is one such device.

Parallelism has long been recognized as a defining feature of Hebrew poetry and is most often used to speak of verse-level cohesion characterized by repetition (recognizable similarity) and also movement (recognizable difference).[4] Various scholars who have investigated the literary features of the biblical text have concluded that both repetition and parallelism are common literary devices used by the biblical authors, even beyond the verse level. For example, J. Muilenburg, in his 1968 SBL presidential address, states that "repetition serves many and diverse functions in the literary compositions of ancient Israel, whether in the construction of parallel cola or parallel bicola, or in the structure of the strophes, or in the fashioning and ordering of the complete literary units."[5] Following this, R. Alter demonstrates that repetition is a primary literary technique of the biblical writers in both narrative and poetry.[6] This repetition, he argues, may serve to connect not only small literary segments to one another, but also larger texts. Word motifs, he says, function "to establish instructive connections between seemingly disparate episodes."[7] Alter observes that in Hebrew poetry, parallelism creates movement not only between parallel lines, but also from verse to verse, and that it shapes the overall storyline.[8] J. P. Fokkelman and B. Weber argue that parallelism can be found at all levels of the poetic text, including verses, strophes, stanzas, and sections.[9] A. Berlin too, in her thorough study of

---

4. R. Alter, *The Art of Biblical Poetry*, 2nd ed. (New York: Basic Books, 2011), 10–11.
5. J. Muilenburg, "Form Criticism and Beyond," *JBL* 88 (1969): 17.
6. Alter, *The Art of Biblical Narrative*, 2nd ed. (New York: Basic Books, 2011), 55–78, 111–42; Alter, *Biblical Poetry*, 1–28.
7. Alter, *Biblical Narrative*, 118.
8. Alter, *Biblical Poetry*, 27–28.
9. J. P. Fokkelman, *Major Poems of the Hebrew Bible: At the Interface of Prosody and Structural Analysis*, vol. 3, SSN 43 (Assen: Royal Van Gorcum, 2003), 61–157; B. Weber, *Werkbuch Psalmen I, Die Psalmen 1–72* (Stuttgart: Kohlhammer, 2001), 99. See also McCann, who argues that repetition is a common feature of Hebrew poetry. McCann, "The Book of Psalms," 653.

Hebrew parallelism, opens the door for parallelism to occur not only on the level of the line, but also on higher literary levels:

> Once we admit smaller segments as being parallel—e.g., words, phrases, even sounds—though the lines to which they belong are not parallel, we raise the incidence of parallelism within a text. And if we do not restrict our search for linguistic equivalences to adjacent lines or sentences, but take a global view, finding equivalences anywhere within a text, we raise the incidence of parallelism still more. [10]

Parallelism can often be expected on the level of the poetic line, however the same is not true when dealing with more distant or larger blocks of text like entire psalms. In the case of the latter, parallel relationships must be identified by repetition. Only then can the reader analyze the difference, or development, that is also present.

LINKING CRITERIA

Several strategies for coordinating psalms across the entire Psalter have been identified by Wilson in his analysis of common ancient Near Eastern editorial devices. Wilson compares the Mesopotamian Hymnic Incipits, the Sumerian Temple Hymns, and the Qumran Psalms scrolls with the Masoretic Psalter and finds the following tacit editorial groupings in the latter: genre, deity addressed, concatenation, lack of superscription, and thematic correspondence. [11] Other scholars, notably D. M. Howard Jr. and his student M. K. Snearly, have applied these criteria to the level of the collection and book within the Psalter. [12] Both Howard and Snearly detect concatenation among psalms through systematic analysis of repeated elements. Howard focuses on key-word links, thematic connections, and structural and genre similarities. Snearly adds to this distant parallelism (e.g., *dis legomena*, parallelism of syntactical construction, and *inclusio*) and common superscripts. [13]

My methodology extends the methods of Howard and Snearly primarily by quantifying the rarity of repetitions and regarding distant parallelism as applicable to all types of linking elements rather than as a

---

10. A. Berlin, *Dynamics of Biblical Parallelism*, rev. ed. (Grand Rapids: Eerdmans, 2008), 3.
11. Wilson, *Editing*, 121–98.
12. Howard, *Structure*; Snearly, *Return*.
13. Snearly, *Return*, 39–53 (esp. 39).

separate criterion. Building on common ancient Near Eastern editorial strategies as well as an understanding of Hebrew parallelism, I propose observing the following criteria for discerning links between psalms:

1. lexical links

2. morphological links

3. phrasal links

4. thematic links

5. structural links

6. superscript links

In addition to these six link types, patterns of the divine names of God will also be discussed as a secondary link type.

In order to determine which psalms within the psalm-group are most closely connected to one another, I use these criteria as a guide to identify every repeated element (i.e., every repeated lexeme, theme, etc.) between each possible psalm-pair in the group.[14] Not all repetitions are significant; I will discuss how to differentiate between these in a later section. Noticing every repetition of each of these kinds between two psalms is the first step to discerning whether two psalms are intentionally linked.

Lexical Links

A lexical link involves the repetition of the root of a word. It is the most common type of link observed by interpreters who are interested in the arrangement of psalms,[15] and for good reason: lexical repetition is

---

14. I.e., Pss 15 and 16; 15 and 17; ... 15 and 24; 16 and 17; 16 and 18; ... 16 and 24; ... and 23 and 24. See appendix 3 for the list of non-incidental lexemes and their variations as found in Pss 15-24.

15. It was common in early rabbinic interpretation to observe lexical links as indicators of textual relationships (see ch. 1). Various subsequent scholars have likewise found it productive, e.g., J. A. Alexander, *The Psalms Translated and Explained*, 6th ed. (New York: Charles Scribner, 1865); Delitzsch, *Psalms*; A. F. Kirkpatrick, *The Book of Psalms: With Introduction and Notes* (Cambridge: Cambridge University Press, 1902); A. Cohen, *The Psalms* (London: Soncino, 1969); Muilenburg, "Form Criticism"; Zimmerli, "Zwillingspsalmen"; Barth, "Concatenatio"; Auffret, "Les Psaumes 15 à 24"; D. H. Hirsch, "Translatable Structure, Untranslatable Poem: Psalm 24," *Modern Language Studies* 12, no. 4 (1982): 21-34; Berlin, *Dynamics*, 64-79; Wilson, *Editing*, 139-98; J. K. Kuntz, "King Triumphant: A Rhetorical Study of Psalms 20-21," *HAR* 10 (1986): 157-76; L. C. Allen, "David as Exemplar of Spirituality: The Redactional Function of Psalm 19," *Biblica* 67 (1986): 544-46; M. E. Tate, *Psalms 51-100*, WBC 20 (Waco, TX: Word, 1990); J. Vermeylen, "Une prière pour le renouveau du Jérusalem. Le Psaume 51,"

a very common feature of Hebrew poetry. In Berlin's study of parallel relationships, she identifies lexical parallelism as one of three aspects of parallelism and demonstrates the prevalence of these repetitions throughout Hebrew poetry.[16] Wilson observes that the Mesopotamian Hymnic Incipits exhibit similar phraseology as a key organizing principle. This increases the plausibility that lexical links play a role in the organization of the Hebrew Psalter.[17] J. F. D. Creach shows how lexical links work on the macro-level by demonstrating that the lexeme *refuge* (חסה) and its semantic field serve an organizational purpose in the overarching structure of the Psalter.[18]

It is important to note that in my identification of lexical links, I do not include conjunctions, prepositions, particles, negative adverbs, or pronouns, since these are often incidental. I will give attention to these lexemes when they contribute to the structure of a psalm or exist as part of a repeated phrase. However, on their own, I find that they do not contribute to cohesion between psalms.

MORPHOLOGICAL LINKS

Morphological links include the repetition of lexemes in corresponding morphological form. For example, the lexeme *lift up* (נשא) occurs in both Psalms 15 and 24 as a *Qal* perfect third-person masculine singular verb,

---

ETL 68 (1992): 257–83; N. Lohfink, "Der Psalter und die Christliche Meditation: Die Bedeutung der Endredaktion für das Verständnis des Psalters," *BK* 47 (1992): 195–200; Hossfeld and Zenger, *Die Psalmen I*; Hossfeld and Zenger, "'Wer darf hinaufziehn zum Berg JHWHs?'"; Mays, *Psalms*; Davis, "Contextual Analysis of Psalms 107–118," 23–26; McCann, "Books I–III," 93–107; McCann, "The Book of Psalms"; Creach, *Yahweh as Refuge*, 74–105; Howard, *Structure*; Zenger, "Composition and Theology," 77–102; G. Barbiero, *Das erste Psalmenbuch als Einheit: Eine synchrone Analyse von Psalm 1–41*, Österreichische Biblische Studien 16 (Frankfurt: Peter Lang, 1999), 20–25; Kimmitt, "The Shape of Psalms 42–49"; Cole, *Shape and Message*, 28–230; J. L. Smith, *Psalms of the Northern Levites: Asaph, Ethan, and the Sons of Korah* (Anchorage, AK: White Stone, 2003); M. Leuenberger, *Konzeptionen des Königtums Gottes im Psalter: Untersuchungen zu Komposition und Redaktion der theokratischen Bücher IV–V im Psalter*, ATANT 83 (Zürich: Theologischer Verlag, 2004), 35; Mitchell, "'God Will Redeem My Soul from Sheol': The Psalms of the Sons of Korah," *JSOT* 30, no. 3 (2006): 365–84; S. K. Ahn, "I Salmi 146–150 come conclusione del Salterio," PhD diss., Pontifical Biblical Institute, 2008; Brown, "Psalms as Collections"; Brown, "'Here Comes the Sun!'"; Sumpter, "Coherence," 186–209; Snearly, *Return*, 37–38; Ho, *Design*.
16. Berlin, *Dynamics*, 64–102. For Berlin, the lexical aspect is composed of both lexical and semantic components, with grammatical and phonological being separate aspects.
17. Wilson, *Editing*, 25–62.
18. Creach, *Yahweh as Refuge*.

and therefore would be a morphological link between the two psalms. Many scholars who identify lexical links between psalms also observe when these lexemes occur in the same morphological form as part of their lexical analysis.[19] Berlin, however, lists morphological parallelism as distinct from lexical parallelism, as a subcategory of grammatical parallelism.[20] I think there is merit to treating repeated lexemes and the forms they occur in separately, because when a word is repeated in the same form, this plausibly creates a stronger link than a repetition in a different form, especially when the morphological form is rare. In addition, repeated words in the same form are more likely to occur in similar contexts, which further binds two psalms. Consider *lift up* of Psalms 15 and 24: following its form as a *Qal* perfect third-person masculine singular verb, both are speaking of a single or paradigmatic human in the third person. Both the form and the context denoted by that form create cohesion.

PHRASAL LINKS

Another type of link closely related to the lexical link is the phrasal link. A phrasal link involves the repetition of at least two corresponding lexemes used within the same clause. Unlike lexical or morphological links, phrasal links may include the following: conjunctions, prepositions, particles, negative adverbs, and pronouns. These will be included on a case-by-case basis if it seems that they are used to construct recognizable corresponding phrases. For example, the phrase made of the negation בל and the verb *shake* (מוט) occurs at the close of Psalm 16, where the psalmist says that with Yhwh at his right hand, *I will not be shaken* (בל־אמוט; v. 8). The same phrase occurs within the early verses of Psalm 17 as בל־נמוטו, where the psalmist says *my feet have not been shaken* (v. 5). These shared phrases create a link between these neighboring psalms, inviting the reader to read them together.

THEMATIC LINKS

Interpreters may also notice that thematic similarities create cohesion among psalms.[21] A theme can be defined as the essential content or sub-

---

19. See n. 15.

20. Berlin divides grammatical parallelism into the two subcategories of syntax (the order of words) and morphology (the form of words). Berlin, *Dynamics*, 36–63.

21. E.g., Howard, *Structure*, 20, 100–102, 183; Davis, "Contextual Analysis of Psalms 107–118," 23, 26–27; Kimmitt, "The Shape of Psalms 42–49," 31–32, 252–73; Cole, *Shape and Message*, 5–14; Leuenberger, *Konzeptionen*, 35; Wilson, *Editing*, 190–93; Zenger,

ject matter of a psalm.[22] Thematic links may consist of repetition of the same idea or an allusion to the same passage in Scripture.[23] The identification of themes is arguably the most subjective of my criteria, because these cannot be concretely identified in the same way that a lexeme can. Yet this can also lead to creative imagination, and it is undeniable that themes create cohesion between psalms in significant ways. For example, *speech* occurs as a major theme only in Psalms 15, 19, and 24 in the collection, creating both cohesion and curiosity, since the theme is used in Psalms 15 and 24 of the righteous worshiper, and in Psalm 19 of the skies.

STRUCTURAL LINKS

By structural links, I mean the correspondences in structure on the level of the whole psalm. Often these correspond with the modern, form-critical categories (e.g., lament, praise, thanksgiving).[24] Structural links certainly occur at the verse level as grammatical parallelism or on the level of the strophe; however, my focus is only on the psalm level, since grammatical correspondences alone between psalms would likely be too distant to create cohesion.

One may also refer to these as "genre links," per the modern, form-critical genres developed by H. Gunkel, C. Westermann, and M. Millard, with an important caveat: only those psalms that also have identifiable corresponding structures will be identified as potential links. For example, thanksgivings and laments follow typical structural patterns, but royal psalms and wisdom psalms do not necessarily. The correspondences between royal psalms or wisdom psalms would be better observed under the "theme" criterion as the theme of "the king" or "creation," etc.

"Psalmenexegese und Psalterexegese: Eine Forschungsskizze," in Zenger, *The Composition of the Book of Psalms*, 31, 77, 91, 94; Ho, *Design*.

22. Davis, "Contextual Analysis of Psalms 107-118," 16-17; see W. G. E. Watson, *Classical Hebrew Poetry: A Guide to Its Techniques*, 2nd ed. (Sheffield: JSOT, 1986), 81.

23. For example, Zenger finds that Pss 138 and 145 both allude to Exodus 33-34. Ps 145:8 quotes the Sinai-formula (Exod 34:6-7) and Ps 145:7, 9 alludes to Exod 33:19. He likewise argues that Ps 138 also has the Yhwh theophany-name event in mind, evidenced in the combination of the lexemes *name* (שם), *glory* (כבוד), *loyal love* (חסד), and *truth* (אמת). Zenger, "Composition and Theology," 94.

24. Gunkel, *Introduction to the Psalms: The Genres of the Religious Lyric of Israel*, trans. J. D. Nogalski (Macon, GA: Mercer University Press, 1998); Westermann, *The Psalms*; Millard, *Die Komposition des Psalters*, 30-32, 35-41, 227-28.

Various scholars have observed that psalms occur in clusters across the Psalter according their genres.[25] Similarly, some scholars have given attention to structural similarities that do not fall into modern form-critical categories. P. Auffret's work is a good example of this type of structural investigation; others include G. Barbiero, Howard, and Snearly.[26]

Wilson found that that genres are grouped together in ancient comparative literature. This supports the plausibility that recognizable genres are clustered together in the Psalter. However, by genre, Wilson referred to the titles in the psalm headings שגיון, מכתם, תפלה, מסכיל, תהלה, and הלליה, rather than their structures.[27] I will give attention to structural links alone in this category but will account for the occurrences of these descriptive words in the lexical-link category. In addition to identifying psalms with corresponding structures, I also give attention to where these psalms differ structurally from one another and what unique emphases the author is making through the breaking of these generic patterns.[28]

SUPERSCRIPT LINKS

A corresponding superscript involves the same designation of author or psalm type, the same non-incidental lexical link, or a combination of these components. While the criterion of superscript link overlaps with that of lexical link, I find it important to analyze superscripts separately for two reasons: First, ancient collections are often grouped by superscripts. Wilson, for example, finds that collections at Qumran are grouped by superscript, both in the identification of the type of psalm (e.g., תפלה) and in the attribution of author (e.g., לדוד).[29] The

---

25. Westermann, "The Formation of the Psalter," 252, 257; Millard, *Die Komposition des Psalters*, 146–51; Leuenberger, *Konzeptionen*, 35; Brueggemann, "Bounded by Obedience and Praise," 79; McCann, "Books I–III," 96.

26. E.g., Auffret, "Les Psaumes 15 à 24"; Barbiero, *Das erste Psalmenbuch als Einheit*, 20–21; Howard, *Structure*, 34–97; Snearly, *Return*, 37–38.

27. Wilson concludes that the Mesopotamian Hymnic Incipits are organized according to the following: (1) genre groupings; (2) arrangement by deity addressed; and (3) juxtaposition by similar phraseology. Wilson, *Editing*, 25–62. Regarding the Qumran scrolls, Wilson finds that "the criteria which are operative in the juxtaposition of psalms would seem to be of two major types: (1) psalm types and (2) functional concerns. The former is divided into two categories: (a) genre-groupings and (b) author-groupings." Wilson, *Editing*, 136.

28. This method aligns with the principles of rhetorical criticism to both identify what is *typical* and also what is *original* in order to understand the author's meaning. See McCann, "The Book of Psalms," 644–45, 651–52.

29. Wilson, *Editing*, 116–38.

grouping of the Songs of Ascents (Pss 120–134), which each begin with the superscript שִׁיר (לְ/ה)מַעֲלוֹת, also implies that superscripts are indicative of collections. The general pattern of Davidic attribution at the beginning and end of the Psalter also indicates movement and grouping in light of superscripts.[30] The second reason it is important to analyze superscripts independently of lexical links is that it shrinks the parameters within which to observe a link. For example, while a particular lexical link in a superscript may not be distinctive in comparison with all other surrounding lexemes, it may be distinctive when compared only with other superscripts. In addition to Wilson, a variety of other scholars have observed superscripts as serving an organizing function in the Psalter.[31]

DIVINE-NAME LINKS

In comparison with other criteria, it is not as common to observe patterns of the divine name as connecting devices among psalms. A handful of scholars, however, consider it productive to observe which divine names are used, where the divine names occur, and how many times divine names occur. Barbiero in particular considers the occurrence of divine names to be important because, as he posits, scribal tradition displays a clear practice of counting.[32] In the Mesopotamian Hymnic Incipits, Wilson regards the name of the deity addressed as an organizing concern, which lends support to the same potential strategy in the Psalter.[33] E. Zenger also demonstrates that the divine name can serve as a central component of a psalm. In his exegesis of Psalm 12, Zenger observes five occurrences of the divine name, each occurring in one of the first five strophes in the psalm, and the central occurrence existing in the middle colon of a tricolon at the chiastic center.[34] In addition, groupings within the Psalter have been designated as Elohistic or Yahwistic,

---

30. Book I contains thirty-seven Davidic psalms; Book II contains eighteen Davidic psalms; Books III and IV contain only three Davidic psalms, and Book V contains fifteen Davidic psalms, concluding with eight psalms of David: Pss 138–145 (Pss 146–150 being considered as the conclusion of the Psalter).

31. E.g., Leuenberger, *Konzeptionen*, 35; Millard, *Die Komposition des Psalters*, 19–46; Davis, "Contextual Analysis of Psalms 107–118," iv; Barbiero, *Das erste Psalmenbuch*, 24–25; Snearly, *Return*, 37–38; Ho, *Design*.

32. Barbiero, *Das erste Psalmenbuch*, 24–25.

33. Wilson, *Editing*, 25–57.

34. Zenger, "Psalm 12, Hilfeschrei zu JHWH, dem Gott der Armen," in Hossfeld and Zenger, *Die Psalmen I*, 92.

depending partially on which name is predominant, which supports a correlation between arrangement and divine names.[35]

I do not include divine-name links in my statistical analysis of the links between psalm pairs for a few reasons. First, the primary way that divine names may create a strong link between psalms—by using a name rare to the collection—will be accounted for by analyzing lexical links. Second, divine names tend to be used primarily to structure individual psalms. Where patterns of divine names do seem to occur, however, I make note of these in my interpretation. Patterns may include any of the following three cases: (1) the occurrence of divine names in structurally significant positions; (2) the occurrence of divine names the same number of times per psalm; or (3) the same designation used for God (e.g., *Yhwh* [יהוה], *Most High* [עליון], *God* [אל], *Lord* [אדני], *God* [אלהים]).

THE STRENGTH OF COHESION BETWEEN PSALM PAIRS

When trying to determine the shape of a collection, the goal is to discover which psalms are most closely linked to which other psalms. When two psalms closely cohere to one another, I call these a psalm pair. Psalms may be arranged so they cohere with neighboring psalms or may even be arranged so that they create an overarching structure—for example, bundles of psalms, or a chiasm, or an ABAB forward movement. The first task is to note every repeated element between every possible psalm pair in a collection. In this case, I will compare Psalm 15 to every other psalm in the collection, then Psalm 16 to every other psalm in the collection, and so on, tracking repeated lexemes, morphologies, phrases, themes, structures, and superscripts.

The second task in determining whether two psalms are intentionally linked together is to determine the rarity of each repeated element, whether it is a lexeme, phrase, theme, etc. Rarity is important for determining intentionality. If a common word is repeated, it's very possible that the repetition is coincidental, rather than intended to link two texts together. But when an extremely rare word is used in two different texts, it becomes more likely that the repetition is intentional, in that the two texts are meant to be read together.

---

35. E.g., Craigie, *Psalms 1–50*, 27–31; McCann, "The Book of Psalms," 653.

THE RARITY OF REPEATED ELEMENTS

Rather than assuming that every repetition is significant, we can analyze the *strength* of each repetition by comparing the rate of the repetition in a psalm pair with its rate in the literary context—in this case,
the collection.[36] When a repeated element occurs at a higher rate in
a psalm pair than its average within the collection, I call it a *distinctive element*. Here's an example: Let's say you notice that Psalms 15 and
19 both use the lexeme *blameless* (תמם; Pss 15:2; 19:7, 13). The root also
occurs in other psalms in the collection of Psalms 15–24. The goal is
to understand whether *blameless* occurs at a higher rate in the psalm-
pair than in the collection. Within Psalms 15 and 19, *blameless* occurs
three times; there are 153 non-incidental lexemes within Psalms 15
and 19 together, so the rate of occurrence of *blameless* is 3/153, or once
every 51 words.[37] Now we can compare this to its average rate in the
collection: *Blameless* occurs eight times in the collection, and there are
1130 lexemes total in the collection, so the average rate of occurrence
overall is 8/1130, or once every 141.25 words. So, in Psalms 15 and 19, the
lexeme *blameless* is distinctive. But *how distinctive?* Dividing the rate
of occurrence in the collection by the rate in the psalm pair yields the
result that the lexeme *blameless* occurs 2.77 times as often in the psalm
pair than in the collection overall. I call this the *strength of cohesion* of
a repeated element.

Here's another example from another set of psalms: The lexeme *save*
(ישׁע) occurs in both Psalms 17 and 22 but is an example of a non-distinc-
tive lexeme. ישׁע occurs three times within those psalms, for an average
of once every 105.67 lexemes. In comparison, it occurs twenty-five times
in the collection as a whole, which averages once every 45.20 lexemes.
Since occurs *less* often in Psalms 17 and 22 than in the collection, this

---

36. In the Psalms, I find it most compelling to use the collection, rather than the book
or the Psalter, for two reasons. First, if authors intend for their audience to notice
links, the more proximate those links are, the more likely it is that they will be noticed. Second, it is likely that many collections existed on their own before being
situated in the Psalter, so we would expect links on this level. Certainly, more editorial shaping took place as collections were arranged into the Psalter, so looking at
the rarity of repetitions on the book or macro-structural level is also helpful. When
repetitions are not as proximate, intentionality is more compelling when there is a
cluster of them.

37. You can find a table of the word count of each possible psalm pair and the collection overall in appendix 3.

lexeme is *not distinctive*, and therefore I do not give further attention to it as I assess the relationship between these psalms.

The Strength of Cohesion between Psalm Pairs

Now, while the mere presence of a distinctive repetition has bearing on interpretation, I am most interested in cases where two psalms contain a high number of these distinctive links in comparison with their surrounding psalms. In such cases, I conclude that two psalms are "parallel" and are meant to be read together and set on analogy to one another.

Identifying distinctive elements and determining their strength of cohesion is one of the distinguishing marks of my methodology and serves as the foundation for identifying parallel psalms. However, that two psalms share a distinctive element does not, on its own, sufficiently indicate that these psalms ought to be paired together as parallel. It is when two psalms share a high number of highly distinctive elements that editorial linking of that kind is likely.

Both the *number* and the *strength* of repeated elements have bearing on whether psalms should be considered parallel. In order to account for both the number and strength of shared elements, I determine the strength of each repeated element within each possible psalm pair per criteria type (e.g., lexical, morphological, etc). By adding all of the strengths of cohesion together within one category (e.g., lexical), we can find the overall strength of cohesion for that link criterion.

In the case of Psalm 15, if we want to find the strength of lexical cohesion it has with every other psalm in the collection, we first identify every lexical repetition and which of those occur at higher rates than their average in the collection (i.e., they are distinctive). When we find the strength of cohesion of each repeated element between two psalms, we can add these together to find the overall lexical cohesion for a psalm pair. If we pair Psalm 15 with every other psalm in the collection—Psalms 16, 17, 18, and so on—we will notice that Psalms 15 and 19 share the highest number of distinctive lexemes, fourteen in all: *tent* (אהל), *amen* (אמן), *acquit* (נקה), *do* (עשׂה), *blameless* (תמם), *fear* (ירא), *heart* (לבב), *eye* (עין), *speak* (דבר), *righteous* (צדק), *make music* (זמר), *glory* (כבד), *David* (דוד), and *Yhwh* (יהוה). Yet, this doesn't necessarily mean these two psalms have the strongest lexical cohesion. When we calculate the strengths of cohesion of each of these lexemes, and then add them together, we find that actually Psalms 15 and 24 share the strongest lexical cohesion. Psalms 15 and 24 share twelve distinctive lexemes—*swear*

(שבע), lift up (נשא), mountain (הר), glory (כבד), forever (עולם), acquit (נקה), holy (קדש), righteous (צדק), make music (זמר), heart (לבב), David (דוד), and Yhwh (יהוה). Their overall strength of lexical cohesion is 54.91—quite a bit higher than that of Psalms 15 and 19, at 43.89. This is due to some of the repetitions between Psalms 15 and 24 being very rare (e.g., *swear* [שבע] occurs only in these two psalms), or occurring at high rates within (*lift up* [נשא] occurs seven of eight times in these two psalms). Below are the numbers and overall strengths of lexical cohesion that Psalm 15 shares with each psalm in the collection:

Table 1. Psalm 15: Degree of Lexical Significance

Psalm Pair	Number of Distinctive Lexemes	Strength of Lexical Cohesion
15 and 16	9	30.50
15 and 17	8	30.54
15 and 18	11	19.67
15 and 19	14	43.89
15 and 20	6	15.33
15 and 21	8	23.97
15 and 22	14	39.01
15 and 23	6	34.11
15 and 24	12	54.91

But lexical cohesion isn't the only type of cohesion. The other plausible link types include morphological, thematic, structural, phrasal, and superscript. Before drawing conclusions about which psalms Psalm 15 is most closely connected to, I analyze the strength of coherence for every other type of linking criteria. These are the results per type:

Table 2. Psalm 15: Strengths of Cohesion per Link Type

Psalm Pair	Lexemes	Themes	Structures	Phrases	Morphologies	Superscripts
15 and 16	30.50	5.99	0.00	15.41	0.00	0.00
15 and 17	30.53	1.83	0.00	3.67	3.56	0.00
15 and 18	19.67	0.00	0.00	0.00	2.50	0.00
15 and 19	43.89	9.72	3.33	0.00	1.29	1.43
15 and 20	15.33	2.69	0.00	0.00	5.95	1.43
15 and 21	23.97	2.94	0.00	4.41	3.67	1.43
15 and 22	39.01	3.35	0.00	4.57	6.84	1.43
15 and 23	34.11	12.77	0.00	0.00	3.54	4.76
15 and 24	54.91	26.27	3.33	29.74	5.93	4.76

At this point, I notice that Psalms 15 and 24 have strong cohesion within each of their categories (highlighted in grey).

What we cannot do yet is compare across categories—as in from lexemes to structures or phrases. Just because the strength of lexical cohesion is represented by a number twice as high as that of thematic cohesion, this does not mean that the thematic connections are only half as strong. Until we scale the columns, comparisons can be done only *within* each criterion (i.e., each column) rather than between them. To scale the columns, I calculate the strengths of cohesion per link type for every possible psalm pair within the collection. In other words, I create the above chart for every psalm in the collection, not just Psalm 15. Once I am able to see which number within its own category, or column, is highest across all charts, I can scale the entire category to that number. The result is that the strongest lexical cohesion would be represented by the number 1.00, and the other strengths of lexical cohesion would be less than 1.00. For example, Psalms 17 and 22 actually have the strongest lexical cohesion of any other possible psalm pair in the entire collection of Psalms 15-24, at 59.99, so I scale each strength of lexical cohesion to this number by dividing by it. The result is that Psalms 17 and 22 have a scaled strength of lexical cohesion of 1.00, and every other psalm pair has a scaled strength of lexical cohesion of less than 1.00. For example, when I divide the lexical cohesion of Psalms 15 and 24 (54.91) by 59.99, this results in a scaled cohesion of 0.91. See the scaled chart of Psalm 15 when paired with every other psalm in the collection:[38]

Table 3. Psalm 15: Strengths of Cohesion (Scaled)

Psalm Pair	Lexemes	Themes	Structures	Phrases	Morphologies	Superscripts	TOTAL
15 and 16	0.51	0.14	0.00	0.52	0.00	0.00	1.17
15 and 17	0.51	0.04	0.00	0.12	0.19	0.00	0.87
15 and 18	0.33	0.00	0.00	0.00	0.14	0.00	0.47
15 and 19	0.73	0.23	0.67	0.00	0.07	0.21	1.91
15 and 20	0.26	0.06	0.00	0.00	0.32	0.21	0.86
15 and 21	0.40	0.07	0.00	0.15	0.20	0.21	1.03
15 and 22	0.65	0.08	0.00	0.15	0.37	0.21	1.47
15 and 23	0.57	0.30	0.00	0.00	0.19	0.70	1.77
15 and 24	0.91	0.62	0.67	1.00	0.32	0.70	4.22

---

38. Find these strengths of cohesion on the tables presented throughout chs. 3-6.

Notice an added column to the right, titled "Total." Now that we have scaled the strengths of cohesion, we can add them across categories to get an idea about which psalms most closely cohere. For example, in order to find the overall strength of cohesion for Psalms 15 and 24, I add the lexical, morphological, phrasal, thematic, structure, and superscript strengths of cohesion. You'll notice above that Psalms 15 and 24 not only have the strongest cohesion in almost every category, but their overall strength of cohesion (4.22) is higher than when Psalm 15 is paired with any other psalm in the collection. Because of this, I view these psalms as parallel, or meant to be read in comparison with each other.

It is important to state at this point that these calculations are merely ways of seeing and quantifying connections in the text. They do not function as proof, but can serve to support and challenge our intuitions and impressions about the uniqueness of certain elements and the resulting cohesion between texts. It is not necessary to perform statistical analysis to discern the shape of collections; one may simply read closely and make observations. But since these strengths of cohesion are derived from the occurrence of various rare elements within psalm pairs, the numbers describe what is likely a unique relationship.[39] In order to assess these unique relationships, I take into account both the overall strength of cohesion as well as the strengths of cohesion per link type. I regard lexemes, themes, and structures as the most significant connective elements, since they account for large portions of each psalm, whereas distinctive phrases, morphologies, and superscripts typically comprise only a few words in a psalm.

READING COHESIVE PSALMS AS PARALLEL TEXTS

As I mentioned above, many scholars have recognized that parallelism exists on various levels of the text, including between entire psalms. When two psalms are set in parallel to one another by the strength and number of their cohesive elements, this is a relationship that involves both repetition and difference. Various scholars argue that Hebrew parallelism is not defined as simply static repetition, but as dynamic movement from the first element to the second, such as heightening,

---

39. As an additional confirmation, I have performed a separate analysis elsewhere of only the *statistically significant* (or extremely rare) elements between psalm pairs by performing a hypothesis test. This analysis confirms the accuracy of the psalm pairs I identify. See Quinn, "Methodology."

intensification, specification, etc. For example, L. Alonso-Schökel writes, "Parallelism can serve to amplify and to concentrate; it can extend the image or explain it … , it can harmonize two things or put them in tension."[40] J. K. Kugel contends that a parallel element in a verse is not simply a repetition, but a modification of the first element.[41] Alter states that parallelism is "a dynamic movement from one verset to the next," since no two words are exact synonyms, and no two contexts are exactly the same.[42] This movement, he says, consists in a "heightening or intensification … of focusing, specification, concretization, even what could be called dramatization."[43] Berlin too describes the various ways in which the second parallel line can go beyond the first linguistically.[44] If parallelism is to be extended to higher literary levels, the same dynamic movement should be expected between larger blocks of material.

In the collection of Psalms 15–24, these blocks of material are entire psalms. I conclude that two psalms are parallel texts when they exhibit a strong cohesion. Parallel psalms, like other parallel texts, are dynamic entities, rather than static. In other words, when elements from one psalm are repeated in its pair, the repetition does not mean the exact same thing but is constituted of intentional differences in use or context that move the narrative strand forward. I use the word *development* to describe this dynamic reuse. My goal in reading psalms as parallel texts is to discern how each latter psalm develops and modifies elements of the former, giving careful attention to how the cohesive elements are dynamically reused. This analysis of the development between parallel psalms is one of the primary ways this study goes beyond previous studies of the shape of the Psalter and could be practiced whether someone calculates the strengths of cohesion or simply performs a close reading.

In order to strategically discern the meaning of parallel psalms, we can compare the corresponding elements of the second psalm with the first to evaluate whether and what kind of developments exist. In Alter's *Art of Biblical Poetry*, he identifies various, specific ways that the second line may go beyond the first. If we apply these criteria to the specific

---

40. "El paralelismo puede sirvir para amplificar y para concentrar, puede ampliar la imagen o explicarla … , puede pacificar dos seres o ponerlos en tensión." L. Alonso-Schökel, *Estudios de Poética Hebrea* (Barcelona: Juan Flores, 1963), 229–30.
41. J. K. Kugel, *Idea of Biblical Poetry: Parallelism and Its History* (New Haven, CT: Yale University Press, 1981), 1–58.
42. Alter, *Biblical Poetry*, 9.
43. Alter, *Biblical Poetry*, 20.
44. Berlin, *Dynamics*, 31–124.

types of correspondences that we are observing between psalms, we can observe developments between corresponding elements in ways like the following:

- **Thematic development**
  » New theme
  » Sequential theme
  » Intensification of theme
  » Change in referent
  » Specification or expansion of place or time
  » Theme moves from general to specific or concrete, or vice versa
  » Chronologically later action
  » Theme is heightened by use of a metaphor

- **Structural development**
  » Different structure to indicate a new emphasis
  » Same structure with differing structural elements to indicate emphasis
  » One component of the structure is intensified

- **Lexical, morphological, and phrasal development**
  » Same element used with new meaning (e.g., new referent, different context, specification, intensification)
  » Same element used more prevalently
  » Superscript development
  » New superscript with plausible explanation

- **Divine name development**
  » Divine name used more prevalently
  » New divine name used

Throughout this study, I will ask the question, *what kind of development is taking place, if any, between these corresponding elements?* I will look for developments like those listed above to help identify the ways the author is using repetition and difference to convey meaning. I will draw attention primarily to those developments that occur *consistently* within the collection, since these most plausibly communicate the main message and storyline.

SUMMARY

In this study, my aim is to investigate the shape and message of Psalms 15–24 through an examination of the cohesion between all possible psalm pairs. In this chapter, I have outlined various processes in order to meet these objectives. I began positing that parallel relationships can occur on any level of the text, and therefore between entire psalms—whether adjacent or non-adjacent. I outlined various criteria for identifying cohesive links between and among psalms—lexemes, morphological forms of lexemes, phrases, themes, structures, and superscripts. I also presented a methodology for calculating the strength of cohesion between psalms. Assessing the strength of cohesion begins with assessing whether shared elements between psalms are distinctive, or rare, and calculating the level of that cohesion. These levels of the cohesion of individual elements are then added together to determine the levels of cohesion per link criterion (e.g., lexical, thematic). The overall strength of cohesion between two psalms equals the sum of each of these levels of distinctiveness. In this study, I perform these calculations for every possible psalm pair in the collection (i.e., 15 and every other possible psalm, 16 and every other possible psalm, etc.) to see which psalms are most closely related to one another. When two psalms exhibit a stronger cohesion when paired together than when paired with other psalms in the collection, I call this a distinctive relationship and conclude that these psalms are parallel to one another. I also outline the methodology for determining whether Psalms 15–24 form a distinctive collection, which involves whether these psalms form a chiasm, the existence of distinctive repeated elements within, and well-defined boundaries around the collection. Finally, I set forth a process for reading psalms as parallel texts, a process that relies both on recognizing repetition but also on the development created by the dynamic reuse of a literary element.

In the remainder of this study, I present my data in various charts and explore the shape and message of the psalm group. In each of chapters 3–6, I analyze the correspondences and development between one pair of parallel psalms, until all of the psalms in the collection are accounted for. In the final chapter, I draw conclusions about the shape and message of Psalms 15–24.

3

From Approach to Arrival: Psalms 15, 19, and 24

When one reads through Psalms 15-24 from beginning to end, it's almost immediately noticeable that Psalms 15 and 24 share some striking features. These two psalms are the only ones in the entire Psalter that contain the twin questions about who may ascend the mountain of Yhwh, which are then followed by an answer describing the righteous worshiper. Several scholars have observed these similarities.[1] In addition, a few scholars have also observed similarities between one or both of these psalms and Psalm 19 at the center of the collection.[2] In the previous chapter, we confirmed mathematically that Psalm 15 is most closely connected with Psalm 24. It remains to be seen whether Psalm 24 is also most closely connected with Psalm 15 and whether these two share any strong connections with Psalm 19. These connections and the resulting meaning are the focus of this chapter.

COHESION AMONG PSALMS 15, 19, AND 24

We saw in the previous chapter that when paired with every other psalm in the collection, Psalm 15 shares the greatest cohesion with Psalm 24 with regard to shared distinctive lexemes, themes, structures, phrases, and superscripts (see table 3, reproduced below).

Table 3. Psalm 15: Strengths of Cohesion (Scaled)

Psalm Pair	Lexemes	Themes	Structures	Phrases	Morphologies	Superscripts	TOTAL
15 and 16	0.51	0.14	0.00	0.52	0.00	0.00	1.17
15 and 17	0.51	0.04	0.00	0.12	0.19	0.00	0.87
15 and 18	0.33	0.00	0.00	0.00	0.14	0.00	0.47
15 and 19	0.73	0.23	0.67	0.00	0.07	0.21	1.91
15 and 20	0.26	0.06	0.00	0.00	0.32	0.21	0.86
15 and 21	0.40	0.07	0.00	0.15	0.20	0.21	1.03
15 and 22	0.65	0.08	0.00	0.15	0.37	0.21	1.47
15 and 23	0.57	0.30	0.00	0.00	0.19	0.70	1.77
15 and 24	0.91	0.62	0.67	1.00	0.32	0.70	4.22

---

1. See ch. 1, n. 25.
2. Auffret, "Les Psaumes 15 à 24," 437; Sumpter, "Coherence," 188–89.

The overall strength of cohesion between Psalms 15 and 24 is also more than two times higher than when Psalm 15 is paired with any other psalm in the collection. In addition, Psalm 15 is also most closely connected with Psalm 24 in every category except for the morphological link type, which still has a relatively strong cohesion (second only to Psalms 15 and 22). The high strengths of cohesion of distinctive lexemes, themes, and structures between Psalms 15 and 24 are especially notable. What is also interesting is that Psalm 15 shows some strong connections with Psalm 19 as well: these two psalms share the second highest total strength of cohesion, and their strengths of lexical, structure, and thematic cohesion are notable. It now remains to be seen whether Psalms 24 and 19 reciprocate this cohesion with Psalm 15.

Perhaps it is not surprising that Psalm 24 shows a strong cohesion with Psalm 15, as table 4 demonstrates:

Table 4. Psalm 24: Strengths of Cohesion

Psalm Pair	Lexemes	Themes	Structures	Phrases	Morphologies	Superscripts	TOTAL
24 and 15	0.91	0.62	0.67	1.00	0.32	0.70	4.22
24 and 16	0.45	0.11	0.00	0.00	0.07	0.00	0.63
24 and 17	0.44	0.04	0.00	0.00	0.00	0.00	0.48
24 and 18	0.53	0.07	0.00	0.10	0.31	0.00	1.00
24 and 19	0.51	0.35	0.67	0.00	0.18	0.21	1.92
24 and 20	0.61	0.23	0.00	0.00	0.52	0.21	1.57
24 and 21	0.66	0.21	0.00	0.00	0.00	0.21	1.08
24 and 22	0.45	0.21	0.00	0.00	0.29	0.21	1.17
24 and 23	0.28	0.22	0.00	0.00	0.14	0.70	1.35

In the table above, you can see not only that Psalm 24 is connected with Psalm 15 at a total strength of cohesion that is more than twice as high as its connection with any other psalm, but that its connection is highest in every category except shared morphologies, where the connection comes in second to that shared with Psalm 20.

What is perhaps surprising is that, like Psalm 15, Psalm 24 also shows a secondary connection with Psalm 19 in overall strength of cohesion, themes, and structures. A question that comes to mind is whether the secondary connection that these two psalms share with Psalm 19 exists because Psalm 19 is connected to various psalms, or because Psalm 19 is

uniquely connected to these two. Let's take a look at Psalm 19's connections within the psalm group in table 5:

Table 5. Psalm 19: Strengths of Cohesion

Psalm Pair	Lexemes	Themes	Structures	Phrases	Morphologies	Superscripts	TOTAL
19 and 15	0.73	0.23	0.67	0.00	0.07	0.21	1.91
19 and 16	0.54	0.04	0.00	0.21	0.45	0.00	1.24
19 and 17	0.86	0.03	0.00	0.00	0.48	0.00	1.37
19 and 18	0.82	0.13	0.00	0.00	0.77	0.30	2.02
19 and 20	0.54	0.10	0.00	0.00	0.14	1.00	1.78
19 and 21	0.58	0.05	0.00	0.00	0.32	1.00	1.95
19 and 22	0.72	0.03	0.00	0.00	0.34	0.51	1.61
19 and 23	0.28	0.11	0.00	0.24	0.07	0.21	0.92
19 and 24	0.51	0.35	0.67	0.00	0.18	0.21	1.92

Table 5 shows that Psalm 19 has a somewhat balanced cohesion with
the other psalms in the collection, with the total strengths of cohesion ranging from 0.92 to 2.02 (this in contrast to the range we see
with Psalm 24, for example, at 0.63 to 4.22). There are a few relationships to note here. First, overall, Psalm 19 is most closely connected to Psalms 18 and 21. The connection with Psalm 18 shows strong
lexical and morphological cohesion, and that with Psalm 21 shows
strong lexical and superscript cohesion. It is notable that Psalm 19 is
linked through superscripts with both Psalms 20 and 21. These connections indicate that Psalms 18-21 are playing a specific role at the
center of the collection. I'll explore this relationship further in the
final chapter.[3]

Also notable is how Psalm 19 is secondarily connected to Psalms
15 and 24 by overall strength of cohesion—1.91 and 1.92 respectively.
This is only slightly lower than the degree of its strongest connections
with Psalms 18 and 21—2.02 and 1.95 respectively. This suggests that
Psalm 19 does in fact share a unique relationship with Psalms 15 and
24 at the outer edges, in addition to its connections at the center of
the collection. Furthermore, when the strengths of cohesion of the
most significant connective elements—distinctive lexemes, themes,
and structures—are added together, Psalm 19 is most closely connected with Psalms 15 and 24. Because of this, I conclude that Psalm 19

3. See ch. 7, "Movement 2: Psalms 18-21."

plays a dual role. It functions in a unique relationship with Psalms 15 and 24 and is also united in a cluster at the center of the collection in Psalms 18–21.

Because Psalms 15 and 24 are most closely connected to one another and secondarily to Psalm 19, and because Psalm 19 is secondarily connected to Psalms 15 and 24, I conclude that these three psalms have a distinct relationship. Because these three psalms exist on the outer edges and in the center of the collection, I will refer to these as the "frame" of the collection, as depicted in figure 1 below.[4]

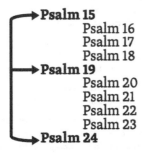

Figure 1. Psalms 15, 19, and 24: The Frame

Because of the connections between Psalms 15, 19, and 24, I view these psalms as parallel texts that can be read together in comparison with one another. Before exploring the connections among these psalms, I will briefly address the shape and message of Psalms 15, 19, and 24 individually, as a foundation for understanding how these psalms relate to one another.

---

4. Language adapted from Sumpter's "The Coherence of Psalms 15–24." While it is possible to refer to Pss 15 and 24 alone as the frame of the collection, their close correspondences with Ps 19 suggest that it too is part of the frame. Auffret anticipated such an idea by observing structural and thematic connections between Pss 19 and 24 (Auffret, "Les Psaumes 15 à 24," 437). He does not, however, include Ps 15 in this analysis. More recently, Sumpter has observed the similarities in tone between Pss 15, 19, and 24. Sumpter argues that these psalms share a theoretical tone, in contrast to the existential or experiential one of the intervening psalms (Sumpter, "Coherence," 188–89).

THE SHAPE OF PSALM 15

Structure 1

Psalm 15[5]

Part			
1	*A psalm of David.* 1a Yhwh, 1b Who may sojourn in your tent? 1c Who may dwell on your holy mountain?		
2		A	2a The walker in blamelessness, 2b and the doer of righteousness, 2c and the speaker of truth in his heart.
		B	3a He has not slandered upon his tongue; 3b He has not done a friend harm; 3c And reproach he has not lifted up against a close one.
	A'		4a The one despised in his eyes is a rejected one; 4b But fearers of Yhwh, he honors.
		B'	4c He swears to [his own] harm, and does not change. 5a His silver he has not given with interest; 5b And a bribe against the innocent he has not taken.
3	5c The doer of these things will not be shaken, ever.		

Following the superscript, Psalm 15 consists of three parts, a question (v. 1), answer (vv. 2–5b), and result or promise (v. 5c). This structure is typically classified as an entrance liturgy.

Part 1 of the psalm begins with an address to Yhwh, and then the double question of who may dwell in Yhwh's presence. Lines 1b and 1c are united by the repeated word *who* (מי), the 3rd person *yiqtol* form of the verb, the ב preposition, and the sound play between *your tent* (אהלך) and *your holy mountain* (הר קדשך). There is progression from 1b to 1c from *sojourning* (גור, involving movement) to *dwelling* (שכן, a stationary and rested position). This indicates that the aim of the psalm is lasting rest in Yhwh's presence.

The second part of the poem, verses 2–5, consists of a description of the perfectly righteous one, in response to the initial question. The description of the righteous worshiper alternates in an ABA'B' forward symmetry, describing what this one does (vv. 2, 4a–b) and does not do (vv. 3, 4c–5b). Unit A (v. 2) consists of a tight bundle of three lines, each beginning with a participle. Righteousness permeates the whole person,

---

5. All translations mine unless otherwise indicated. I've performed a more formal translation to reveal repeated words and sentence structures.

involving both the external (*doer of righteousness* v. 2b) and internal (*speaker of truth in his heart*, v. 2c). There is a movement within this bundle from general to specific acts of righteousness, from *walking* to *doing* to *speaking*.

Speaking (v. 2c) provides the transition to unit B (v. 3), which focuses on what the righteous one does *not* do, especially in regard to slanderous speech. These three lines are joined together as a bundle in a few key ways: they each contain the negation לֹא followed by a *Qal* third-person masculine singular form. This is both structural similarity and sound play. Lines 3a and 3c are further joined through the sound play of *upon his tongue* (עַל לְשֹׁנוֹ) and *against a close one* (עַל קְרֹבוֹ), and lines 3b and 3c are joined through the sound play of *he has not done* (לֹא עָשָׂה) and *he has not lifted up* (לֹא נָשָׂא). There is a progression among these lines from any person to a neighbor to a close one, with the result that this one does not withhold righteous speech or deeds from anyone.

But this does not mean the righteous one is unwise when it comes to the character of others. Unit A' (vv. 4a-b) returns to the positive description of the righteous one, this time focusing on the right nature of their perception of others. In other words, they are wise; they see others rightly. This unit consists only of two lines, joined by inverted parallelism.

The final lines of the answer, unit B' (vv. 4c-5b) again focus on what the righteous one does not do, using the negation-verb form familiar from unit B. The repeated word *harm* (רָעָה/רֵעַ) also connects units B and B', but there is an intensification from unit B. Not only does this one not do *harm* to others (v. 3b), he takes the hit—he swears to his own *harm* and does not change [his commitment/oath] (v. 4c). This idea is continued in lines 5a and 5b.

Part 3 of this psalm consists of the result or promise, including just one brief line: *The doer of these things with not be shaken, ever* (v. 5c). *These things* seems to refer to the entirety of the description of the righteous worshiper (vv. 2-5) by harkening back to the participle form of unit A and the negation-verb form of units B and B'. It also recalls the opening question in part 1 by the *yiqtol* form of the verb.

Overall, Psalm 15 is a highly structured poem that describes the perfectly righteous one who may access Yhwh's presence. The description of the righteous worshiper may leave readers with the question, "How could one attain such perfection?" Later in this chapter, we will see how the reuse of distinctive elements in Psalm 19—especially the theme of *speech* and lexemes related to *righteousness*—provides an answer to this question.

THE SHAPE OF PSALM 19

Structure 2

Psalm 19

Part			
			¹ᵃ *Of the director. A psalm of David.*
1	**A**	1	²ᵃ The skies are recounting the glory of God; ²ᵇ And the work of his hand, the sky-dome is declaring.
		2	³ᵃ Day to day, it pours out speech; ³ᵇ And night to night, it declares knowledge.
		3	⁴ᵃ There is no speech; ⁴ᵇ And there are no words; ⁴ᶜ Without sound is their voice.
	B	1	⁵ᵃ Into the whole earth, it has gone out, their line, ⁵ᵇ and to the extremity of the world, their words.
		2	⁵ᶜ For the sun, he has set a tent in them; ⁶ᵃ It is like a bridegroom going out of his chamber; ⁶ᵇ And it exults like a mighty one to run the path.
		3	⁷ᵃ From the extremity of the skies is its going out, ⁷ᵇ and its circuit, to the extremity. ⁷ᶜ And there is nothing hidden from its heat.
2	**A'**	1	⁸ᵃ The law of Yhwh is blameless, reviving the soul; ⁸ᵇ The testimonies of Yhwh are to be trusted, making wise the simple.
		2	⁹ᵃ The instructions of Yhwh are right, gladdening the heart; ⁹ᵇ The commandment of Yhwh is pure, enlightening the eyes.
		3	¹⁰ᵃ The fear of Yhwh is clean, standing forever; ¹⁰ᵇ The judgments of Yhwh are truth; they are righteous together.
		+1	¹¹ᵃ —More desirable than gold, and much refined gold; ¹¹ᵇ —And sweeter than honey, and flowing honey from the comb.
3	**B'**	1	¹²ᵃ Also, your servant is admonished by them; ¹²ᵇ to keep them the result is great.
		2	¹³ᵃ Errors who can discern? ¹³ᵇ From hidden ones, acquit me. ¹⁴ᵃ Also, from insolent ones, keep your servant; ¹⁴ᵇ May they not rule over me! ¹⁴ᶜ Then I shall be blameless; ¹⁴ᵈ And I will be innocent of great transgression.
		3	¹⁵ᵃ May it be according to your favor, the speech of my mouth, ¹⁵ᵇ and the meditation of my heart, before your presence, ¹⁵ᶜ Yhwh, my rock and my redeemer.

After its title, Psalm 19 can be structured into three parts: the first focuses on the communication of creation (vv. 2–7); the second focuses on the communication and character of Torah (vv. 8–11); and the third is about the servant's alignment with creation and Torah (vv. 12–15).[6] The lexeme

---

6. It is also possible to structure this poem into two parts that focus on creation and Torah respectively (vv. 2–7 and 8–15)—in other words, parts 2 and 3 as I've identified

speak (אמר) creates an inclusio that governs the entire poem, occurring at the beginning of part 1 (vv. 3a, 4a) and in the final unit of part 3 (v. 15a). This lexeme introduces a main theme of the poem: speech. The word *hide* (סתר) also creates a frame around the middle part of the psalm (vv. 7c, 13b).

Part 1 consists of two units of three subunits each (vv. 2, 3, 4; and vv. 5a-b, 5c-6, 7); part 2 consists of three parallel units with an added element to form a "three-plus-one" structure[7] (vv. 8, 9, 10, 11); and part 3 consists of three units (vv. 12, 13-14, 15). Another structure is overlaid on top of these three parts, and that is an ABA'B' forward symmetry, which pairs verses 2-4 and 8-11 (as A and A'), and verses 5-7 and 12-15 (as B and B'). It is quite common in biblical texts that two or more structures exist to highlight different correspondences. A simple example of this would be a set of two parallel lines, *aa'bb'*, where the first and last lines also function as a frame, *abb'a'*. In the case of Psalm 19, part 1 can be broken up into two units (A and B respectively). Part 2 corresponds to A' and part 3, B'. This ABA'B' structure highlights some of the correspondences between the words of creation (A) and the words of Torah (A') and then the activity of the sun (B) and the activity of Yhwh (B'). I will give attention to both of these structures as I explore the shape of this psalm.

Part 1 of the psalm contains an inclusio in the word *skies* (שמים; vv. 2a, 7a). As I mentioned before, this part consists of two units, which can be called A and B (vv. 2-4; 5-7). Units A and B begin with *skies* (שמים) and *land* (ארץ) respectively (vv. 2a, 5a), to emphasize that creation's witness is comprehensive. These two units are joined together at their seam with the sound play of קולם and קום, *voice* and *line* (vv. 4c-5a). Unit A exhibits internal coherence especially in its emphasis on *speech* and in Genesis 1 creation imagery (*skies* [שמים], *sky-dome* [רקיע], *work* [עשׂה], *day* [יום], *night* [לילה], and *speaking* [אמר]). The idea seems to be that God's ordering and sustaining work continues and is evident in the daily functioning of the created world. Imagery from the Eden narrative of Genesis 2-3 is also employed here in the words *God* (אל), *knowledge* (דעת), *sound/breath* (נשׁמת/נשׁמע), and *voice* (קול). The effect is that just as with the tree in the garden, God continues to offer his presence and knowledge consistently to humans.

---

them on the Torah and the servant would be combined into one. I find a three-part structure to be more compelling because of the strong shift in subject and imagery between each of the three parts from creation to Torah to the servant. In addition, three-part structures are very common within the Hebrew Bible and in this psalm-group in particular. Other close structural correspondences between Pss 15, 19, and 24 also make it more likely that Ps 19 has a three-part structure. (Refer to figure 4.)
7. I elaborate on this structure shortly.

Within unit B (vv. 5-7), there is an internal repetition of the words *go out* (יצא) and *extremity* (קצה) to describe how active, persistent, and effective the communication of the skies is. It is precisely because these two words are used in both verses 5 and 7 that I think verse 5 has stronger cohesion with vv. 6-7 than with what comes prior. The primary image used to make the point of the active communication of the skies is the consistent, determined, and pervasive path of the sun: it goes from extremity to extremity, and nothing is hidden from its heat. We will see how the persistent and pervasive activity of the sun is analogous to Yhwh's activity when we get to its parallel text, B' (i.e., part 3).

Now we arrive at the second part of the psalm (vv. 8-11), which is made up of three tightly bound sets of synonymous or echoing lines[8] and an additional element (v. 11). This can be referred to as a "three-plus-one" structure, which takes its cues from the creation story on the first lines of the Genesis scroll (Gen 1:1-2:3).[9] There, we can see a grouping of the six days of creation in three pairs, corresponding to one another as *abca'b'c'*, and then followed by an additional or "plus-one" element (+1), the seventh day, which stands out structurally and for significance.

Day 1 (*a*)	Day 4 (*a'*)
Day 2 (*b*)	Day 5 (*b'*)
Day 3 (*c*)	Day 6 (*c'*)

Day 7 (+1)

Figure 2. The Beginning of the Three-Plus-One Structure

This structure sets a pattern for many like it that follow, including what seems to be happening in verses 8-11 in Psalm 19. The three sets

---

8. I use the word "echoing" rather than "synonymous" throughout to describe parallelism that is characterized by repetition of the same or similar grammatical structures or semantic content in consecutive or nearly-consecutive lines. The choice of "echoing" emphasizes that the second line does not merely repeat the first, but goes beyond it in some way.

9. The "three-plus-one" or "three ... and for four" structure is a common literary device in the Hebrew Scriptures. For extensive treatments see Y. Zakovitch, *"For Three ... and for Four": The Pattern of the Numerical Sequence Three-Four in the Bible*, 2 vols. (Jerusalem: Makor, 1979 [Hebrew]); S. M. Paul, *A Commentary on the Book of Amos*, Hermeneia (Minneapolis: Fortress, 1991), 27-30; S. Talmon, "The Topped Triad in the Hebrew Bible and the Ascending Numerical Pattern," in *Literary Motifs and Patterns in the Hebrew Bible: Collected Studies* (University Park: Penn State University Press, 2021), 77-124; and S. J. Golani, "Three Oppressors and Four Saviors—The Three-Four Pattern and the List of Saviors in 1 Sam 12,9-11," *ZAW* 127, no. 2 (2015): 294-303.

of parallel lines (vv. 8-10) together describe Yhwh's Torah, or instruction, but are imbued with creation imagery (including the three-plus-one structure). They are closely bound in form and content with each line beginning with a description of a positive quality of Yhwh's Torah, consisting in form of a construct noun, Yhwh's name, followed by a verb describing how it affects the worshiper—*reviving the soul, making wise the simple*, etc. These six lines are closely bound not only in form but also in a six-fold repetition of the name *Yhwh* and by the lexical frame of the word *true* (אמן; vv. 8b, 10b). The additional element, verse 11, describes the immeasurable worth of the Torah of Yhwh in two echoing lines. Together, verses 8-11 are united by imagery that recalls the tree of knowledge: It is said that the Torah can make one *wise* (חכם) and that the *commandment* (מצוה) enlightens the *eyes* (עינים; vv. 8b, 9b). These three words harken back to the fruit of the tree in Genesis 3:16-17, which was pleasing to the *eyes* (עינים) and desirable for gaining *wisdom* (using a synonym, שכל) and which God had issued a *command* (צוה) about. The idea is that Yhwh's Torah here is like that desirable tree. Verse 11 homes in on the desirability of Torah, using the same lexical root used to describe the *desirability* of the tree of the knowledge in Genesis 2:9: חמד.[10] This imagery of the tree closely binds verses 8-11.

Part 2 (also referred to as A') echoes its counterpart, unit A, in its use of words reminiscent of the tree of knowledge. In addition, both texts are all about speech. Reading A and A' together creates an analogy between the communication of the skies and the communication of Yhwh's Torah. Both texts emphasize communication going out, though a major difference is that the speech of the skies is *without words* (v. 3) whereas the Torah is not so. There is a consistency and order present in both: the skies pour out speech every day and night (v. 2), and the Torah is described with words like *trustworthy, truth,* and *standing forever* (vv. 8b, 9). The comparison with the tree of knowledge depicts both creation and Yhwh's Torah as sources of wisdom for humans, freely offered and accessible.[11]

---

10. חמד is used as a Niphal verb only in four places in the Hebrew Bible: Gen 2:9 and 3:6 to describe the tree, our text (Ps 19:11) to describe Torah, and the treasure of the wise (חכם) in Prov 21:20.

11. S. L. Klouda describes Ps 19 as an interplay between creation and Torah that undermines the view of wisdom in the ancient Near East as discovered in nature only. For Israel, creation provides wisdom, but this is not distinct from the fear of Yhwh or obedience to the covenant. Comprehension of the person of Yhwh comes both through "seeing" and "hearing," themes that Klouda points out are used in ways that

The emphasis on Torah's benefit and worth to the worshiper in part 2 provides a smooth transition to part 3 of the psalm, which further describes the benefit to the worshiper. What is ambiguous at this point is *what* it is that the worshiper benefits from. The text reads, *your servant is admonished by them* (בהם; v. 12a). At first glance, בהם seems to refer to Torah in the previous unit. But it is curious that the only other time בהם is used in the psalm is in reference to the skies, where Yhwh has set a tent for the sun: *he has set a tent in them* (בהם; v. 5c). It will become clearer throughout this section that the psalmist seeks to align himself with both creation and Torah, suggesting that the ambiguity at this point is intentional.

Part 3 uniquely focuses on the servant as the subject. *Servant* (עבד) is first used in the psalm in the first unit of this part (v. 12a). This first unit is linked to the previous unit by its use of the lexeme *much/great* (רב; vv. 11a, 12b), and focuses on the benefit to the human as both *admonishment* and *reward*. *Great* (רב) and *your servant* (עבדך) occur again in the next unit (vv. 13–14), binding these first two units of part 3 closely together.

The second unit of part 3 (vv. 13–14) is framed by the word *acquit/innocent* (נקה; vv. 13b, 14d). This unit can be further divided into three subunits: a question about who can discern errors (v. 13a), which is answered in the next three lines in a prayer that God would discern, acquit, and keep the servant from sin (vv. 13b–14b). The result is given in the following lines: the blamelessness and innocence of the servant (vv. 14c–d). In verses 13–14 we can detect a comparison between Yhwh and the sun of vv. 5–7: The psalmist asks Yhwh to make him innocent of *hidden* (סתר) errors, recalling how the sun reaches to every corner of the earth: *nothing is hidden from its heat*. Just as the sun goes to the extremities, Yhwh too is the one who can discern all errors. Lest this sound too terrifying, the psalmist is asking God to do so in order to *acquit* him, not allow sin to *rule over him* (words that recall the story of Cain in Gen 4:7), and that this process of discerning and acquitting results in *blamelessness* (תמם) and *innocence* (נקה; v. 14).

The positive benefit for the servant continues in the final unit of part 3 (v. 15), where the prayer of the psalmist is that his own words and heart would be pleasing to Yhwh. He uses words that recall both parts 1 and 2, praying that his *speech* would be pleasing (recalling the *speech* of

---

defy reader expectations in Ps 19. Klouda, "The Dialectical Interplay of Seeing and Hearing in Psalm 19 and Its Connection to Wisdom," *BBR* 10, no. 2 (2000): 184–85, 192.

creation, v. 3a) and that his *heart* would be pleasing (recalling how the Torah affects the *heart*, v. 9a). In other words, the psalmist is praying that the quality of his words and character would align with all creation and with Yhwh's Torah. These two ideas—creation and Torah—were already mapped onto one another by the ABA'B' structure, which paired the speech of creation and the words of Torah. Now we see the psalmist pray for alignment with both. His desire for *blamelessness* (תמם; v. 14c) also creates a close relationship between the character of the servant and the character of Torah, which was also called *blameless* (v. 8a).

REUSE AND DEVELOPMENT IN PSALM 19

Recall from the previous chapter that parallelism is defined not by static repetition, but by dynamic movement from the first element to the second, such as heightening, intensification, and specification. My goal in reading the psalms as parallel texts is to discern how each latter psalm develops and modifies elements of the former, giving careful attention to how the distinctive linking elements are dynamically reused (these are the elements that occur at a higher rate in two psalms than in the collection). In what follows, I draw conclusions about the meaning of parallel psalms, based on the distinctive elements they share, beginning with Psalms 19 and 15. Of course, there are many more correspondences between these psalms, but I focus here on only the distinctive connections, since these are the ones that have the highest probability of being intentional.

Psalms 15 and 19 share distinctive lexemes (*tent* [אהל], *blameless* [תמם], *do/work* [עשׂה], *innocent* [נקה], *trust* [אמן], *fear* [ירא], *heart* [לבב], *eye* [עין], *speak* [דבר], *righteous* [צדק], *sing* [זמר], *glory* [כבד], *David* [דוד], *Yhwh* [יהוה]); morphological forms of lexemes (*psalm* [מזמור]); the themes of *speech, righteousness,* and *Yhwh's presence;* and a corresponding macro-structure.[12] You'll recall that Psalm 15 is all about defining the righteous one who may access Yhwh's presence. But how could one attain such righteousness that they could dwell in the presence of Yhwh himself? Psalm 19's reuse of the themes and lexemes related to *righteousness* and *speech* from Psalm 15 help to clarify.

Speech is a major theme only in Psalms 15, 19, and 24 across the collection, classifying it as a distinctive theme. The way this theme is

---

12. I will explore macro-structural correspondences among Pss 15, 19, and 24 together in the following section on Ps 24.

developed from Psalm 15 to 19 provides a clue as to how one becomes
the righteous worshiper of Psalm 15. In Psalm 15, the speech is that of
the righteous one. In Psalm 19, speech is that of creation and Torah. The
development from the *righteous one's speech* in Psalm 15 to *creation's* and
Torah's speech in Psalm 19 implies that in order to become the righteous
worshiper of Psalm 15, one has resources in Yhwh's created order and
in his Torah (Ps 19). Psalms 15 and 19 also share significant lexemes related to righteousness. Psalm 15 uses the lexemes *blameless* (תמם) and
truth (אמת) to describe the righteous worshiper,[13] but Psalm 19 reuses
them to describe Torah. The point again is that Torah is one of the resources a person has for attaining the righteousness required for access to Yhwh's presence.

But what if a person is *not* righteous? Have they lost the privilege of
communing with God? Psalm 19 reuses the distinctive lexemes *innocent*
(נקה) and *blameless* (תמם) in the psalmist's prayer to shed light on how
one who is not innocent may become so (vv. 12–13). The psalmist prays
for Yhwh to search out his hidden sins and *acquit* him (from נקה), so
that this (along with keeping from sin) will make him *blameless* and
innocent. In other words, one may become the *blameless one* of Psalm
15 through the forgiveness of sin by Yhwh (Ps 19). This is a significant
development, since Psalm 15 depicts only a perfectly righteous human
as able to enter Yhwh's presence.

The lexeme *tent* (אהל) is another distinctive link between Psalms 15
and 19 that further elaborates on how relentless Yhwh is in his forgiveness and deliverance of his people. In Psalm 19, it is the sun that dwells
in a *tent* (v. 5c); *tent* is a distinctive lexeme used elsewhere in the psalm
group only of God's dwelling (Ps 15:1), implying an analogy between God
and the sun. Internal coherence within Psalm 19 further supports this
conclusion. Within Psalm 19, Yhwh's activity is united with that of the
sun thematically and through the lexeme *hidden* (סתר): Just as the sun's
activity extends from extremity to extremity, and *nothing is hidden from
its heat* (vv. 5c–7c), Yhwh actively discerns all parts of a human heart,
including the *hidden* errors (vv. 12–13). This analogy depicts Yhwh as relentless to deliver his people from sin to present them as blameless and
innocent before him (v. 14).

---

13. *Truth* is also a significant morphological link, occurring only two places in the
whole collection as אמת.

So, Psalm 15 opens the collection with the desire to dwell in Yhwh's presence and describes the righteousness required to ascend to his dwelling place. It concludes with a promise of finality and stability. When we reach Psalm 19, we again find themes of Torah righteousness along with the new theme of creation. Psalm 19 reveals that to dwell in Yhwh's presence as the righteous one of Psalm 15, one has resources in the created order, in God's instruction, and in his relentless forgiveness. Psalm 24 furthers the storyline of entering Yhwh's presence in significant ways; it is to that psalm that we now turn.

THE SHAPE OF PSALM 24

Structure 3

Psalm 24

Part		
		Of David. A psalm.
1		1a The land is Yhwh's, and its fullness, 1b the world, and the dwellers in it. 2a For he, on the seas, founded it; 2b And upon the rivers, he established it.
2	1	3a Who may ascend the mountain of Yhwh? 3b And who may stand in his holy place?
	2	4a [The one] of clean hands and a pure heart, 4b who does not lift up to treachery his soul, 4c and does not swear deceitfully.
	3	5a [This one] bears blessing from Yhwh, 5b and justice from the God of his salvation.
	+1	6a This is the generation of the searchers of him, 6b the seekers of your face, 6c Jacob. *Selah.*
3	A	7a Lift up, O gates, your heads; 7b Be lifted up, O doors of old; 7c And may he come in, the glorious king.
	B	8a Who is this glorious king? 8b Yhwh strong and mighty; 8c Yhwh mighty in battle.
	A'	9a Lift up O gates, your heads; 9b And lift up, O doors of old; 9c And may he come in, the glorious king.
	B'	*a* 10a Who is he, this glorious king? *b* 10b Yhwh of hosts— *a'* 10c He is the glorious king. *Selah.*

Psalm 24 consists of three parts (vv. 1-2, 3-6, 7-10), each with distinct themes and structures. Part 1 focuses on creation, part 2 on the righteous one who may enter Yhwh's presence, and part 3 on Yhwh's entry to his holy temple.

The entire poem is framed by the name Yhwh (יהוה; vv. 1a, 10b) and the pronoun he (הו; vv. 2a, 10a, c), a link that closely unites parts 1 and 3. In both uses, he refers to Yhwh. In the first occurrence, he created, and in the second, he is the glorious king. There are also a variety of repetitions between parts 2 and 3. First, there is a double use of the pronoun who (מי) in each part, the first wondering "who may ascend?" and the second asking, "who is the king?" This reveals an emphasis on identity and entry in the poem—both of the people and the glorious king. Communion between the two is the aim. Parts 1 and 3 are also united by repetition of the word this (זה)—first used of the people (v. 6a), then of Yhwh (vv. 8a, 10a)—again, identity and communion are the aim. Finally, the word lift up (נשא) is used of the people (vv. 4b, 5a), and then also of the gates (vv. 7a, 9a), uniting humanity and creation in their acts of welcoming the king Yhwh.

Part 1 of the psalm consists of two sets of echoing parallel lines and centers on Yhwh's sustaining power and authority over creation (vv. 1–2). These verses employ creation imagery from Genesis 1–2 through the use of land (ארץ), seas (ים), and rivers (נהר). The reference to the land and seas in particular recalls day three of creation, when God separates the seas from the land so that life can thrive there (cf. Gen 1:9–13).

Third-day creation imagery provides a transition to the next part of the psalm, which begins with the line who may ascend the mountain (הר) of Yhwh? (Ps 24:3). The land appearing out of the sea on day three creates an image of that land being a mountain, rising up out of the waters and creating a sacred space for life above the chaotic seas.[14] The question who may ascend the mountain of Yhwh? is matched by a parallel line, who may stand in his holy place? This double question introduces the question-answer-result structure about who may enter Yhwh's presence, as we saw in Psalm 15 (vv. 3–5). The answer consists of a brief description of the righteous one, who is holistically righteous (hands [כף], heart [לבב], soul [נפש], speech, as שבע, v. 4). Two positive characteristics—clean hands and pure heart—are followed by two negations: he does not lift up to treachery his soul, and does not swear deceitfully. This structure is briefer than in Psalm 15 but is very similar to the alternation between positive

---

14. That the dry land can be envisioned as a hill is also evidenced in the rivers that flow out of Eden, presumably downward (Gen 2:10–14) and how this creation imagery is later repurposed in the flood narrative with the waters receding from the land (Gen 8:3).

characterizations and negations in the entrance liturgy we find there
(vv. 2–5). Just as in Psalm 15, this description is followed by the promise, or result, and this one will bear or bring blessing and justice from
Yhwh—a description that depicts the role of the priest or king extending blessing and justice to the community.[15] The question-answer-result
structure forms a tightly woven and distinct three-unit part. And yet
there is an additional set of lines to follow. Just as we saw in Psalm 19:11,
this seems to be an additional element (v. 6) that together with verses
3–5 forms another "three-plus-one" structure.

The significance of the additional element ought not be underesti-
mated: In verse 6, it is surprising to find that the identity of this "righteous one" is not the priest or king, but the entire community of those
who seek Yhwh's *face* or *presence* (פנה). This verse is set off slightly from
the previous in its shift to the plural. It also coheres with the question
of verse 3 by its emphasis on the presence of Yhwh. Here we see that
the righteous ones are defined as a whole community, characterized
through echoing parallelism as the *searchers for him, the seekers of his face,*
and *Jacob,* which in this psalm group is another designation for God's
people Israel (Pss 20:1; 22:23).[16] Part 2 concludes with *Selah* and transitions to a new subject, Yhwh's arrival.

The third and final part of the psalm follows an ABA'B' forward symmetry (vv. 7, 8, 9, and 10, respectively), which culminates in Yhwh's arrival. Units A and A' (vv. 7, 9) are verbatim repetitions, save one form of a
word (the change from the *Niphal* to the *Qal* form of נשׂא). Verses 8 and 10
begin with the exact same question and have a slightly different answer.
Verse 10 is the climax of the psalm, with the identity of Yhwh as *Yhwh
of hosts* being framed by an *aba'* structure by the question and answer
about the glorious king:

---

15. See, e.g., Num 6:23–27; 2 Sam 8:15; 1 Kgs 10:9; 1 Chr 18:14. The lexeme נשׂא could
mean "carry" or "bring," as it has often been translated in this verse. However, when
נשׂא is followed by the preposition מן, it most likely means "to receive." נשׂא מן is used
thirty-two other times in the Hebrew Bible (with up to two words in between). In
sixteen cases, it means "to physically carry or bring something from one place/per-
son to another." Other uses include "to lift," "to take for oneself," or "to uproot," none
of which make more sense in context.
16. I find it most compelling to read "Jacob" in echoing parallel structure with
"searchers" and "seekers" rather than to refer to God (i.e., "God of Jacob," where "God
of" was omitted). Hebrew parallelism often uses ellipses, and it is a striking feature
of this very psalm (e.g., vv. 1–2). Moreover, Jacob is throughout Book I of the Psalter
to refer to the people rather than to God (Pss 14:7; 20:1; 22:23).

> Who is he, this glorious king?
>   Yhwh of hosts—
> He is the glorious king. *Selah.*

In comparing the different parts of the psalm, we can see that identity and community are central concerns in the poem, with the questions of who may enter (v. 3) and who is the king (vv. 8, 10) being answered: the righteous community (vv. 4–6) and Yhwh, the mighty and glorious king (vv. 8, 10). We can also see the analogy created between creation (vv. 1–2), the mountain (v. 3), and the temple (vv. 7, 9) as sacred spaces. The Genesis 1–2 imagery in the first verses of the poem recalls when Yhwh dwelt among humanity, and we see this portrayed again in the final verse of the poem when he arrives among the community. It is fitting that when he arrives, he is called *Yhwh of hosts*, a designation that echoes his authority over all heavenly beings in his creation of the inhabitants of the cosmos in the creation account.[17]

Reading Psalm 24 as the culmination of the collection raises various questions. For example, what is it that brings about Yhwh's arrival at the end of the collection? How does the storyline develop from the first "entrance liturgy" (Ps 15) to the last (Ps 24)? And what is the significance of the communal identity in this final psalm? I will begin to address questions such as these by examining how Psalm 24 reuses distinctive elements from both Psalms 15 and 19.

REUSE AND DEVELOPMENT IN PSALM 24

Psalms 15 and 24 share a high number of distinctive elements. Both psalms contain the twin questions about who may ascend Yhwh's holy mountain (Pss 15:1; 24:3).[18] The lexemes *holy* (קדש) and *mountain* (הר) are distinctive, and when paired with the interrogative *who* (מי), they become distinctive phrases matched only with one another. These opening phrases frame the entire collection with the distinctive theme of entering Yhwh's presence. These psalms share additional distinctive lexemes (*innocent* [נקה], *swear* [שבע], *lift up* [נשא], *glory* [כבד], *ever* [עולם], *righteousness/justice* [צדק], *sing* [זמר], *David* [דוד], and *Yhwh* [יהוה]), morphological forms of lexemes (*holy* [קדש], *mountain* [הר], *psalm* [מזמור],

---

17. Gen 1:14–19; 2:1; cf. Deut 4:19; 17:3.
18. Various scholars have observed that Pss 15 and 24 uniquely correspond to one another as the only two entrance liturgies in the Psalter. See ch. 1, n. 25.

and *he lifts up* [נשׂא]), phrases (*he does not lift up* [לא־נשׂא]), themes (*righteousness, speech, finality/forever,* and *entering Yhwh's dwelling*), and a corresponding macro-structure. These significant elements create a noticeably strong cohesion between Psalms 15 and 24.

Psalms 15 and 24 characterize the collection's aim as accessing Yhwh's presence and describe the requisite character of righteousness. The shared distinctive lexemes and themes of the two psalms center on an inward and outward character of righteousness.[19] Thematically, the result of this righteous character is security and blessing—namely, access to Yhwh's presence (Pss 15:5; 24:5). The tie between Psalms 15 and 24 is further strengthened by the inverted superscripts—*A psalm of David* (מזמור לדוד) in Psalm 15:1 and *Of David, a psalm* (לדוד מזמור) in Psalm 24:1—which further suggests that these two psalms function as bookends that mirror one another. As two psalms closely bound, Psalms 15 and 24 function as an inclusio framing the collection and thereby set the trajectory of the storyline as accessing Yhwh's presence through righteous character.

Psalms 19 and 24 also share distinctive lexemes (*world* [תבל], *clean/innocent* [נקה], *glory* [כבד], *mighty* [גבר], *result/Jacob* [עקב], *pure* [בר], *heart* [לבב], *earth* [ארץ], *soul* [נפשׁ], *Yhwh* [יהוה], *righteousness* [צדק], *sing* [זמר], and *David* [דוד]); morphological forms of lexemes (*psalm* [מזמור] and *mighty one* [גבור]); the themes of *Yhwh's presence, righteousness, speech, Yhwh as a mighty warrior,* and *creation imagery*; and a corresponding macro-structure. These connections create a strong cohesion among these three parallel psalms so that together, they function to frame the collection with a particular emphasis.

You'll recall that parallelism does not involve simply static repetition but dynamic reuse of shared elements. In order to explore how the author has crafted Psalm 24 to develop storyline, it will be helpful to examine the overarching structures of these three psalms together.

Structure: A Developing Narrative

Psalms 15, 19, and 24 share structural correspondences that are distinctive within the collection. As I mentioned previously, Psalms 15 and 24

---

19. The distinctive lexemes related to righteousness that are shared by Pss 15 and 24 include the following: נשׁא, שׁבע as a *Qal* perfect third-person masculine singular noun, קדשׁ, נקה as a masculine singular construct noun, צדק, and לבב. See appendix 2 for further data.

can be classified as entrance liturgies with regard to modern form-critical categories by their question-answer-result structure—the only two of their kind in the entire Psalter. Psalm 19 is often designated by form-critical categories as a wisdom or Torah psalm.[20] Although wisdom psalms do not have a defined structure, the structural correspondences between Psalms 15, 19, and 24 are striking.[21]

To see the correspondences that Psalms 15 and 24 share with Psalm 19, we must begin by comparing Psalms 15 and 24:

Psalm 15	Psalm 24
	Creation (vv. 1-2)
Righteousness (vv. 1-5)	**Righteousness** (vv. 3-6)
1. Question	1. Question
2. Answer (ABA'B')	2. Answer
3. Result	3. Result
	+1 Community
	Arrival (ABA'B'; vv. 7-10)

Figure 3. Structural Correspondences between Psalms 15 and 24

The question-answer-result structure makes up the entirety of Psalm 15. The central concern is on the righteousness required to enter Yhwh's presence. In Psalm 24, the question-answer-result structure contains the added element of the community, creating a "three-plus-one" structure in that section. It is also preceded by creation imagery and followed by the arrival of Yhwh.

---

20. My methodology recognizes as links those genres that also have corresponding structures. To my mind, "wisdom" or "Torah" are better suited for and analyzed within the "theme" category rather than "genre/structure." See "Structural Links" in ch. 2.

21. This is especially true when compared to the other psalms in the 15–24 psalm group, which are structurally very different from 15, 19, and 24. They include songs of trust (Pss 16 and 23), laments (Pss 17 and 22), thanksgiving (Ps 18), and community petition and praise (Pss 20–21).

When we compare these two psalms with Psalm 19, we can see how the latter bridges their content:

Psalm 15	Psalm 19	Psalm 24
	Creation (AB) (vv. 2-7)	**Creation** (vv. 1-2)
Human Righteousness (vv. 1-5)	**Torah Righteousness** (A') (vv. 8-11)	**Human Righteousness** (vv. 3-6)
1. Question	*3+1 structure*	1. Question
2. Answer		2. Answer
3. Result	**Human Righteousness** (B') (vv. 12-15)	3. Result
		+1 Community
		Yhwh's Arrival (ABA'B') (vv. 7-10)

Figure 4. Structural Correspondences between Psalms 15, 19, and 24

Notice in figure 4 above how the structures of these three psalms parallel one another, but how each psalm carries the narrative strand of the collection forward with additional sections. Psalm 19, like both 15 and 24, focuses on righteousness and the result of such righteousness for the human (in Psalm 19 the result is the section called "human righteousness"). The structure of Psalm 19 bridges the content of Psalms 15 and 24 through its similarities with Psalm 24: both Psalms 19 and 24 begin with an entire part about creation, each contains an ABA'B' structure, and each contains a "three-plus-one" structure. It is worth noting that "human righteousness" in both Psalms 15 and 24 is fleshed out by the relationship between the Torah and the human in Psalm 19. The addition of "Yhwh's arrival" in Psalm 24 is unparalleled in Psalms 15 and 19.

THE RIGHTEOUS ONE MAY ENTER

At the close of the collection, Psalm 24 echoes and develops the content of Psalms 15 and 19. Like Psalm 15, Psalm 24 returns to the question of who may ascend. Since the question has been thoroughly explored in

Psalms 15 and 19, Psalm 24 provides only a brief summary (v. 4), reusing distinctive lexemes to describe the righteous one: *clean* (בר), *heart* (לבב), *lift up* (נשא), and *swear* (שבע). Like Psalm 15, both the *speech* and *action* of the worshiper are the focus. The lexeme *lift up* (נשא) occurs as part of a distinctive phrase in both psalms to describe how this one does *not lift up* (לא־נשא) his soul to treachery (Pss 15:3; 24:4).

Psalm 19 is related to Psalms 15 and 24 primarily through distinctive vocabulary and themes that emphasize righteous character, as well as by its focus on creation. Psalm 19 uses many of the distinctive lexemes of Psalms 15 and 24 to create a tie between it and the righteous character expounded in Psalms 15 and 24. Recall how those distinctive words and themes that describe the human character in Psalms 15 and 24 describe Yhwh's Torah in Psalm 19. Whereas Psalms 15 and 24 characterize the collection's aim as accessing Yhwh's presence through righteousness, Psalm 19 shows that Yhwh and his Torah are able to transform the worshiper to enable dwelling in his presence (Ps 19:8–15, especially vv. 13–14).

The way the distinctive lexemes *innocent/clean* (נקה) and *blameless* (תמם) are reused in Psalm 24 exemplifies the development in the theme of righteousness from Psalm 15 to 19 to 24. Recall how Psalm 15 had defined the righteous one as *blameless* (תמם; v. 2a). Psalm 19 developed the narrative strand by showing that Yhwh, through offering his *blameless* (תמם) Torah (v. 8a) and *acquitting* (נקה) of sin (v. 13b), would make the worshiper *blameless* (תמם) and *innocent* (נקה; v. 14c–d). Now in Psalm 24, this worshiper stands with *innocent/clean* (נקה) hands before the gate of Yhwh (v. 4a). Taken together, these three psalms portray a Torah-obedient figure who will dwell in Yhwh's presence.

While Psalm 19 may have originated as two separate psalms, a creation hymn (vv. 1–7) and a Torah psalm (vv. 8–15),[22] in its present form, it can best be classified broadly as a wisdom psalm. In fact, creation imagery and veneration of Torah are two characteristics of wisdom psalms.[23]

---

22. See, for example, Gunkel, *Introduction to the Psalms*, 2, 13; Gerstenberger, *Psalms: Part 1*, 100–103; Kraus, *Psalms*, 268–69; G. von Rad, *Wisdom in Israel* (London: Bloomsbury T&T Clark, 1972); G. Fohrer and E. Sellin, *Introduction to the Old Testament* (Nashville: Abingdon, 1968), 28.

23. McCann, "The Book of Psalms," 751; Clifford, *Psalms 1–72*, 26; Wilson, *Psalms*, vol. 1, NIVAC (Grand Rapids: Zondervan, 2002), 72–74; Craigie, *Psalms 1–50*, 180; C. G. Bartholomew and R. P. O'Dowd, *Old Testament Wisdom Literature: A Theological Introduction* (Downers Grove, IL: InterVarsity Press, 2011), 32–36; Ross, *Commentary on the Psalms*, 143–44. In his study on words that are characteristic of the wisdom genre, R. B. Y. Scott has demonstrated that Psalm 19 uses as much wisdom vocabulary

As a wisdom psalm with a didactic tone, the function of Psalm 19 is to provide instruction. Because Psalm 19 is closely connected with Psalms 15 and 24, which define the ultimate aim as accessing Yhwh's presence, Psalm 19 provides instruction regarding that goal.

Creation Imagery and Spatial Expansion

The theme of creation in Psalms 19 and 24 is a significant development from Psalm 15. This imagery seems to play two important roles in the development of the storyline of the collection. The first, which I alluded to earlier, is that the cohesion between each part of Psalm 19 indicates that when one aligns oneself with Yhwh's Torah, one is aligning oneself with the created order (vv. 2-7, 8-11, 12-15). When humans live rightly, they are fulfilling their original design as Yhwh's partners, as described in the creation narratives of Genesis 1-2.

The creation imagery of Psalms 19 and 24 plays another significant role in the storyline of Psalms 15-24. It develops the narrative strand of the collection through spatial expansion. Within the frame of the collection, there is spatial expansion from Psalm 15 to 19 to 24: The setting of Psalm 15 is the holy mountain in Jerusalem (v. 1). In Psalm 19, the revelation of Yhwh goes out into all creation (vv. 2-7), and in Psalm 24, all of creation is under his dominion (vv. 1-2). The shift in structure from Psalm 15 to Psalms 19 and 24 also indicates spatial expansion. Psalm 15 follows a question-answer-result structure in its entirety, focusing on Torah-like character. Psalm 19 expands this focus to include a description of Torah as influential of that character (vv. 12-15 and 8-11 respectively) and also adds a large section containing creation imagery, unparalleled in the psalms that precede it (vv. 2-7). Like 15 and 19, Psalm 24 also contains the theme of Torah, even following the same format of question-answer-result that Psalm 15 does. But like Psalm 19, Psalm 24 also adds the element of creation, using the same lexemes, *earth* (ארץ) and *world* (תבל), as Psalm 19. This added theme of creation in Psalms 19 and 24 extends the locality of Psalm 15, the holy mountain, to the whole world. Psalm 24 maps creation imagery (vv. 1-2) and temple imagery (vv. 7-10) onto one another as the setting of Yhwh's arrival,

---

as Pss 37 and 49, which are traditionally recognized as wisdom psalms. Scott identifies 77 words that are characteristic of the wisdom genre. Ps 119 uses 28; Pss 15, 32, and 94 each use 13; Pss 25 and 55 use 12; and Pss 19, 37, and 49 use 11. Scott, *The Way of Wisdom in the Old Testament* (New York: MacMillan, 1971), 121.

resulting in a picture of all creation as Yhwh's temple, or dwelling place, calling back to the original purpose of creation in Genesis 1.[24]

EXPANSION FROM THE INDIVIDUAL TO THE COMMUNITY

Psalms 15, 19, and the first part of 24 (through v. 5) use singular verbs and focus on the individual. In Psalms 15 and 24, this one is the Torah-obedient one, and in Psalm 19, this one is called the servant (vv. 12a, 14a). Is this one the anointed king, or any righteous individual? It is interesting that all three psalms are titled *of David* (לדוד), indicating some association with the anointed king. Additionally, this one is one who may approach Yhwh's holy dwelling, indicating a priestly or kingly role (Pss 15 and 24), and in Psalm 24:5, this one is described as one who brings blessing and justice from Yhwh his God, depicting a ruler who extends Yhwh's benefits to all as his earthly representative.[25] And yet the description of righteousness throughout all three psalms is not specific to a ruler or king. This is one who acts and speaks with love and justice toward those around him and who loves Yhwh's instruction. Furthermore, there is a clear inclusion of the entire community in the description of the righteous at the end of the collection in Psalm 24:6: *This is the generation of the searchers of him, the seekers of your face.*

What is clear is that there is a progression in the frame from a focus on the individual in Psalms 15 and 19 to inclusion of the community in Psalm 24. Verse 6 functions much like a hinge in the psalm, extending the Torah-obedient character of verses 3–5 to include the community and identifying the subjects of Yhwh's kingdom, who are present at his arrival in verses 7–10. Such an expansion within the psalm itself invites us to reread verses 3–5 as a description of anyone who seeks Yhwh, rather than a description of a specific someone. This theme of *community* in Psalm 24 is a development within the structures of Psalms 15, 19, and 24 (refer to figure 4 above). It is fitting that the significant lexical root of Jacob, עקב, is the same root used in Psalm 19:12b to speak of the *result* or *reward* of keeping Torah.[26] The reuse implies that it is now this Torah-

---

24. See Walton's work on the cosmic temple in *The Lost World of Genesis 1: Ancient Cosmology and the Origins Debate* (Downers Grove, IL: InterVarsity Press, 2009).
25. See n. 15.
26. It's likely that this root also recalls the use of *Jacob* in Ps 22, where all of Israel and the nations gather to feast with Yhwh after the human king is delivered from death by the glorious king Yhwh.

keeping community, called *Jacob*, who are rewarded by the arrival of king Yhwh (Ps 24:7–10).

In their diachronic study on Psalms 15–24, F.-L. Hossfeld and E. Zenger contend that Psalm 24:6 indicates that the community is defined as "David." They argue that Psalms 15 through 24 as a whole reflect the process of constituting a collective identity. This, they argue, is visible in the question that opens Psalm 15, is reiterated in Psalm 24:3, and is answered in Psalm 24:6 in a way that includes the community and defines that community by the Davidic identity. They conclude that it is this community's identification with David that will enable the entrance of the majestic king (24:7–10).[27]

I agree that the entire community is in some way associated with David and included at the arrival of Yhwh. And yet there still does seem to be an individual in view. To my mind, these psalms primarily portray the king, David (because of the superscript, approaching of God's dwelling, and role in spreading blessing and justice; Ps 24:6), and yet David's identity, experiences, and wisdom resonate with and are assimilated by the people as they read the psalms together in community. So, the individual worshiper is invited to identify with David, and yet there is also a specific and differentiated role that the Davidic king seems to play. This specific role is hinted at in these psalms only in Psalm 24:5, where he is the one who brings God's blessing and justice, but this more nuanced role will be clarified as we examine the intervening psalms. At this point, it is sufficient to note that there is an expansion from the individual to the community from Psalm 15 to 24 and that both the people and the human king are in view.

The Arrival of Yhwh as King

A final and significant progression within the frame is the identification of Yhwh as king and his arrival among his people. Whereas Psalm 15 focuses on righteousness and Psalm 19 on creation and righteousness, Psalm 24 goes beyond both of these psalms by introducing an entirely new section proclaiming Yhwh's arrival at the temple in the presence of the community (vv. 7–10). This is a new development; the theme of Yhwh's kingship is not found in Psalms 15 or 19 at all. However, in Psalm 24, Yhwh's identity as king is revealed with full force.

---

27. Hossfeld and Zenger, "Wer darf hinaufziehn zum Berg JHWHs?," 168.

The arrival of Yhwh as *the glorious king* (מלך הכבוד) in Psalm 24:7-10 is the climax of the plot in the collection and also reuses distinctive lexemes introduced earlier, especially from Psalm 19. In this culminating section of Psalm 24, Yhwh is called the king of *glory* (כבד) and *mighty* (גבור) multiple times. *Glory* is an echo from Psalm 19,[28] where it is used in tandem with creation imagery to describe the constant activity of Yhwh. The description of Yhwh as the *mighty one* is the same word used in Psalm 19 of the sun. Just as the sun's influence reaches to the ends of the earth in Psalm 19, so God's kingdom does in Psalm 24 (Pss 19:6-7; 24:1-2).[29] Daily and consistently, the sun is as active as a *mighty man* running, just as God is *mighty* (Ps 19:3, 6-7; 24:8, 10). The sun is said to dwell in a *tent* (אהל), just as God does in Psalm 15 (Pss 15:1; 19:5c). Like the sun, God is glorious. Like the sun, God is daily and consistently active. The analogy portrays God as one who actively delivers his people from sin to present them as blameless and innocent before him. This glorious king is also described in Psalm 24 by the words *strong* (עזוז), *mighty in battle* (גבור מלחמה), and *Yhwh of hosts* (יהוה צבאות). The parallels between Psalms 19 and 24 suggest that God is consistently active as a warrior and that his activity as such is tied to his arrival as king on earth. To understand the significance of Yhwh as the warrior king in the plotline of this collection, we will have to explore connections between the intervening psalms in later chapters (see especially chapter 7).

SUMMARY

Beyond the observation of the entrance liturgy form, Psalms 15 and 24 correspond closely in terms of their many distinctive elements. Second only to their correspondence with one another, Psalms 15 and 24 correspond closely with Psalm 19 at the center of the collection. Taken together, these three psalms frame the collection with the goal of entering Yhwh's presence and dwelling with him forever. These psalms reveal that only the righteous may do so, but that God is an active participant in delivering his people and making them blameless before him. The

---

28. Brown notes this connection, as well, in Brown, "Psalms as Collections," 98–99.
29. The imagery of the sun in Ps 19 is used for God elsewhere. God is described as a "sun" in Ps 84:12, as a joyful bridegroom (see Ps 19:6) in Isa 62:5, and as a mighty warrior in Ps 24:8. See J. R. Wagner, "From the Heavens to the Heart: The Dynamics of Psalm 19 as Prayer," *CBQ* 61, no. 2 (1999): 252; Brown, "'Here Comes the Sun!,'" 273–75.

story ends with this delivering, cosmic king arriving on his holy mountain and dwelling with all those who seek his presence, forever.

While the frame of the psalm group, Psalms 15, 19, and 24, establishes the goal of accessing Yhwh's presence, the collection does not end exactly where it began. Rather, there is a significant progression in Psalm 24 in Yhwh's arrival as king. His identity is revealed as the glorious warrior king, and the plot culminates in his arrival. There are also significant expansions, including an expansion to the community—from the righteous individual in Psalms 15 and 19 to the inclusion of the entire community of the righteous in Psalm 24—and spatial expansion—from Jerusalem in Psalm 15 to all of creation in Psalms 19 and 24. Yhwh dwelling as king in his place (the whole earth) and with his people is a depiction of the consummation of his kingdom on earth. The community of those who seek Yhwh's face (Ps 24:6) stand before the glorious warrior king as he enters the gates. The collection closes by recalling the promise in Psalm 15 that the righteous worshiper would dwell in Yhwh's presence *eternally* (עוֹלָם; Ps 15:1, 5c): the *eternal* doors are lifted up (Ps 24:7, 9) so that Yhwh and all those who seek him would dwell together.

Certainly, Yhwh's arrival is a fitting conclusion to a collection that has as its goal dwelling in his presence. Now that we can see where the storyline is headed, we are left wondering about other key components of the plot. What in the plot, if anything, initiates this progression toward the kingdom? Will the other pairs of parallel psalms also exhibit similar developments toward the kingdom and communal and spatial expansion? In light of the idealistic vision of the kingdom and of the righteousness required to access his presence, what wisdom, if any, does this psalm group offer in the present realities of human suffering? The next pair of parallel psalms, 16 and 23, will offer some reflections on the latter two questions.

4

Awaiting the Arrival with Confidence: Psalms 16 and 23

In the previous chapter, we explored how Psalms 15 and 24 frame the collection with the ultimate goal of accessing Yhwh's presence, and how Yhwh calls his human partners to right relationships with himself and others. We saw in Psalm 19 how humans have resources in the ordered world, Yhwh's instruction, and Yhwh's own transformational and delivering work on their behalf to make them blameless. The collection ends with Yhwh's arrival as king among his righteous community, where he will dwell forever. As our investigation moves forward to Psalm 16, I will seek to quantify with which psalms it is most closely connected and how these connections move the storyline forward.

COHESION BETWEEN PSALMS 16 AND 23

When paired with every other psalm in the collection, Psalm 16 exhibits the most cohesion with Psalm 23 in terms of its distinctive elements (i.e., those elements used at higher rates in the psalm pair than in the collection). The total strength of cohesion between Psalms 16 and 23 can be represented by the number 2.56, in the column titled "Total" on table 6 below. The high cohesion is especially due to the close thematic and structural correspondences between the two psalms. In fact, Psalms 16 and 23 have the strongest thematic and structural cohesion of any two possible psalm pairs in the collection, represented by the number 1.00 in those columns. The two psalms do not have a strong lexical or morphological correspondence, and yet of the nine lexemes they do share, every single one of them is distinctive.

Table 6. Psalm 16's Strengths of Cohesion
with Every Other Psalm in the Group

Psalm Pair	Lexemes	Themes	Structures	Phrases	Morphologies	Superscripts	TOTAL
16 and 15	0.51	0.14	0.00	0.52	0.00	0.00	1.17
16 and 17	0.83	0.09	0.00	0.11	0.81	0.00	1.83
16 and 18	0.55	0.04	0.00	0.00	0.07	0.00	0.66
16 and 19	0.54	0.04	0.00	0.21	0.45	0.00	1.24
16 and 20	0.72	0.12	0.00	0.00	0.11	0.00	0.95
16 and 21	0.98	0.23	0.00	0.12	0.36	0.00	1.69
16 and 22	0.75	0.06	0.00	0.00	0.15	0.00	0.96
16 and 23	0.49	1.00	1.00	0.00	0.07	0.00	2.56
16 and 24	0.45	0.11	0.00	0.00	0.07	0.00	0.63

Other significant connections in the table include Psalm 16's cohesion with its neighboring psalm, Psalm 17. This, we will see, occurs often throughout collections. Even when two distant psalms are most closely linked, neighboring psalms tend to be linked especially by shared lexemes, morphologies, and phrases (e.g., the repeated phrase *not shaken* [בל/לא מוט] that binds Psalms 15, 16, and 17). This seems to be an editorial strategy used to arrange neighboring psalms into a story that can be read linearly.[1]

It now remains to discover whether Psalm 23 reciprocates the most coherence with Psalm 16 when compared with other psalms in the collection. Table 7 displays the distinctive correspondences between Psalm 23 and every other psalm:

Table 7. Psalm 23: Strengths of Cohesion

Psalm Pair	Lexemes	Themes	Structures	Phrases	Morphologies	Superscripts	TOTAL
23 and 15	0.57	0.30	0.00	0.00	0.19	0.70	1.77
23 and 16	0.49	1.00	1.00	0.00	0.07	0.00	2.56
23 and 17	0.32	0.21	0.00	0.00	0.12	0.00	0.65
23 and 18	0.24	0.10	0.00	0.00	0.27	0.00	0.60
23 and 19	0.28	0.11	0.00	0.24	0.07	0.21	0.92
23 and 20	0.51	0.14	0.00	0.00	0.13	0.21	1.00
23 and 21	0.57	0.41	0.00	0.29	0.35	0.21	1.83
23 and 22	0.44	0.18	0.00	0.00	0.21	0.21	1.05
23 and 24	0.28	0.22	0.00	0.00	0.14	0.70	1.35

---

1. In chapter 7, I perform such a reading.

Psalm 23's strongest cohesion is with Psalm 16, especially due to its thematic, structural, and lexical correspondences. It is also notable that Psalm 23 shares high correspondences with Psalm 21, which I will briefly explore later in this chapter.

Because Psalm 23 reciprocates the close relationship with Psalm 16, I consider these two psalms to form a distinctive psalm pair. So far, the structure of this collection can be depicted as follows in figure 5, where the bold connecting lines represent the frame, and the thin lines, other parallel psalms:

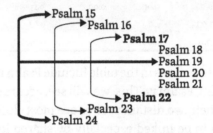

Figure 6. The Frame, Psalms of Confidence, and Laments

THE SHAPE OF PSALM 16

After the title, Psalm 16 has three parts, each expanding in length (vv. 1, 2–4, 5–11). Part 1 contains only one verse and consists of the initial call for Yhwh's preservation and a declaration of trust, indicated by the word *refuge* (חסה). The remainder of the psalm expresses confidence in the fulfillment of what the psalmist here asks Yhwh to do. As such, this psalm can be classified as a psalm of trust, or confidence.

Part 2 of the psalm consists of verses 2–4. That verse 2 begins a new section is indicated by the speech marker *I say* (אמרת) and the repetition of the designated recipient of the speech, Yhwh (cf. v. 1a, where the psalmist has already addressed God). Part 2 is made up of two units (vv. 2, 3–4), united by the repetition of the negation *not* (בל; vv. 2c, 4b, 4c) and governed by the theme introduced in verse 2: the psalmist worships Yhwh alone, and there is no good apart from him. Verse 2c could also be translated as *my good is not over you*; in other words, even the benefits and blessings the psalmist has do not compare to Yhwh. Either way, verse 2 affirms the supreme value of Yhwh to the psalmist. Verses 3–4 elaborate on this theme: In verse 3, the psalmist expresses his delight in

Structure 4

Psalm 16

Part		
		A miktam of David.
1		1a Watch out for me, God, 1b for I take refuge in you.
2		2a I say to Yhwh, 2b "My Lord you are; 2c My good does not exist apart from you." 3a Concerning the holy ones who are in the land, 3b they are the majestic ones of all my delight (in them). 4a Their suffering will multiply, [if] another they go after; 4b I will not pour out their drink offerings of blood; 4c And I will not bear their names on my lips.
3	A	5a Yhwh, the portion of my share and my cup; 5b You grasp my lot. 6a Lines have fallen for me in pleasant places; 6b Indeed, [my] inheritance is beautiful for me.
	B	7a I will bless Yhwh who counsels me; 7b Indeed, at night my gut admonishes me. 8a I set Yhwh before me always; 8b Because [he is at] my right hand, I will not be shaken.
	A'	9a Therefore, my heart is glad; 9b And my whole self rejoices; 9c Indeed, my body will dwell securely. 10a For you will not abandon my being to *Sheol*; 10b You will not give your loyal one to see the pit. 11a You make known to me the way of life; 11b —an abundance of gladness in your presence; 11c —pleasures in your right hand, forever.

those who follow Yhwh, or *the holy ones* (קדושים). Though perhaps not intuitive in many individualistic societies today, it seems that association with Yhwh naturally involves association with his righteous community. This also seems to be an intentional link to the previous psalm, where right judgment and association with others is a descriptor of the righteous one (Ps 15:4).

The final verse of part 2, verse 4, continues to describe the psalmist's association with others, this time those who do not follow Yhwh (just as Ps 15:4 does). This verse expands further on the theme that good does not exist apart from Yhwh by describing how *others* (אחר)—(presumably gods—bring *multiplied suffering*.[2] *Suffering/difficulty* as עצבת is a word that only occurs in the Psalms (4x) and in Job (1x), but its root, עצב, is a common

---

2. I've translated מהרו as "they go after" to capture the meaning of the *Qal* form of this verb as "to acquire by paying a purchase-price," especially in marriage (BDB §5083). With different vowel markings it is also possible that this verb could be a *Piel* perfect 3cp and mean "to hasten after." The Hebrew consonants appear with this

one. Its use alongside *multiply* (רבה) here echoes the failure narrative of Genesis 3, where Yhwh says to the woman that he will *greatly multiply* (רבה; 2x) her *difficulty* (עצבון) in conceiving, just as the man will work the ground with *difficulty* (עצבון; Gen 3:16–17). Going after others, then, is both meant to be seen as the common, human predicament, and also patterned after the template for failure. The second two lines of verse 4 begin with *not* (בל), are tightly bound in syntactic structure, and are related to the first by consequence: it is because of the suffering associated with other gods that the psalmist commits to not make offerings to them or *bear their names* (from נשא and שם), a phrase that echoes the covenant relationship between Yhwh and his people in the ten commandments (Ex 20:7). In echoing the ten commandments, it is clear that the psalmist is committed to uniting with Yhwh alone in covenant relationship.

Verse 5 begins a new section, indicated by another address to Yhwh, using his name and the pronoun *you* (אתה), just as in the beginning of the previous part (cf. v. 2a). Verses 5–11 constitute the third and final part of the psalm, which is made up of three units (vv. 5–6, 7–8, and 9–11). Part 3 is unified by repeated words and themes associated with delight, security, Yhwh's guidance, provision, satisfaction, and joy. Repeated words and shifts in tense give part 3 an ABA' structure: the word *pleasant/pleasures* (נעים) occurs in units A and A' (vv. 5–6, 9–11); and there is a shift from addressing Yhwh in the second person in units A and A' to speaking of him in the third person in unit B in the center (vv. 7–8). Units A and A' speak of the physical provision of security for the psalmist—namely, inheritance and life—while unit B at the center emphasizes the intimate nature of Yhwh's counsel and guidance, even at night. Additional structurally significant repetitions among these three units include the word *right hand* (ימין), which concludes both units B and A', and *glad* (שמח), which forms an inclusio around unit A' (vv. 9a, 11b).

Working through part 3 one unit at a time, we begin with verses 5–6. These verses consist of two sets of echoing lines expressing the psalmist's confidence that Yhwh will watch over him, as requested in the opening line of the psalm. Verses 5 and 6 continue the theme introduced in verse 2, that good exists in Yhwh alone, by providing a contrast to the inheritance of suffering that those who follow other gods experience. Here, the psalmist experiences a delightful inheritance from Yhwh, which is a

---

meaning in 2 Chr 24:5; Ps 106:13; Isa 49:17, and this is how the LXX understands this word. The translation "they go after" also captures this potential meaning.

major theme in this unit and is expressed with the vocabulary of *portion* (מנת), *share* (חלק), *cup* (כוס), *lot* (גורל), *boundary lines* (חבל), and *inheritance* (נחל). There is also sound play with first-person suffixes throughout, which connects these two verses closely.

Like verses 5–6, verses 7–8 continue to describe the security experienced by the psalmist, but now in the form of guidance and comfort. Verse 7 is a tight unit of inverted parallelism where *counsel* and *admonish* are paired, as are *Yhwh* and *the gut*, literally *kidneys* (כליה). The psalmist is connected to Yhwh in his innermost thoughts and being even in the darkest moments, signified by the word *night* (לילה). Even then, Yhwh's instruction is never ceasing. The reference to *night* recalls how the righteous one of Psalm 1 (who is also the king of Ps 2) meditates on Torah day and night. The psalmist there declares his faithfulness and dependence on Yhwh at all times, as prescribed for the righteous king of Israel. The theme of perpetuity continues into the next line (v. 8b), with the result of security: because Yhwh is ever present (*at the psalmist's right hand*) the psalmist will not be shaken—language that recalls the promise to the righteous one who seeks Yhwh in Psalm 15:5c.

The final unit of the psalm expresses themes of satisfaction, life, and joy. Verse 9 emphasizes through three lines of echoing and inverted parallelism that the *heart*, *self*, and *body* rejoice and are secure. Verse 10 provides the reason for this in two more echoing lines: Yhwh will not abandon the psalmist to death. Instead, as verse 11 expounds through three additional echoing lines, Yhwh brings *life*, *gladness*, and *pleasures* in connection with himself, *forever*.

THE SHAPE OF PSALM 23

Following its Davidic superscript, the structure of Psalm 23 can be understood as three parts (vv. 1–3, v. 4, and vv. 5–6), with the outer two each consisting of two units (vv. 1, 2–3 and vv. 5, 6) and the middle consisting of one (v. 4). The outer parts contain mirrored images of the provision of a shepherd and the provision of a feast, respectively, and there is a shift in setting from a field (part 1) to Yhwh's house (part 3). The central part stands out in form in its two uses of כי (as *even* and *for*) that surround a climactic inner line: *I will not fear harm* (לא אירא רע). As such, Psalm 23 can be understood as an ABA' structure with unit B also displaying a smaller level aba' chiastic structure, where the central subunit expresses the utmost confidence of the psalmist: *I will not fear harm*. The entire psalm is framed by an inclusio of the only two uses of the divine name in the entire psalm (vv. 1a, 6b).

Structure 5

Psalm 23

Part				
				A psalm of David.
				^{1a} Yhwh is my shepherd; ^{1b} I do not lack.
1	A			^{2a} In pastures of vegetation, he causes me to lie down; ^{2b} Over waters of rest, he leads me; ^{3a} My life, he restores; ^{3b} He guides me on paths of righteousness for his name's sake.
2	B	a		^{4a} Even if I walk in a valley of death-shadow,
			b	^{4b} I will not fear harm,
		a'		^{4c} for you are with me; ^{4d} Your rod and your staff, they comfort me.
3	A'			^{5a} You arrange before me a table in the presence of my enemies; ^{5b} You anoint with oil my head; ^{5c} My cup overflows.
				^{6a} Surely goodness and loyal love will pursue me all the days of my life; ^{6b} And I will return to the house of Yhwh for length of days.

Part 1 of the psalm finds cohesion in its imagery of Yhwh as the psalmist's shepherd. The first set of lines introduces this image (v. 1a) and its consequence, that the psalmist lacks nothing (v. 1b). From the first verse to the second and third, there is movement from this general statement to specific examples of Yhwh's provision. Verse 2 contains a tight bundle of echoing lines in which *pastures of vegetation* and *waters of rest* are paired, as well as *he makes me lie down* and *he leads me*, the latter two of which involve the sound play of the *yiqtol* form with the first-person suffix (ירביחני and ינהלני).

Imagery from the creation narrative and flood (de/re-creation) narratives are used in verse 2 to depict a life of humanity united with Yhwh. The word for *vegetation* (דשא) occurs only sixteen times in the Hebrew Bible and is initially used to describe God's creative work on the third day of creation in bringing forth plants yielding seeds and fruit trees, so that life could thrive (Gen 1:11–12). Surrounded by vegetation, the psalmist is able to thrive and rest, or *lie down* (רבץ) in repose.[3] The echo of Genesis 1 depicts the psalmist as dwelling with God as intended in his original creation. The next line, *over waters of rest, he leads me*, also activates the rest intended in the creation narrative which concludes on the seventh day with a never-ending rest of God and humanity together.[4] The refer-

---

3. BDB §8880.
4. The seventh day seems to have an enduring quality in that it does not end with the formula "and then there was evening, and then there was morning." The root for *rest*

ence to deliverance through *waters of rest* simultaneously activates the narrative pattern of God's rescue of his chosen one through the suffering (often expressed as waters), and out the other side to life.[5] It is also significant that the word *rest* as a noun in Psalm 23, מנוחה, recalls the promised land of inheritance from Numbers 10:33. There, we see that Yhwh goes before the people in the desert, guiding them toward a place to *rest* (מנוחה). The point is that the ultimate aim of humanity dwelling with Yhwh, as depicted in creation, re-creation after the flood, and settling in the land, is fulfilled in the image of Yhwh as shepherd.

The next verse begins with *my life, he restores*, further activating the theme of deliverance, from which we can learn that the intended rest of the previous verse is not exclusive of suffering (v. 3a). The two words *life* (נפש) and *restores/returns* (שוב) also recall Psalm 19, which uses the same words to describe Yhwh's instruction as the restorer of life. In other words, the psalmist's well-being is connected to meditation on Yhwh's Torah (cf. Pss 1; 19:7–9). The following parallel line (v. 3b) specifies that this restoration involves walking in Yhwh's way of righteousness, which is precisely the role of God's ideal human partner set out in Genesis 1.

The second and central part is indicated by a switch from speaking of Yhwh in the third person to speaking directly to him. It is also demarcated by two כי-clauses that encompass a central statement, which itself is tightly woven through sound play: *I will not fear* (לא אירא רע; v. 4b). The reason is provided in the next set of parallel lines, bound through sound play of the Hebrew for *with me* (עמדי) and *they comfort me* (ינחמני): Yhwh is with the psalmist and his rod and staff comfort the psalmist. While staff (משענת) can be a generic term for a walking stick helpful for supporting someone, rod (שבט) is a word with kingly overtones,[6] suggesting that Yhwh's authority as king and his allegiance with the psalmist is the ultimate comfort. The word for *comfort* (the *Piel* form of נחם) recalls once again the story of Noah, who was intended to bring *comfort* (נחם) from suffering, carrying forward that theme of the chosen one delivered

---

in Ps 23:2 is נוה. While the seventh-day *rest* is the word שבת in Gen 2:2–3, the root נוח is used in Gen 2:15 when the first human is *rested* in the garden in Gen 2:15.

5. There seems to be a recurring pattern in the story of Scripture beginning with Noah in Gen 6–9: God's chosen one goes through suffering, often portrayed as waters, and comes out the other side to new life, often making intercession or sacrifice.

6. The first time *rod* (שבט) is used in the Hebrew Bible it is in parallel construction with *ruler's staff* (חקק) and refers to a future king (Gen 49:10). The second time שבט is used in this way is in Num 24:17, another significant poem that refers to a future ruler. See also the uses of שבט in 2 Sam 7:7; Pss 2:9; 45:7; Isa 14:5; Ezek 19:11, 14; Amos 1:5, 8; Zech 10:11.

from great suffering (Gen 5:29). The placement of this psalm of comfort on the heels of the suffering of Psalm 22 furthers this idea as well.[7]

Verses 5 and 6 constitute the third and final part of the psalm, made up of two units that correspond to their verse numbers. This new part is indicated by the change in imagery to a feast, by the change in setting to the house of Yhwh, and by a variety of new themes focusing on satisfaction, life, and joy.

Feast imagery, second-person verbs, and first-person pronouns unite verse 5 in meaning and sound (especially ראשי//כוסי). The word *table* (שלחן) is used in a generic way throughout Scripture to speak of abundant feasting,[8] often at the table of a king or leader,[9] or of God's table in his holy place.[10] The phrase *to arrange a table* (ערך שלחן) is used in the Psalms only in one other place, Psalm 78:19, where the phrase refers to Yhwh's acts of provision of food and water. It is likely that abundant provision is what the psalmist has in mind in Psalm 23.

What is interesting is that this feast seems to have both priestly and kingly overtones for the human. Pouring *oil* (שמן) on the *head* (ראש) is a sign of anointing a priest or king throughout Scripture.[11] Dwelling in the house of Yhwh is mentioned in the last line of the psalm, potentially associating the *table* with the table of God's house where the priest would minister. The table also has kingly overtones: Psalm 23 is associated with king David in its superscript. The table is arranged before the psalmist's enemies, and it is there that his *head* is anointed with *oil*, which recalls Psalm 2:9, where the enemy kings are humbled before the anointed one. In Psalm 2, it is this anointed king who is installed on Yhwh's holy mountain, an image echoed in Psalm 15:1 and again here in Psalm 23:6, where the psalmist will return to the house of Yhwh to dwell forever. Another notable facet of the use of *table* throughout Scripture is that "to eat at the same table" means to be associated with one another in some way.[12] It is curious that Psalm 23:6 mentions that this *table* is arranged before

---

7. See "Movement 3: Psalms 22–24" in ch. 7.

8. See Pss 69:22; 78:19; 128:3; Prov 9:2.

9. This is the way the word is used in the story of David (1 Sam 20:29, 34; 2 Sam 9:7–13; 19:29; 1 Kgs 2:7) and Solomon (1 Kgs 5:7; 7:48; 2 Chr 9:4), of future kings (Dan 11:27); and of influential leaders (1 Kgs 18:19; Isa 21:5; Neh 5:17).

10. This is the way the word is used throughout Exodus in the instructions for the tabernacle (Exod 25–40). See also Lev 24:6; Num 3:31; 4:7; Ezek 40; 44:16; Mal 1:7, 12; 2 Chr 4:8, 19; 13:11; 29:18.

11. See Exod 29:7; Lev 8:12; 14:18, 29; 21:10; 1 Sam 10:1; 2 Kgs 9:3, 6; Ps 133:2)

12. Eating at the same table seems to involve association with and sometimes receiving the benefits of the one to whom the table belongs. See 2 Sam 9:7–13; 19:29; 1 Kgs 2:7; 5:7; 18:19; Neh 5:17; Ps 128:3; Prov 9:2; Isa 65:11; Ezek 23:41.

the psalmist's enemies. Reading this verse on its own, one might imagine that the table is simply a sign of honor in the face of enemies. But reading *table* in light of its uses elsewhere, it seems there is a stronger association now between the enemies and the psalmist—perhaps the obedience of enemy kings to the true king, as described in Psalm 2.

Verse 6 concludes part 3 with a summary statement of the goodness that will follow the psalmist, where we see that Yhwh's goodness and love will *pursue* (רדף) the psalmist (v. 6a). *Pursue* is used throughout Scripture to describe the activity of enemies.[13] In context of this poem, rather than the enemies of verse 5 pursuing the psalmist, it is Yhwh's love. This description creates an inclusio with the first verse: Yhwh both goes before the psalmist as a shepherd and goes behind him in loyal and loving pursuit. Verse 6 is made up of two lines; the latter halves of each closely parallel one another in the phrases *all the days of my life* (כל ימי חיי) and *for length of days* (לארך ימים). This correspondence invites us to also map the first halves of the lines onto one another, so that the phrase *goodness and loyal love* (טוב וחסד) is parallel to *Yhwh's house* (בית יהוה). In other words, *goodness and loyal love* are not distinct from Yhwh as something the psalmist has earned, but are found in his presence. *Loyal love* (חסד) itself is a relational term, often used to describe Yhwh's covenant with the human king.[14]

REUSE AND DEVELOPMENT IN PSALM 23

Psalms 16 and 23 are the only two psalms in the collection that can be classified thematically as songs of trust or confidence.[15] While "song of trust" is a genre classification based on theme rather than structure, we will also see how these two psalms have highly distinctive and corresponding structures. Their high cohesion is also indicated by their many shared distinctive themes: *righteousness; trust in Yhwh; safety/protection/comfort/refuge; Yhwh guides/leads; forever/finality; provision/inheritance; and life/delight/goodness.* As mentioned above, these two psalms have the strongest thematic cohesion of any two possible psalm pairs in the collection. These shared themes are supported by shared lexemes. In fact, all of the lexemes shared by these two psalms are distinctive: *cup* (כוס), *good* (טוב), *name* (שם), *being* (נפש),

---

13. BDB §8930.

14. See 2 Sam 7:15; 22:51; 1 Kgs 3:6; 2 Chr 6:42; Pss 18:51; 21:8; Isa 16:5; 55:3.

15. See, e.g., Gunkel, *Introduction to the Psalms* (, 190. Although Ps 16 does begin with an initial plea, which can indicate a lament, the plea is very general and there is no sense of specific distress in the rest of the psalm, so that it is still best understood as a psalm of trust.

Table 8. Structural Parallels between Psalms 16 and 23

Topic	Psalm 16
General statement of trust, based on Yhwh's identity	¹ᵃ Watch out for me, God, ¹ᵇ for I take refuge in you. ²ᵃ I say to Yhwh, ²ᵇ "My Lord you are;
Statement of all good found in Yhwh, using a negation	²ᶜ My good does not exist apart from you." *(vv. 3–4 expand)*
Description of provision using land imagery	⁵ᵃ Yhwh, the portion of my share and my cup; ⁵ᵇ You grasp my lot. ⁶ᵃ Lines have fallen for me in pleasant places; ⁶ᵇ Indeed, [my] inheritance is beautiful for me.
Yhwh as the psalmist's guide	⁷ᵃ I will bless Yhwh who counsels me; ⁷ᵇ Indeed, at night my gut admonishes me.
Security within distress because of Yhwh's presence	⁸ᵃ I set Yhwh before me always; ⁸ᵇ Because he is at my right hand, I will not be shaken. ⁹ᵃ Therefore, my heart is glad; ⁹ᵇ And my whole self rejoices; ⁹ᶜ Indeed, my body will dwell securely. ¹⁰ᵃ For you will not abandon my being to *Sheol*; ¹⁰ᵇ You will not give your loyal one to see the pit.
Everlasting joy and satisfaction in Yhwh's presence	¹¹ᵃ You make known to me the way of life; ¹¹ᵇ —an abundance of gladness in your presence; ¹¹ᶜ —pleasures in your right hand, forever.

live (חיה), David (דוד), face (פנה), all (כל), Yhwh (יהוה). Of these lexemes, *being* is also morphologically distinctive, occurring as נפשי. The result of all of these correspondences is that Psalms 16 and 23 are joined together as psalms expressing trust in Yhwh and emphasizing security in his presence even when trouble, described as death in both psalms, is very near.[16]

STRUCTURAL CORRESPONDENCES

Psalms 16 and 23 have distinctive and corresponding structures when it comes to the topics addressed, as displayed in table 8.

The corresponding structures of Psalms 16 and 23 are based on the order of the topics addressed. You'll notice that this is different from the structures I previously identified for each psalm.[17] That multiple structures overlay one another is quite common in biblical texts. Various structures and linking devices are used for different purposes. I would argue that these psalms each have a three-part structure (which I identified

---

16. לא תעזב נפשי לשאול (Ps 16:10); גם כי אלך בגיא צלמות (Ps 23:4).
17. See "The Shape of Psalm 16" and "The Shape of Psalm 23" earlier in this chapter.

Table 8. Structural Parallels between Psalms 16 and 23

Topic	Psalm 23
General statement of trust, based on Yhwh's identity	[1a] Yhwh is my shepherd;
Statement of all good found in Yhwh, using a negation	[1b] I do not lack.
Description of provision using land imagery	[2a] In pastures of vegetation, he causes me to lie down; [2b] Over waters of rest, he leads me;
Yhwh as the psalmist's guide	[3a] My life, he restores; [3b] He guides me on paths of righteousness for his name's sake.
Security within distress because of Yhwh's presence	[4a] Even if I walk in a valley of death-shadow, [4b] I will not fear harm, [4c] for you are with me; [4d] Your rod and your staff, they comfort me.
Everlasting joy and satisfaction in Yhwh's presence	[5a] You arrange before me a table in the presence of my enemies; [5b] You anoint with oil my head; [5c] My cup overflows. [6a] Surely goodness and loyal love will pursue me all the days of my life; [6b] And I will return to the house of Yhwh for length of days.

in the previous two sections), but that the author(s) has/have also intentionally arranged the topics addressed within these psalms to create a striking correspondence between them. Table 8 displays how each component is addressed in the exact same order, from the opening statement of trust to the concluding statement of everlasting joy.

There are additional corresponding structural components worth mentioning here as well. The concluding verse of each psalm creates a phonological link: *path of life* (ארח חיים; Ps 16:11a) and *length of days* (ארך ימים; Ps 23:6b). Both psalms contain an ABA' structure:

Structure 6

Psalm 16	Psalm 23
A (vv. 5–6)	A (vv. 1–3)
B (vv. 7–8)	B (vv. 4)
A' (vv. 9–11)	A' (vv. 5–6)

The central, or 'B', element in each psalm focuses on the presence of Yhwh in a dark time. In Psalm 16, this is described as *night* (v. 7), and in

Psalm 23, this image is intensified to *the valley of death-shadow*. In both cases, the psalmist declares his confidence in that moment.

The divine name *Yhwh* is also used in structurally prominent positions in both psalms: In Psalm 16, the name occurs at the beginning of multiple sections (Ps 16:2, 5, 7, 8). In Psalm 23, the name occurs as an inclusio around the entire psalm. The centrality of the name *Yhwh* contributes to the theme of the psalmist placing all of his confidence in him. In both psalms, the psalmist addresses Yhwh with the second-person pronoun, *you* (אתה), further indicating the theme of trust in him (Pss 16:2, 5; 23:4).

INTENSIFIED TRUST IN PSALM 23

While Psalms 16 and 23 correspond in structure and theme, there is also significant development between these psalms. Like the intensifying development among the frame (Pss 15, 29, and 24), Psalm 23 also intensifies the security and satisfaction that characterizes Psalm 16. The intensification of confidence can be detected at various points, including development of corresponding structure, themes, and lexemes. For example, although both psalms are songs of trust with corresponding structures, Psalm 16 begins with an opening petition for deliverance, while Psalm 23 instead begins on a note of confidence. In Psalm 23, trouble is not in view in the opening verses, which indicates that the psalmist has no fear. This increased security is made explicit in verse 4, which begins with *I will fear no harm*. In addition, Psalm 23 shifts the psalmist's elaboration of his allegiance to Yhwh (Ps 16:1-2) to a statement actualizing this allegiance as the present experience of life under the reign of Yhwh (Ps 23:1).[18] This shift creates a sense that the psalmist is both more secure in his relationship with Yhwh and that the reign of Yhwh is realized. Structurally, Psalm 23 exhibits increased security in Yhwh and a shift to a more theocentric focus, since the psalmist's role in his security is absent while Yhwh's role becomes central.

This increasing theocentric focus in Psalm 23 is indicated by the lexeme *name* (שם) and the theme of righteous ways. In Psalm 16, *name* is used in the commitment of the psalmist to not take up the *names* of other gods on his lips. In Psalm 23, it is God who is active rather than the

---

18. In Ps 16:3, it seems best to take "holy ones" to refer to the holy people in the land, rather than to heavenly beings who rebelled against God. This reading is most coherent with the preceding psalm, 15, which provides an example of the ability to judge between the righteous and the wicked as a characteristic of the righteous one.

psalmist: he leads the psalmist on right paths for *his name's sake*. The theme of righteous ways in Psalm 23 has ethical overtones that recall the commitment to righteousness in Psalm 16:3–4. In Psalm 23, rather than the psalmist committing to righteousness, it is Yhwh who leads in righteousness. These developments indicate a shift in perspective from the psalmist's role in his security to Yhwh's role in providing security for the psalmist.

The way that various lexemes are reused in Psalm 23 also contributes to heightened confidence. One example involves the lexemes *good* (טוב) and *live* (חיה). In Psalm 16, the psalmist affirms that his "*good* does not exist apart from [Yhwh]" (v. 2), and that " [Yhwh] makes known to [him] the path of *life*" (v. 11). This language is heightened in Psalm 23, where the psalmist does not merely *know* about this *good* and this *life*, but Yhwh's *good* actively pursues the psalmist all the days of his *life* (v. 6). Likewise, the corresponding theme of forever/finality also indicates fulfillment from Psalm 16 to Psalm 23: in Psalm 16, the psalmist knows that pleasures forever exist in Yhwh's presence (v. 11); in Psalm 23, the receipt of satisfaction forever is at hand (v. 6).[19] The reuse of the lexeme *being* (נפש) also indicates increased serenity and safety in Psalm 23: in Psalm 16, the *soul* is not forsaken (v. 10); in Psalm 23, not only is the *soul* not forsaken, the *soul* is refreshed (v. 3). This positive affirmation enhances the serenity.

Trust in Yhwh is also intensified in Psalm 23 through the use of land imagery. Land and inheritance imagery are central to both psalms (Pss 16:5–6; 23:2–3), but in Psalm 23, the land imagery is notably more broad, dynamic, and serene. In Psalm 16, the inheritance imagery can be described as static and localized, using lexemes associated with the allotment of the land under Joshua, like *portion* (חלק), *lot* (גורל), *boundary line* (חבל), and *inheritance* (נחל).[20] In comparison, the inheritance imagery of Psalm 23 is more expansive, using the spatially broader terms *pastures of vegetation* (נאות דשא), *waters of rest* (מי מנחות), and *paths* (מעגלי; Ps 23:2–3).[21] As noted earlier, *pastures of vegetation* and *waters of rest*

---

19. Concerning the idea of eternality in these psalms, it is my view that rather than the psalmist referring to life after death in Ps 16:11, the psalmist is expressing a general hope of an unbroken relationship between Yhwh and life. On this view, see Mays, *Psalms*, 88; McCann, "The Book of Psalms," 737.

20. See Lev 6:16–18; 7:33; Num 18:20; Josh 17:14; 18:6, 10; 19:9, 51.

21. Sumpter argues that in God himself is the space of union/communion in Ps 23, in "Coherence," 200. I see this as true in both psalms to an extent. In Ps 16, the psalmist says that Yhwh is his portion and share, in language reminiscent of the allotment of

activate the images of the livable land and waters that Yhwh created in Genesis 1. They are not limited in scope, but cosmic and expansive. Both images depict an idyllic and serene existence, in contrast to the allusion to conquering the land in Psalm 16. Psalm 23 also neglects the tumultuous allusion to other competing gods included in Psalm 16:3-4, but depicts complete rest and repose in the presence of Yhwh (Ps 23:2). Psalm 23 returns us to the Genesis 1 ideal, but projects it out into a future *forever* (Ps 23:6). The land imagery of Psalm 23 also seems to have a dynamic quality to it, in that a variety of words are associated with the exodus out of Egypt and journey through the wilderness, including *lead* (נהל), *pasture* (נוה), and *rest* (מנוחה).[22] I will discuss the language of journey in Psalm 23 later in this chapter.

Trust in Yhwh is also enhanced in Psalm 23 by the introduction of the new image of Yhwh as the shepherd, who not only provides (Ps 23:1), but also protects (Ps 23:2-4) and guides (Ps 23:3b). The shepherd's protection and guidance are both indicated by the reference to the rod and staff in verse 4 and by the association of shepherding with bravery and ruthlessness in the Hebrew Bible.[23] That Yhwh is the shepherd imparts courage to the psalmist and the subsiding of all fear (Ps 23:4).[24]

The theme of trust in both psalms is deepened by the accompanying theme of distress. In both psalms, there is trust in Yhwh in the face of *death*, evidenced by the lexemes *Sheol* (שאול; Ps 16:10) and *death-shadow* (צלמות; Ps 23:4), and because Yhwh protects *life* (נפש; Pss 16:10; 23:3-4). B. L. Tanner suggests that it is the existence of a threat in both psalms that makes the confidence more meaningful, calling Yhwh and the valley of deep darkness "dueling presences."[25] It is death that evokes

---

the priests in Num 18:20. In Ps 23, this is certainly an idyllic picture of union with God in both realms of peace and fear. However, both psalms do use specific land language to describe these metaphorical realities, and the difference I am noting here is not that one is concrete and the other metaphorical, but that one (Ps 16) is more static and less expansive and the other (Ps 23) more dynamic, expansive, and serene.

22. Exod 13:17, 21; 15:13; 32:34; Num 10:33; Deut 32:12; Pss 77:21; 78:14, 53. See P. Milne, "Psalm 23: Echoes of the Exodus," *Studies in Religion/Sciences Religieuses* 4 (1974-1975): 237-47; D. N. Freedman, "The Twenty-Third Psalm," in *Michigan Oriental Studies in Honor of George G. Cameron*, ed. L. L. Orlin (Ann Arbor: University of Michigan Press, 1976), 139-66.

23. See Delitzsch, *Psalms*, 330; E. Power, "The Shepherd's Two Rods in Modern Palestine and in Some Passages of the Old Testament," *Biblica* 9 (1928): 434-42.

24. נחם carries a connotation greater than comfort and also involving courage. See deClaissé-Walford, Jacobson, and Tanner, *The Book of Psalms*, 244.

25. deClaissé-Walford, Jacobson, and Tanner, *The Book of Psalms*, 178, 238.

fear, yet it is Yhwh's presence in both psalms that evokes trust and even provides security despite the threat of death (Pss 16:8, 10; 23:4, 6).

Psalm 23's emphasis on the presence of Yhwh with the psalmist is an intensification of that same theme found in Psalm 16. In Psalm 23:4, the statement *I will not fear* communicates trust in the face of death, and this confidence is because of Yhwh's presence: *for you are with me.* Various commentators identify the statement about Yhwh's immediate presence in verse 4 as the center of the psalm, since verse 4 shifts in person to speak to Yhwh rather than about him.[26] The distress in this verse of the poem is tangible: it is in the darkest valley that this shift occurs and that Yhwh's presence is most realized. Yhwh's presence with the psalmist in the midst of his distress in Psalm 23 is central. Tanner writes that the setting of the poem is "the existential space of being in the presence of something that is terrifying, ... and a space in which, according to the witness of the poem, the Lord can also be found."[27] Yhwh's presence is that place. Psalm 23 capitalizes on the themes of trust in Yhwh's presence in the midst of distress, and Yhwh's presence becomes the space of safety in distress on the journey to the permanent dwelling in his presence, depicted in the following psalm.

INCREASED SATISFACTION IN PSALM 23

In addition to and closely related to the theme of trust in Psalm 23 is the theme of joyful satisfaction in Yhwh's presence, which M. D. Futato calls "the final fruit of trust."[28] Both Psalms 16 and 23 emphasize the satisfaction and goodness found in Yhwh's presence, as demonstrated by the lexemes *name* (שם) and *good* (טוב) in both psalms: in Psalm 16, *good* (v. 2) is not found in the *names* (v. 4) of idols; in Psalm 23, Yhwh guides the psalmist for his *name's* sake (v. 3), and the result is *good* pursuing the psalmist forever (v. 6).

Psalm 23 not only continues the theme of joyful satisfaction from Psalm 16, but also intensifies the theme. Greater satisfaction in Yhwh's presence is exhibited by use of the most distinctive lexeme in these psalms, *cup* (כוס). This lexeme occurs in only three places in all of Book

---

26. See, e.g., McCann, "The Book of Psalms," 768; R. E. Tappy, "Psalm 23: Symbolism and Structure," *CBQ* 57, no. 2 (1995): 260; Futato, *The Book of Psalms*, 102; K. Schaefer, *Psalms*, 58; deClaissé-Walford, Jacobson, and Tanner, *The Book of Psalms*, 239.

27. deClaissé-Walford, Jacobson, and Tanner, *The Book of Psalms*, 239. Sumpter argues something similar, saying that God himself is the space of union or communion.

28. Futato, *The Book of Psalms*, 79.

I of the Psalter.[29] Furthermore, it occurs here with the exact same morphology, including the same suffix, as *my cup* (כוסי). This exact morphology occurs only in Psalms 16 and 23 in the entire Psalter, which increases the distinctiveness of the word and the strength of the connection. *My cup* is used in both psalms as an expression of trust to indicate satisfaction in Yhwh's provision. *Cup* is a metaphor in both psalms, but is taken to the second power in Psalm 23 by the phrase *my cup overflows*. In this phrase, the *cup* stands for overflowing satisfaction, which is metonymically equivalent to the contents, which are *overflowing*. In Psalm 23, the idea of the cup is also related to the new theme of feasting, which is itself imbued with immense joy and satisfaction. Yhwh is depicted as the host who provides in abundance for the psalmist. In addition to indicating satisfaction, the feast also indicates honor for Yhwh's guest, as do the themes of anointing the guest's head with oil and the locality of the feast in the presence of the guest's enemies (Ps 23:5).[30] Psalms 16 and 23 both indicate great satisfaction in Yhwh's presence, with satisfaction overflowing in abundance in Psalm 23.

The honor that Yhwh bestows on his guest in Psalm 23 seems to be that due to a king, an impression supported by a word cluster shared between Psalms 23 and 21. You may recall from table 7 earlier in this chapter that after its cohesion with Psalm 16, Psalm 23 is most closely connected with Psalm 21. Psalms 21 and 23 share stronger lexical, thematic, morphological, and phrasal cohesion than when Psalm 23 is paired with any other psalm in the collection.[31] Moreover, there is a cluster—a group of lexemes used within the confines of just a few verses—of shared distinctive lexemes that indicate intentional linking. The following distinctive lexemes are used within the confines of Psalms 21:4-8 and 23:5-6: *good* (טוב), *head* (רוש), *loyal love* (חסד), *day* (יום), *live* (חיה), and *length* (ארך). In addition, the phrase *length of days* (ארך ימים) is

---

29. Pss 11:6; 16:5; 23:5.

30. Craigie connects the feast idea with the exodus by similar language in Ps 78:19, where Yhwh spreads a table in the desert for his people. He also connects this idea with the feast of the future declared by the prophets, especially Isa 25:6. The connection with the exodus supports the conclusions above about shepherding indicating a journey. Allusion to a future feast exhibits similarity with Ps 24, which seems to indicate a full consummation of Yhwh's presence on earth. Craigie, *Psalms 1–50*, 204–9.

31. Distinctive corresponding lexemes include: ארך, טוב, רעע, יום, זמר, ראש, חסד, פנה, חיה, and דוד. The lexemes יום, טוב, and ראש are also distinctive morphologically. Pss 21 and 23 also share the distinctive phrase ארך ימים. See appendix 2 for all data.

used within these verses with the same morphology. The first word of this phrase, אֶרֶךְ, is highly distinctive, occurring in only these two places in all of Book I of the Psalter, which further strengthens the link.

Each of the six words above and the phrasal link *length of days* are used with regard to the human king in Psalm 21 and of the banquet guest in Psalm 23, indicating that this is the same person: *Good* (טוב) blessings are given to the king in Psalm 21 and this same *goodness* pursues the psalmist in Psalm 23. A crown is placed on the *head* (רוש) of the king in Psalm 21; similarly, God anoints the *head* with oil in Psalm 23. The king is referred to as the recipient of Yhwh's *loyal love* (חסד) in Psalm 21, indicating he is a partner in covenant with Yhwh. In Psalm 23, Yhwh's *loyal love* pursues the psalmist. In Psalm 21, *length* (אֶרֶךְ) and *days* (יום) indicate an unending period of blessing for the king; this same idea is applied to the psalmist in Psalm 23. *Life* (חי) is given to the king in Psalm 21 and describes the period of blessing for the psalmist in Psalm 23. In addition to this word cluster being applied to both the king of Psalm 21 and to the psalmist in Psalm 23, some of these words are most naturally associated with a king in general. For example, placing honor on one's *head*, whether in the form of a crown or anointing oil, depicts that one as a leader. In addition, the lexeme *loyal love* and the phrase *length of days* (and the corresponding line *all the days of my life* in Ps 23:6) carry covenantal overtones. While the covenant certainly applies to all of Yhwh's people, it also applies in a focused way to the king, whose covenantal faithfulness affects the people. The effect of this shared word cluster is that it provides a persuasive reason to view the banquet guest of Psalm 23 as the king of Psalm 21. This identification is also consistent with the title of Psalm 23 as *a psalm of David* (מזמור לדוד). That Psalm 23 is about the human king is significant for understanding the storyline and primary character of the collection.

ROYAL AND COMMUNAL DIMENSIONS IN PSALM 23

There is another royal figure in Psalm 23 in addition to the human king. Like Psalm 24, Psalm 23 also introduces new themes of the divine king Yhwh and his community. While both of these themes are subtle in Psalm 23, if similar developments exist in surrounding psalms, their existence here is more plausible.

One indication that Yhwh is portrayed as the king in Psalm 23 is in his designation as *shepherd* (רעה). This designation is used in various places throughout the Hebrew Bible as well as in other ancient Near Eastern literature to characterize a king or someone in authority.[32] Psalm 23 pairs this image with the lexeme *rod* (שֵׁבֶט; v. 4), which also contains royal connotations.[33] Psalm 23 also ends with a description of returning to the house of Yhwh to dwell forever, a theme that is picked up in Psalm 24 at the arrival of Yhwh as king in his dwelling place.

Like the expansion to the community that takes place from Psalm 15 to 24, Psalm 23 also alludes to the community, although more subtly. The communal dimension in Psalm 23 may be encompassed in the imagery of the shepherd.[34] In many places throughout the Hebrew Bible, the community of Israel is compared to a flock of sheep.[35] Often, the people of Israel are specifically referred to as Yhwh's sheep, so that when the imagery of shepherd is used here, it likely has a communal dimension.[36] Even in places where shepherds are not linked with a group of people, they are often mentioned in tandem with a group of sheep, which still imbues the imagery of shepherding with a group.[37] The reference to Yhwh as *my shepherd* (רֹעִי) in Psalm 23 and the first-person singular pronoun used throughout the psalm do not negate the communal aspect of shepherding; rather, they indicate an intensely personal experience of Yhwh's presence. The communal dimension in Psalm 23 is consistent

---

32. See, for example, 2 Sam 5:2; 7:7; 24:17; 1 Kgs 22:17; 1 Chr 11:2; 17:6; 21:17; Isa 44:28; Jer 23:1–4; Ezek 34:1–16, 23–24; Mic 5:2–4; Ps 78:70–72. See "The Laws of Hammurabi," where Hammurabi and other kings are called the shepherds of the people. For the use of *shepherd* with divine connotations, see *ANET* 69, 71–2, 164, 337, 387–88. The shepherd's provision of peaceful waters is likely also a royal allusion, since, as Tanner points out, Marduk is described as providing peaceful waters for his people in *ANET*, 69. Tanner, "King Yahweh as the Good Shepherd," in *David and Zion: Biblical Studies in Honor of J. J. M. Roberts*, ed. B. F. Batto and K. L. Roberts (Winona Lake, IN: Eisenbrauns, 2004), 274.

33. See n. 6.

34. McCann makes note of an additional allusion to the community in Ps 23: "The house of Yhwh" in v. 6. He argues that "the house of Yhwh" contains a communal dimension, especially following Ps 22. See McCann, "The Book of Psalms," 769.

35. E.g., the community is compared to a flock in the following passages: 2 Sam 5:2; 7:8; 24:17; 1 Kgs 22:17; 1 Chr 11:2; 17:6; 21:17; 2 Chr 18:16; Pss 28:9; 44:22; 78:71–72; Isa 13:14; 53:6; 63:11; Jer 23:4; 50:6; Ezek 34:2, 23–24; 36:37; Mic 2:12; Zech 10:2. In addition to these passages, sheep represent a community of people in Ps 49:14, Mic 7:14, and Nah 3:18.

36. Israel is referred to as Yhwh's flock in the following verses: Num 27:17; Pss 77:20; 78:52; 79:13; 80:1; 95:7; 100:3; Isa 40:11; Jer 23:1–2; 31:10; Ezek 34:5, 7–10, 12, 16; Zech 9:16; 10:3.

37. In addition to the verses above, the following serve as an example: Gen 29:3, 9; 46:34; Exod 2:17, 19; Lev 27:32; 1 Sam 17:20; 2 Sam 7:8; 1 Chr 17:7; Isa 13:20; 61:5; Jer 6:3; 10:21; 25:35–36; 33:12; 51:23; Amos. 7:15; Zeph 2:6; Zech 11:4–9, 15–17; 13:7.

with the gathering of the community in the following psalm, which suggests a recurring development of communal inclusion from the first half of the psalm group to the second.

JOURNEY IMAGERY

That Psalm 23 is moving toward this great arrival of the king is not only indicated by the royal allusions inherent in the imagery of the shepherd and Psalm 23's placement before Psalm 24, but also by language that indicates that Psalm 23 involves a journey. I have already made note of the increasingly expansive and dynamic imagery of Psalm 23.[38] The psalm also includes additional language associated with movement, such as *guide* (נחה), *walk* (חלך), and *path* (מעגל; Ps 23:2–4). In addition, the imagery of shepherding itself may depict a journey, since shepherding typically involves movement as the flock grazes the land.[39] The effect of this dynamic language in Psalm 23 provides a sense of journey or pilgrimage under the guidance of Yhwh. And the last line of the psalm specifies the destination: *And I will return to the house of Yhwh for length of days* (Ps 23:6).[40] This language of movement in Psalm 23 depicts a journey whereby Yhwh leads the psalmist toward Yhwh's arrival at the consummation of his kingdom; in other words, "God is the psalmist's destination."[41]

SUMMARY

Psalms 16 and 23 are closely related to one another as psalms of trust, and yet Psalm 23 goes beyond its counterpart by intensifying the security and satisfaction provided by Yhwh's presence, even in the midst of the valley

---

38. See "Intensified Trust in Psalm 23" earlier in this chapter.

39. Shepherding usually occurs in the *wilderness* (מדבר)—a land that cannot sustain sheep long term. Goldingay, *Psalms*, 349. Some commentators also see the shepherding imagery as referring to specific journeys, such as the exile or the return from exile. See, e.g., *The Targum of Psalms: Translated, with a Critical Introduction, Apparatus, and Notes*, trans. D. M. Stec (Collegeville, MN: Liturgical Press, 2004), 61; Freedman, "The Twenty-Third Psalm," 139–66; M. L. Barré and J. S. Kselman, "New Exodus, Covenant, and Restoration in Psalm 23," in *The Word of the Lord Shall Go Forth*, ed. C. L. Meyers and M. O'Connor (Winona Lake, IN: Eisenbrauns, 1983), 97–127.

40. I understand ושבתי here as "and I will return" from root שוב rather than from root ישב, since this exact form of שוב occurs seven other places in the Hebrew Bible (Gen 28:21; Jer 29:14; 30:3; 48:47; Ezek 16:53; 29:14; Amos 9:14), whereas ישב never occurs as ושבתי. The b-preposition that follows שוב is rare, and may indicate that the psalmist has both returning and dwelling in mind, i.e., "I will return to the house of Yhwh with the purpose of dwelling there forever."

41. deClaissé-Walford, Jacobson, and Tanner, *The Book of Psalms*, 245.

of death. Like Psalm 24, Psalm 23 alludes to Yhwh as king, yet also seems to have the human king in view. Through its dynamic imagery, Psalm 23 depicts a journey toward the arrival of Yhwh and his kingdom.

The greater confidence in Psalm 23 is maintained even in the face of great distress. This is because the psalmist finds peace and protection in Yhwh's presence in the midst of his distress, indicated by the intensification of the theme of Yhwh's presence in the central statement in verse 4: *For you are with me.* McCann points out that joy and trust within the realities of suffering make sense only in light of the certainty of Yhwh's reign as king.[42] The reality of suffering in Psalm 23 indicates that the arrival of Yhwh's kingdom is future; yet at the same time, God's kingship is experienced here and now in his presence as the shepherd. Psalm 23 exemplifies that the appropriate attitude through times of suffering is confidence in Yhwh's coming kingdom and refuge in his presence in the interim.

Through its emphasis on Yhwh as the shepherd king and its imagery of the human king, Psalm 23 functions as a hinge between focus on the human king in Psalm 21 and focus on the divine king in Psalm 24. Furthermore, the identification of Yhwh as king in Psalm 23 is consistent with the development from Psalm 15 to Psalm 24, which suggests that perhaps this is a larger development throughout this collection. Like the psalm pair of 15 and 24, Psalms 16 and 23 also show a development of inclusion of the community through the shepherding motif and a development from the specific imagery of the land to the spatially broader terms of *green pastures, waters of rest,* and *right paths.* In other words, like Psalms 15 and 24, these two psalms also show communal and spatial expansion.

Psalms 16 and 23 envelop the inner psalms, 17–22, in confidence. The collection is ultimately framed by the depiction of Yhwh's kingly presence on earth (Pss 15 and 24), and Psalms 16 and 23 express confidence in the prospect of Yhwh's arrival at the end of the journey. Psalms 16 and 23 express confidence in the ideals set forth by the frame, Psalms 15, 19, and 24. In this sense, they serve as a bridge between these ideal psalms and the other psalms within (Pss 17, 18, 20, 21, and 22), which we will see are more descriptive of the human experiences of suffering. These psalms of trust thereby teach that the way to appropriate the ideals of Psalms 15, 19, and 24 in the midst of distress is to *trust* in Yhwh until his

---

42. McCann, "The Book of Psalms," 667.

final installment as king.[43] As this study progresses further, it remains to investigate whether parallel psalms continue to form a discernible structure. It also remains to discover whether the thematic intensification and the progressions toward the kingdom and the community prove to be consistent developments throughout the entire collection. If the communal, kingly, and cosmic dimensions are consistent developments, the question arises, *What, in the storyline, initiates this progression toward the kingdom?*

---

43. Sumpter has argued that all of the intervening psalms, 16–18 and 20–23, are "existential." Sumpter, "Coherence," 188. To my mind, Pss 16 and 23 serve as a bridge between the more experiential psalms and the ideal frame.

5

A Twist in Plot:
Suffering in Psalms 17 and 22

Up to this point in Psalms 15–24, the content has been primarily hopeful and optimistic, expressing joy in Yhwh's presence and confidence in his arrival. We have seen how Psalms 15 and 24 are integrally connected as the outer frame of the collection, and also secondarily are connected to Psalm 19 at the center of the collection. These three psalms together frame the collection with their ideal vision of the righteous ones dwelling in the presence of Yhwh, a vision that is realized in Psalm 24 at Yhwh's arrival as king. In Psalm 24, Yhwh's kingdom extends beyond the individual to include the entire community and is expanded into the entire cosmos. Just within this outer frame are Psalms 16 and 23, which express confidence in this ideal vision. Like the development from Psalm 15 to 24, the development from Psalm 16 to 23 is also one of intensification and revelation of Yhwh's identity as king.

As the investigation moves inward toward the center of the collection, Psalms 17 and 22 create disequilibrium between the ideals and confidence of the outer psalms and the reality of suffering within them. Psalm 16 transitions smoothly to Psalm 17 through the reuse of shared lexemes, phrases, and morphologies.[1] Yet these shared elements used to express trust and confidence in Psalm 16 often express the experience of suffering in Psalm 17. So, beginning in Psalm 15, there is progression from the stated ideal (Ps 15) to trusting in that ideal (Ps 16) to the "on-the-ground" experience of trusting in the midst of suffering (Ps 17). Psalm 16 is a psalm expressing confident trust in Yhwh's presence, while Psalm 17 is a lament based on those confident expectations being let down and tested. The phrase *not shaken* as בל אמוט or בל נמוטו is a good example of reuse that

---

1. Pss 16 and 17 are connected by their distinctive themes of righteousness and trust in Yhwh and by eighteen distinctive lexemes (דוד, לבב, חיה, ארץ, אמר, חסד, פנה), שפה, חלק, ארח, חסה, מוט, לילה, נפש), six morphological connections (חלק, שפה, שמר, לבב, אל, חיה), and one distinctive phrase (בל/לא מוט).

exhibits a progression toward the experience of the psalmist: In Psalm 15, this phrase functions as a sure promise to the righteous (v. 5). In Psalm 16, the phrase expresses confidence that the psalmist *will not be shaken* (i.e., his righteousness will continue because of the sustaining power of Yhwh; v. 8). In Psalm 17, however, the psalmist uses this phrase to motivate Yhwh to deliver him from his distress; because the psalmist's feet *have not been shaken* (i.e., he has remained righteous; v. 5), the psalmist urges God to deliver him. The development between these psalms is one from confidence to the experience of trust in deliverance within a dire situation.

While Psalms 17 and 22 correspond superficially in terms of their distress, it remains to show whether these psalms are statistically connected through analysis of distinctive elements. Moreover, if these psalms are parallel to one another, it remains to discover in what ways Psalm 22 goes beyond Psalm 17 and whether it continues the patterns of intensification and development toward the kingdom found in the outer psalms.

COHESION BETWEEN PSALMS 17 AND 22

Psalms 17 and 22 are each more closely connected with one another than with any other psalm within the collection. Their total strength of cohesion with one another is significantly high when compared with the strengths of cohesion with other psalms, suggesting that the author/editor intended them to be read in light of each other.

The strengths of cohesion per element type between Psalm 17 and every other psalm within the collection are displayed in table 9:[2]

Table 9. Psalm 17: Strengths of Cohesion

Psalm Pair	Lexemes	Themes	Structures	Phrases	Morphologies	Superscripts	TOTAL
17 and 15	0.51	0.04	0.00	0.12	0.19	0.00	0.87
17 and 16	0.83	0.09	0.00	0.11	0.81	0.00	1.83
17 and 18	0.88	0.05	0.00	0.00	0.64	0.00	1.57
17 and 19	0.86	0.03	0.00	0.00	0.48	0.00	1.37
17 and 20	0.59	0.21	0.00	0.00	0.00	0.00	0.80
17 and 21	0.95	0.15	0.00	0.10	0.36	0.00	1.56
17 and 22	1.00	0.23	1.00	0.36	0.40	0.00	3.00
17 and 23	0.32	0.21	0.00	0.00	0.12	0.00	0.65
17 and 24	0.44	0.04	0.00	0.00	0.00	0.00	0.48

---

2. See appendix 2 for further data.

Of all possible psalm-pair combinations, the total strength of cohesion between Psalms 17 and 22 is rather high. This is due to their strong cohesion in terms of shared distinctive lexemes, themes, structures, and phrases—each strongest when paired with one another rather than with other psalms in the collection. The number 1.00 in the lexeme and structure columns indicates that of every other possible psalm pair in the collection, these two share the strongest cohesion in these categories. It is also significant that Psalms 17 and 22 have more phrases in common than when paired with any other psalm, since repeated phrases are easily noticed by readers and so would have the effect of closely binding these psalms together in the mind of the reader.[3] You may also notice on the table above that Psalm 17 is secondarily connected to Psalm 16, due to its strong morphological cohesion. Psalms 16 and 17 are linked together as neighboring psalms through the use of repeated words in the same distinctive form, but in terms of lexemes, themes, structures, and phrases, Psalm 17 is most closely connected with Psalm 22.

The strengths of cohesion between Psalm 22 and every other psalm within the collection are displayed in table 10:[4]

Table 10. Psalm 22: Strengths of Cohesion

Psalm Pair	Lexemes	Themes	Structures	Phrases	Morphologies	Superscripts	TOTAL
22 and 15	0.65	0.08	0.00	0.15	0.37	0.21	1.47
22 and 16	0.75	0.06	0.00	0.00	0.15	0.00	0.96
22 and 17	1.00	0.23	1.00	0.36	0.40	0.00	3.00
22 and 18	0.83	0.00	0.00	0.07	0.87	0.30	2.06
22 and 19	0.72	0.03	0.00	0.00	0.34	0.51	1.61
22 and 20	0.59	0.16	0.00	0.00	1.00	0.51	2.26
22 and 21	0.48	0.18	0.00	0.00	0.47	0.51	1.64
22 and 23	0.44	0.18	0.00	0.00	0.21	0.21	1.05
22 and 24	0.45	0.21	0.00	0.00	0.29	0.21	1.17

Like table 9, table 10 demonstrates that Psalm 22 is much more closely connected with Psalm 17 than with any other psalm within the collection.

---

3. See appendix 2. The distinctive corresponding phrases in Pss 17 and 22 are constructed from the following lexical combinations: נפשי and חרב; טרף and אריה; and, קרא, ענה, and אל.

4. See appendix 2 for further data.

The two psalms share the strongest lexical, thematic, structural, and phrasal connections. Table 9 also shows that Psalm 22 has some strong cohesion with Psalm 20 due to corresponding morphologies and also with Psalm 18 due to corresponding morphologies and lexemes. I will briefly address the significance of these secondary connections later in this chapter.

In light of the strong cohesion between Psalms 17 and 22, we can conclude that these two psalms are parallel to one another and continue the pattern of parallel psalms observed thus far in the collection, as represented in figure 6:

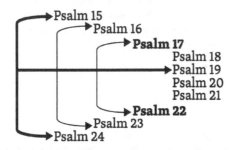

Figure 6. The Frame, Psalms of Confidence, and Laments

From figure 6, it seems that a chiastic pattern is emerging within this psalm group, though it remains to investigate whether and how this pattern continues for Psalms 18, 20, and 21, especially since there is an odd number of psalms remaining. In what follows I will explore the shape and message of Psalms 17 and 22 and then how Psalm 22 develops the distinctive elements it shares with Psalm 17.

THE SHAPE OF PSALM 17

Psalm 17 can be broken up into three parts (vv. 1-5, 6-12, 13-15), depicted on the next page and in figure 7. Each part begins with a unit of petition to God (vv. 1-2, 6-9, 13-14b), which is followed by a second unit. These second units vary per each part. First is motivation (vv. 3-5), then distress (vv. 10-12), and finally, confidence (vv. 14c-15), respectively. Each of these second units moves the storyline of the psalm forward from plea to confidence.

Structure 7
Psalm 17

Part		
		A prayer of David.
	A	¹ᵃ Hear, Yhwh, righteousness; ¹ᵇ Give attention to my cry. ¹ᶜ Give ear to my prayer, ¹ᵈ [made] without lips of treachery. ²ᵃ From your presence, may my judgment go out; ²ᵇ Your eyes, may they see uprightness.
1	B	³ᵃ You tested my heart; ³ᵇ You visited at night. ³ᶜ You refined me, but you have not found [anything]; ³ᵈ I have purposed [that] my mouth will not transgress. ⁴ᵃ As for the works of humanity, by the word of your lips, ⁴ᵇ I have kept [from] the paths of the violent. ⁵ᵃ Grasping my steps to your tracks, ⁵ᵇ they do not totter, my footsteps.
2	A'	⁶ᵃ I call to you, ⁶ᵇ for you answer me, God. ⁶ᶜ Incline your ear to me; ⁶ᵈ Hear my word. ⁷ᵃ Wondrously show your loyal love, ⁷ᵇ savior of those who take refuge from those who rise up, at your right hand. ⁸ᵃ Keep me as the pupil of the daughter of the eye; ⁸ᵇ In the shadow of your wings, you shall hide me, ⁹ᵃ from the presence of the wicked, who destroy me, ⁹ᵇ the enemies of my being surround me.
	C	¹⁰ᵃ Their fat, they close; ¹⁰ᵇ Their mouth, they speak with majesty. ¹¹ᵃ Our steps, now they surround me; ¹¹ᵇ Their eyes, they set to bend to the ground. ¹²ᵃ His likeness is as a lion; he longs to tear; ¹²ᵇ And like a young lion, sitting in hiding.
3	A'	¹³ᵃ Arise, Yhwh! ¹³ᵇ Confront his face! ¹³ᶜ Cause him to bow! ¹³ᵈ Deliver my being ¹³ᵉ from the wicked [by] your sword; ¹⁴ᵃ from men [by] your hand, Yhwh; ¹⁴ᵇ from men of the world.
	D	¹⁴ᶜ Their portion is with the living; ¹⁴ᵈ And [with] your treasure you fill their belly. ¹⁴ᵉ They are satisfied, their sons; ¹⁴ᶠ and they cause to rest the excess with their children. ¹⁵ᵃ I—in righteousness—I will see your face; ¹⁵ᵇ I will be satisfied upon waking [with] your likeness.

Following the title, *a prayer of David,* part 1 consists of a petition to Yhwh to hear the psalmist's plea (A) and then a section of motivation for Yhwh to intervene (B), which describes the righteousness of the psalmist. The psalmist trusts that Yhwh responds to righteousness justly and so puts forth the ways that he has lived rightly in order to motivate Yhwh to act in accordance with his character.

Part	Vv.	Units		
1	1-2	Petition		
	3-5		Motivation	
2	6-9	Petition		
	10-12		Distress	
3	13-14b	Petition		
	14c-15			Confidence/Fulfillment[5]

Figure 7. The Structure of Psalm 17

Each of these units, petition and motivation, consists of two subunits (vv. 1, 2; vv. 3, 4–5). The first subunit of the petition consists of three parallel clauses, all beginning with synonyms for *hear* in the form of an infinitive, followed by a noun (vv. 1a–c). Yhwh's name is used in the first line only, as the addressee: *Hear, Yhwh, righteousness.* The second two lines are closely joined semantically, morphologically, and in sound by רנתי and תפלתי—*my cry* and *my prayer.* Because of the echoing parallelism, it is likely that *righteousness* (צדק) in the first line also refers to the psalmist's prayer, describing its nature. The final line (1d) modifies the prayer of the third line by saying that it is made *without lips of treachery.* This line recalls the first line by specifying a characteristic of righteousness, creating an inverted *abb'a'* structure to this verse. It is because the psalmist's prayer is righteous that he then asks that God will judge him in the next verse (v. 2). He trusts that God's judgment is right. Verses 1–2 together are also united by imagery of God's eyes and ears. Verse 2 continues the petition of verse 1 but shifts in form. It is made up of two lines, united by their imperfect verb form and language of Yhwh's discernment. The plea for God to judge the psalmist in verse 2 serves as a bridge to verses 3–5, which go into detail about the psalmist's righteousness.

Verses 3–5 (B) consist of two subunits, the first about how God has tested the psalmist and found nothing (v. 3) and the second elaborating

---

5. This section of confidence indicates fulfillment by its repetition of three lexemes from vv. 1–14b: righteousness (צדק), see (חזה), and presence (פנה). In vv. 1–14b, these lexemes are used as supplication; here they are used as confidence in the fulfillment of the supplication. See also Auffret, "Les Psaumes 15 à 24," 414.

on how the psalmist keeps the ways of God (vv. 4–5). These verses show that in motive (v. 3a), speech (v. 3d), and action (vv. 4–5), the psalmist is righteous. Verse 3 is made up of two sets of parallel lines. The first two lines form a tight bundle, indicated by their same verb form, *you tested* (בחנת) and *you visited* (פקדת), and paronomasia in the nouns that follow: *heart* (לבי) and *night* (לילה). The echoing structure elucidates that the purpose of Yhwh's *visit* is to *test*. Yhwh's visiting at night both connotes that he is ever present in his testing and also recalls the kind of righteousness explicated in Psalm 1: it is a day-and-night meditation on Yhwh's instruction. The third line of verse 3 transitions from the previous lines by using a synonym for testing—*refining* (צרף)—but it adds a new element: *You will not find [anything]* (בל תמצא), in other words, no sin (v. 3c). This new element is paralleled in the fourth line by the negation *not* (בל) and the sound play between צרפתני and זמתי—*You refined me* and *I have purposed* (v. 3d). This final line provides the reason that Yhwh will find nothing: the psalmist has purposed that his mouth will not transgress, which recalls the opening petition, which says that the psalmist's prayer is made without lips of treachery (v. 1d).

Verse 4 picks up on the imagery of the mouth, but this time it is the word of Yhwh's lips that is the focus. Verses 4 and 5 are unified by anthropomorphic language used of God and also specify the righteous ways of the psalmist, this time contrasting them with the ways of the violent. *The works of humanity* (פעלות אדם) seem to describe simply the deeds that God will see, rather than carrying an inherently negative or positive connotation.[6] These verses have an *aba'b'* structure, where parts *a* and *a'* reference Yhwh's words and tracks, using the second-person suffix to end both lines with the same sound (ך); parts *b* and *b'* describe what the psalmist does *not* do—join the paths of the violent or totter. There is also a contrast between *ab* and *a'b'*, between the *paths of the violent* (ארחות פריץ; v. 4b) and the *tracks of Yhwh* (מעגלותיך; v. 5a). The result of *keeping from* (שמר) the violent and *holding fast* (תמך) to God's ways instead is that the psalmist will *not totter* (בל מוט)—just as stated in the promise of Psalm 15:5c.

Part 2 of the psalm begins with another petition (A'). Whereas the opening petition had two subunits, this second petition intensifies by expanding to three subunits (vv. 6, 7, 8–9). The first subunit picks

---

6. See Prov 24:12; Job 34:11.

up the imperative verb forms from the petition of part 1 and also re-uses some of the same lexemes: *hear* (שׁמע) and *ear* (אזן; v. 6). This sec-ond petition shows a bit more confidence in Yhwh's answer, perhaps because the psalmist trusts that Yhwh will respond justly to his righ-teousness just described. The second subunit of the petition intro-duces the distress of enemies and pleads for Yhwh to show his *loyal love* (חסד) to those who *take refuge* (חסה) in him—a word that recalls the command to kings in Psalm 2 to take refuge in the son (v. 7). The third subunit of the petition (17:8–9) requests that Yhwh would pro-tect the psalmist in the same way that we would protect one of our most vulnerable parts, *the pupil of the eye*. This is paired and bound by inverted parallelism with the image of Yhwh as a mother hen who hides her chicks with her wings. Together these are two images dis-playing the vulnerability and dependency of the psalmist on Yhwh. Verse 9 specifies what it is that the psalmist needs protection from: his powerful enemies.

The second unit of part 2 (C; vv. 10–12) consists of three sets of par-allel lines that describe the enemies and the distress they cause to the psalmist. These lines reuse lexemes from earlier units to create con-trasts between the enemies and the psalmist and between the enemies and God. Verses 10–12 stand in stark contrast with verses 3–5, where the psalmist described his own righteousness, reusing the lexemes *mouth* (פה), *speak* (דבר), and *step* (אשׁר) from that section: whereas the psalmist purposed his *mouth* would not transgress and he would keep the *speech* of Yhwh, the enemies use their *mouth* to *speak* with majesty, or arrogance; whereas the psalmist's *steps* held fast to God's tracks, now the enemy surrounds his *steps*. The enigmatic line *their fat, they close* (חלבמו סגרו) may also be elucidated by the contrast between verses 3–5 and 10–12. In the former, the psalmist is characterized by openness to Yhwh's testing, specifically using the language of testing the heart. It is likely that the fat closing is indicating that the enemies' hearts are closed to God, encased in their own sense of sufficiency, which will be the focus of the final unit of the poem. Verses 10–12 also reuse the lexemes *eye* (עין) and *hide* (סתר) from verses 8–9 to create a contrast between the ways of the enemies and the ways of God. These lexical contrasts created between God and the enemies and the psalmist and the enemies align the psalmist with God. The enemies are depicted as beasts, as a *lion* (ארי) and *young lion* (כפיר). Such an image subverts the Genesis 1 ideal of humans ruling over the animals by showing that when humans turn against God, they become beasts themselves.

The third and final part of the psalm consists of a petition (A″; vv. 13–14b) followed by a section of confidence (D; vv. 14c–15). The petition consists of one extended unit from 13–14b. The first four lines (13a–d) consist of short cries to God and are united by imperative verbs for deliverance from enemies. There is a sequential progression from *arising* (קום) to *confronting* (קדם) to *causing to bow* (כרע) and the result, *delivering* (פלט). The following three lines are phrases that stand in parallel to one another. Each begins with *from* (מן) and has as its object the *wicked* and *men* (מתים/רשע). Following suit, this petition also reuses lexemes from the previous petition (vv. 7–9): the psalmist calls on Yhwh to *arise* (קום), confront his *face* (פנה), and deliver his *being* (נפשי) from the *wicked* (רשע; v. 13), recalling the description of the enemies as *those who rise up* (קום) and the *presence* (פנה) of the *wicked* (רשע) who surround the psalmist's *being* (נפש; vv. 7–9).

The final unit of part 3 creates a curious contrast between the fate of the enemies and the fate of the psalmist. These verses begin with what seems like a positive fate for the enemies: they have a portion in this life, Yhwh's treasures fill their bellies, and their children are both satisfied and have excess (v. 14). The description functions both as a cry against the injustice of such a situation and also as a statement of confidence when contrasted with the next set of parallel lines (v. 15): in contrast to the wicked who are *satisfied* (שבע) in this life with abundance, the psalmist will be *satisfied* upon waking with Yhwh himself.[7] This contrast maps *in this life* (בחיים) onto *upon waking* (בהקיץ) for comparison, suggesting that even if the psalmist suffers the worst fate, death, this will be met with waking in the presence of Yhwh. Such a contrast continues the theme of the previous psalm pair that Yhwh's chosen one will encounter suffering, even death, but will be delivered and brought to new life out the other side.[8]

---

7. Yhwh's *face* (פנה) and Yhwh's *likeness* (תמונה) stand in parallel construction here, presumably referring to the same thing, his presence.
8. Death and new life are often referred to in terms of sleeping and waking (see Isa 26:19; Dan 12:2).

THE SHAPE OF PSALM 22

Structure 8

Psalm 22

Part				
				¹ᵃ *Of the director. Upon the doe of the dawn. A psalm of David.*

	A		²ᵃ My God, my God, why have you abandoned me? ²ᵇ Far from my salvation, my words of my roaring. ³ᵃ My God, I call daily, but you do not answer. ³ᵇ And at night—no repose for me.

1

B

    a

⁴ᵃ But you are holy,
⁴ᵇ seated on the praises of Israel.
⁵ᵃ In you, our fathers trusted.
⁵ᵇ They trusted and you delivered them.
⁶ᵃ To you they cried out, and they escaped.
⁶ᵇ In you they trusted and they were not ashamed.

    b

⁷ᵃ But I am a worm, and not a man,
⁷ᵇ a reproach of humanity and a despised one of people.
⁸ᵃ All who see me mock me.
⁸ᵇ They separate the lip.
⁸ᶜ They shake the head.
⁹ᵃ "Commit to Yhwh!"
⁹ᵇ "Let him deliver him.
⁹ᶜ Let him rescue him, for he delights in him."

    a'

¹⁰ᵃ For [it was] you, bringing me forth from the belly,
¹⁰ᵇ Causing me to trust upon the breast of my mother
¹¹ᵃ upon you I was cast from the womb
¹¹ᵇ From the belly of my mother, my God you [are].

A'

¹²ᵃ Do not be far from me,
¹²ᵇ for distress is near;
¹²ᶜ for there is no helper.

2

C

    a

¹³ᵃ Great bulls have surrounded me.
¹³ᵇ Strong ones of Bashan have encircled me.
¹⁴ᵃ They open at me their mouths,
¹⁴ᵇ lions, tearing and roaring.

    b

¹⁵ᵃ Like water, I am poured out,
¹⁵ᵇ and divided are all my bones.
¹⁵ᶜ My heart has become like wax.
¹⁵ᵈ It melts in the midst of my inward parts.
¹⁶ᵃ It is dried up like earthenware, my strength.
¹⁶ᵇ And my tongue is being made to cling to my gums.
¹⁶ᶜ And in the dust of death, you set me.

    a'

¹⁷ᵃ For dogs have surrounded me;
¹⁷ᵇ An assembly of evil ones has encompassed me,
¹⁷ᶜ like a lion, my hands and my feet.
¹⁸ᵃ I recount all my bones.
¹⁸ᵇ They look, they see me.
¹⁹ᵃ They have apportioned my garments among themselves.
¹⁹ᵇ For my clothing, they have cast lots.

A"
²⁰ᵃ But you, Yhwh, do not be far!
²⁰ᵇ My help, to my aid, come quickly!
²¹ᵃ Rescue from the sword my being,
²¹ᵇ from the hand of the dog, my only one!
²²ᵃ Save me from the mouth of the lion!
²²ᵇ From the horns of the wild ox, you have answered me.

a
²³ᵃ I will recount your name to my kin.
²³ᵇ In the midst of the congregation, I will praise you.
²⁴ᵃ Fearers of Yhwh, praise him!
²⁴ᵇ All offspring of Jacob, honor him!
²⁴ᶜ And revere him, all offspring of Israel!

b
²⁵ᵃ For he has not despised and he has not detested the affliction of the afflicted.
²⁵ᵇ And he did not hide his face from him.
²⁵ᶜ But his crying for help to him, he heard.

a'
²⁶ᵃ Because of you is my praise in the great congregation.
²⁶ᵇ I will fulfill my vows before those who fear him.

3

D

a
²⁷ᵃ The afflicted ones will eat and be satisfied.
²⁷ᵇ They will praise Yhwh, the seekers of him.
²⁷ᶜ May your hearts live forever.
²⁸ᵃ They will remember and turn to Yhwh, all the ends of the earth.
²⁸ᵇ And they will worship before your face, all the families of the nations.

b
²⁹ᵃ For to Yhwh is the kingship.
²⁹ᵇ He is ruler of the nations.

a'
³⁰ᵃ They will eat and they will worship, all the fat of the earth.
³⁰ᵇ And before his face, they will bow, all who go down to the dust.
³⁰ᶜ Even [the one who] his being he cannot preserve.

+1
³¹ᵃ Offspring shall serve him.
³¹ᵇ It will be recounted of the Lord to the [next] generation.
³²ᵃ They will come and they will declare his righteousness,
³²ᵇ to a people who will be born, that he has done [it].

The structure of Psalm 22, as with many texts, has at least two structures overlaying one another to highlight different components. First, notice in the translation above and also in figure 8 below how the psalm can be understood as three parts, each beginning with a unit of petition (A, A' and A") and followed by a unit with an *aba'* structure (B, C, and D).⁹

---

9. These *aba'* structures do not correspond to one another between parts. I.e., subunit *a*, "Motivation," in part 1 (vv. 4–6) does not correspond to subunit *a*, "Distress (Outer)," in part 2 (vv. 13–14). '*aba*' is just the simplest designation to describe the threefold structure where the first and third subunit correspond, without introducing multiple new letters (if we did this, it could look like *aba'* in part 1; *b'cb"* in part 2; and *ded'*, *d"e'd"'*, and f in part 3).

Part 3 intensifies this structure in that it has a second *aba'* structure, followed by one additional element, called here a "plus-one" (+1) element.[10]

Part	Vv.	Units/Subunits		
1	2-3	Petition		
	4-6		(a) Motivation	
	7-9			(b) Distress
	10-11		(a') Motivation	
2	12	Petition		
	13-14			(a) Distress (Outer)
	15-16			(b) Distress (Inner)
	17-19			(a') Distress (Outer)
3	20-22	Petition		
	23-24			(a) Confidence (Praise)
	25			(b) Confidence (Reason)
	26			(a') Confidence (Praise)
	27-28			(a) Confidence (Implication)
	29			(b) Confidence (Reason)
	30			(a') Confidence (Implication)
	31-32			(+1) Confidence (Forever)

Figure 8. The Structure of Psalm 22

A second way to understand the structure of Psalm 22 is to begin by looking at the central part, part 2. I have already drawn attention to the *aba'* structure in unit 2 here—a mini-chiasm (vv. 13-19). This chiasm continues outward (see figure 9); on either side of it, there is a petition (v. 12; vv. 20-22), and there are also some verbal correspondences and a reversal of the initial distress to deliverance in the remaining larger sections (vv. 2-11; vv. 23-32). So, the structure could be understood as chiastic as follows:

A - Initial petition and distress (vv. 2-11)
   B - Petition (v. 12)
      C - Outer distress (vv. 13-14)
         D - Inner distress (vv. 15-16)
      C'- Outer distress (vv. 17-19)
   B - Petition (vv. 20-22)
A' - Reversal of distress, praise (vv. 23-32)

Figure 9. Psalm 22 as a Chiasm

---

10. See figure 2, "The Beginning of the Three-Plus-One Structure" in ch. 3.

This second structure highlights how the initial distress is completely undone by the end of the psalm. Both of these structures are compelling. Because the three-part structure shows strong correspondences with Psalm 17, I will use the three-part structure as my starting point and then address the chiastic elements and the reversals they indicate as necessary.

Psalm 22, like Psalm 17, goes beyond a typical lament to include *three* petitions (vv. 2-3, 12, 20-22), which structure the psalm into three parts (vv. 2-11, 12-19, 20-32). In figure 8 above, notice how each part begins with a unit of petition, followed by a unit that shows a progression in content: following the petition of part 1 (A), we find distress with motivation (B; vv. 4-11); following the petition of part 2 (A′), we have intensified distress (C; vv. 13-19); and following the petition of part 3 (A″), we have confidence and praise, which concludes the psalm (D; vv. 23-32).

Part 1 begins with a petition (vv. 2-3) and introduces the tragic theme of abandonment, or the farness of God. The farness of God and the pleas for him to draw near indicate the theme of his presence in this psalm, as in many others in the collection. It is important to note that God's presence (or lack thereof) is not merely a sense of companionship for the psalmist but an act of deliverance on his behalf. This is evidenced especially in the psalmist's contrast later on between his present state of abandonment with past deliverance of the ancestors (vv. 2-6) and also in the paralleling of the verbs *answer* with *save* and *rescue* in the final petition (v. 22). The psalmist is depicted as in so much pain that he *roars* (שאג), much like a lion (v. 2b). The problem introduced is that God does not *answer* (ענה); this word will come up again as the turning point in verse 22. These four lines (2a, 2b, 3a, 3b) exhibit both an *aa′bb′* structure and an *aba′b′* structure: 2a and 2b are joined morphologically and phonologically by the first-person suffixes throughout; 2a and 3a are joined by the cry *my God* (אלי/אלהי); and 3a and 3b are joined by the merism *day* (יום) and *night* (לילה) and their negation לא.

After the petition comes the first of four *aba′* structures in the psalm (B). The central subunit, *b*, describes the distress of the psalmist (vv. 7-9), but this distress is couched in God's past examples of faithfulness (*a* and *a′*, vv. 4-6, 10-11), which serve as motivation for God to answer now (i.e., to be faithful to his proven character). The focus of subunit *a* is the people of Israel's past trust in God and his faithfulness to deliver them. This verse stands in sharp contrast to the abandonment experienced by the psalmist. Verse 4 is a general statement of Israel's praise for Yhwh, which is followed by the reason in verses 5-6: the fathers trusted

Yhwh and he delivered them. Verses 5-6 show a sequential movement from trust (v. 5a), deliverance (v. 5b), escape (v. 6a), and then a summary—they were not ashamed (v. 6b). Verses 5-6 are also framed by *in you* (בך) and *they trusted* (בטחו), creating a tightly bound bundle.

A new subunit (part *b* of the *aba'* structure) is indicated in verses 7-9 by the introduction of the pronoun *I* (אנכי) and the shift in content. In verse 7a, the psalmist questions his worth and compares himself to another animal—a lowly worm. In a parallel line (v. 7b), he then contrasts himself to the fathers, who trusted and were delivered, saying that he is *a reproach of humanity* (חרפת אדם) *and despised of the people* (ובזוי עם). In other words, he does not see himself within this group whom Yhwh delivers. Verse 8 describes the activity of others in three parallel lines using imperfect third-person masculine plural verbs: they mock him, separate the lip (either mouths gaping in shock or open in slander), and shake their head.[11] Verse 9 describes their mocking speech, reusing vocabulary from how Yhwh *delivered* (פלט) the fathers, further dissociating the psalmist from the surrounding people.

The final subunit of part 1, *a'* (vv. 10-11) returns to using the second person pronoun *you* (אתה), echoing subunit *a*. It also returns to the theme and language of trust, but this time focusing on how Yhwh has sustained the psalmist since birth, expressing trust that his present state won't continue. Verses 10 and 11 consist of two sets of echoing lines (the second set is inverted), and the outer verses also form a frame with the words *you* (אתה) and *from the belly* (מבטן). Verse 11b also recalls the first word of the petition in its use of *my God* (אלי), creating a frame that demarcates part 1.

Part 2, like part 1, begins with a petition where the psalmist pleads that God not be *far* (רחוק; A"; v. 12, cf. v. 2b). Two reasons are provided as כי-clauses: distress is near, and there is no helper (vv. 12b-c). In part 2, the focus is primarily on the immense distress of the psalmist, indicated by the brevity of the petition (it is as if the immediacy of the distress takes over) and by the lack of statements of past trust as found in part 1 (called "motivation" in figure 8). The shift to focus only on distress indicates that the distress is so intense that there is room for nothing else.

The distress is described with an *aba'* structure, where subunits *a* and *a'* focus on the outer distress, or the beast-like enemies who surround

---

11. The Hebrew word גלל (typically translated as *roll*) that begins this section has the sense of "commit" here, as it also does in Ps 37:5 and Prov 16:3.

the psalmist (vv. 13-14, 17-19). The psalmist previously described himself like an animal—a lion roaring in pain (v. 2b) and a debased worm (v. 7a)—and now his enemies are compared to bulls and lions in subunit *a* and dogs and lions in *a'*. When the psalmist previously spoke of the enemies' mouths in verse 8, it was their separated lips. Here in verse 14, the image is intensified to describe their open mouths, like lions, tearing and roaring (v. 14). There is a zooming-in movement in verses 13-14, from seeing the animals surround the psalmist to seeing them open their mouths and roar.

Subunit *b* at the center focuses on the inner psychological and physiological distress of the psalmist (vv. 15-16). If the structure of Psalm 22 is viewed chiastically as indicated in figure 9, this inner distress is also the center of the chiasm of the entire psalm, making it stand out for emphasis. This subunit is made up of seven lines that have a sequential movement. First, the whole body loses its structure: the psalmist is poured out like water (v. 15a) and his bones are divided (v. 15b). Then the description of melting focuses inward even deeper as the psalmist compares his heart to wax (v. 15c) that melts in his inward parts (v. 15d). The imagery of melting wax naturally evokes imagery of heat or fire, a thought picked up in the next line: the psalmist's strength is all dried up and compared to brittle earthenware (v. 16a). It's as if extreme heat has dried up all the moisture of the body. The image then goes further, focusing on the tongue, which in complete dryness is stuck to the gums (v. 16b). The psalmist describes his ultimate withering away in the final line: God lays him in the *dust of death* (עפר מות), *dust* recalling the image of the dried-up earthenware, now ground to a powder (v. 16c).

The final subunit of this part, *a'* (vv. 17-19), reuses the lexeme *lion* (ארי) and the morphological form of סבב as *they surround me* (סבבוני) from subunit *a* (vv. 13-14) but amplifies the distress by expanding the length of the description from four lines to seven lines and by echoing both the outer and inner distress of the two previous subunits *a* and *b* (vv. 13-14 and 15-16). These seven lines show a sequential movement, much like subunit *b*, just prior. First, the psalmist is surrounded by dogs (v. 17a), who are then further identified as evil people (v. 17b). The circle gets tighter around the psalmist in the next line, when he says *like a lion [they surround/encompass] my hands and my feet* (v. 17c).[12] The center line

_____

12. I interpret כארי in Ps 22:17c as "like a lion," following the MT, and understand the verb to be implied from the previous line through ellipsis: "Dogs have surrounded me // an assembly of evil ones has encompassed me // like a lion, (they have

stands out in both its verb form[13] and by its echo of the previous subunit focused on inner distress: *I recount all my bones* (כל עצמותי; v. 18a, cf. v. 15b).[14] It is as if the psalmist has suddenly recalled how exposed and vulnerable his body is in the midst of these wild beasts. Then, it's as if these beast-like enemies come to this same awareness: they *see* (ירא־) or stare at the psalmist (v. 18b), and as a result they apportion his belongings for themselves (v. 19a–b). In so doing, they anticipate his certain death before the psalmist's eyes. Part 2 closes on this note of deep despair.

In part 3, the psalmist musters one last and long petition, echoing the two previous ones: in the first, the psalmist cried out to God because he was *far* (רחק) from his *salvation* (ישועה; vv. 2–3); in the second, he pleads that God not be *far* and says that there is no *help* (עזר; v. 12); and here, he pleads that God not be *far* and prays that God would *help* (עזר) and *save* (vv. 20–22). This petition is made up of three sets of parallel lines. The first addresses *Yhwh//my help* and petitions that he *not be far//come quickly*. It is notable that the psalmist first uses the name of Yhwh here in the psalm, to be taken up four more times in the following sections! The second set of parallel lines focuses on rescue from death. These two lines begin a semantic pattern that is followed and then subverted by the next set of lines in an important way: the first of these two lines, 21a, begins with a *Hiphil* imperative masculine singular verb (*rescue*), followed by *from* (מן) and the objects (*the sword, my being*); the second line begins with *from* and the indirect object (*the hand of the dog*), followed by the direct object (*my only one*; v. 21b); the verb is omitted but implied. The next set of parallel lines, 22a–b, follows the pattern by beginning

---

encompassed/surrounded) my hands and my feet." Hebrew poetry commonly uses ellipses, as is evident from the very first verse of this psalm; "like a lion" is consistent with the pairing of lion and dogs in vv. 21–22; lions are mentioned throughout this poem in vv. 14, 17, and 22, and also in the parallel psalm, 17. For further survey of opinions and history of interpretation of this verse, see the following: G. Vall, "Psalm 22:17b: 'The Old Guess,'" *JBL* 116 (1997): 45–56; J. Linville, "Psalm 22:17B: A New Guess," *JBL* 124 (2005): 733–44. It is worth noting that whether one adopts the translation of "lion" or not, the animal imagery is still preserved and the point is that this one is surrounded and oppressed by beast-like humans.

13. Verse 18a uses an imperfect first-person common singular verb, in contrast to the perfect third-person masculine plural verbs in the rest of the unit (vv. 17, 18b, 19).

14. This line focusing on the psalmist's inner distress, v. 18a, at the center of this subunit (vv. 17–19), mirrors how the psalmist's inner distress stands at the center between the descriptions of outer distress in this unit (vv. 13–19) in an *aba'* structure. This is a good example of how structures are mirrored on different levels of the text and teach the reader what to expect.

with a *Hiphil* imperative masculine singular verb (*save me*) followed by *from* and the indirect object (*the mouth of the lion*). The final line begins as expected with *from* and the indirect object (*the horns of the wild ox*) but then subverts the pattern: rather than implying the verb *save me* by ellipsis, or even including an imperative verb, the text reads *you have answered me* (עניתני), using the *Qal* perfect form of the verb ענה. This incohesive verb form does not seem accidental, since what follows in the remainder of the psalm is a description of immense praise to Yhwh for his rescue of the afflicted one. In other words, something has happened in this verse that initiates this praise. All of the subsequent verbal forms and themes shift their focus to the future. Whether one interprets עניתני as a past event or a certain future event, there is one thing that is clear: the axis upon which the shift from lament to praise rests is what Yhwh does for the psalmist in *answering* him, a verb that echoes the initial cry of the psalmist that Yhwh does *not answer* him (v. 2).

Just as the petitions of parts 1 and 2 are followed by *aba'* structures, part 3 follows suit but is an amplified version, consisting of *two aba'* structures (D; vv. 23–26, 27–30). Rather than focusing on distress, these *aba'* structures consist of immense confidence and praise for the positive implications that the deliverance of the afflicted one has on all humanity.

Subunit *a* of the first *aba'* structure is made up of two sections (vv. 23, 24). The first is a set of inverted echoing lines describing how the psalmist will praise Yhwh in the congregation (v. 23). The reuse of the word *recount* (ספר) in the *Piel* imperfect here is significant: rather than *recounting* all his bones (v. 18a), the psalmist will *recount* Yhwh's name in the congregation, indicating a reversal of circumstances. The next section is comprised of three parallel lines that command the whole congregation—called *fearers of Yhwh, offspring of Jacob*, and *offspring of Israel* (ישראל)—to *praise* (הלל; v. 24). It is significant that the psalmist now identifies himself firmly within the people of Israel, whereas before he distanced himself from participating in the *praises* (הלל) of *Israel* (ישראל) because of his afflicted state (v. 4b). His isolation has been reversed and he finds himself at the head of the community, orchestrating their praise to Yhwh.

Subunit *b* (v. 25) begins with a כי-clause and consists of three lines describing the reason for praise. The first line stands alone as an *aa'bb'* structure of two negated verbs and two words for the object: *he has not despised and he has not detested* (לא בזה ולא שקץ) *the affliction of the afflicted* (ענות עני). The word *despised* (בזה) also indicates a reversal of the psalmist's previous state as a *despised one* among the people (v. 7b), and the root of *affliction* and *afflicted* is the same as that of *answer*, עָנָה, defining the affliction in terms of the lack of answer from Yhwh and also resolving the initial conflict of the farness of God with his answer (vv. 2–3). The next two lines are tightly bound with inverted parallelism and exhibit a movement from the general—not despising or detesting (v. 25a)—to specific: God did not hide his face, but heard his crying (v. 25b–c).

Subunit *a′* (v. 26) recalls subunit *a* (vv. 23–24) in the reuse of the words *praise* (הלל), *congregation* (קהל), and *fear* (ירא), and in returning to the theme of communal praise. This communal aspect becomes the main focus of the final unit of the psalm (vv. 27–32), where the benefits experienced by the *afflicted one* (עָנִי; v. 25a) are extended to all *afflicted ones* (עֲנָוִים; v. 27a).

The second *aba′* unit within part 3 elaborates on the implications for the community. Subunits *a* and *a′* mirror one another in their use of the words *eat* (אכל), *worship* (חוה), *earth* (ארץ), and *life/preserve* (חיה); in the use of two *Qal* imperfect third-person masculine plural verbs within one line (vv. 27a, 28a, 30a); and in the repetitive use of *all* (כל) to identify the subjects (vv. 28, 30). Subunit *a* of the *aba′* structure consists of two sections (vv. 27 and 28), the first made up of three lines and the second of two even more tightly bound echoing lines. Both sections begin with a line with two *Qal* imperfect third-person masculine plural verbs describing the benefits of the community: *they will eat* (יאכלו), *they will be satisfied* (וישבעו; v. 27a), *they will remember* (יזכרו), and *they will turn* (וישבו; v. 28a). This unit (vv. 27–30) shows an expansion in theme from the previous unit (vv. 23–26): not only is there an expansion from the individual *afflicted* (עָנִי) to the *afflicted ones* (עֲנָוִים), but there is an expansion from focus on Israel/Jacob (v. 24) to the more generic *seekers of him* (דרשיו; v. 27b), *the ends of the earth* (אפסי ארץ), and *all families of the nations* (כל משפחות גוים; v. 28). In other words, all humanity will benefit from the deliverance of the afflicted one and return to worship Yhwh. The phrase *all families of the nations* recalls God's promise to Abraham in Genesis 12:3 that God would bless *all families of the earth* (כל משפחת האדמה) through him. The expansion from the *afflicted* to *afflicted ones* and from *Israel* to the *nations* in Psalm 22 is one example of many where God's blessing comes to the one for the benefit of the many.

Just as in the prior *aba′* structure, *b* here begins with a כי-clause and provides the reason for satisfaction and worship: Yhwh is the king, even over the nations (v. 29). Following this, *a′* consists of three lines

(v. 30). The first two lines show an echoing structure, using imperfect third-person masculine plural verbs to describe how all will *eat* (אכלו), *worship* (ישתחוו), and *bow* (יכרעו) before Yhwh. *All the fat of the earth* and *all who go down to the dust* are paired as a merism to show that everyone— from the well-off to the dying—are the recipients of Yhwh's benefits, and in this, there is equity. The final line amplifies this claim: *even [the one who] his being he cannot preserve*—in other words, the dying or the dead. Just as God's dominion expands horizontally to *the ends of the earth* (v. 28a), so it also extends downward to the realm of the dead. The words *dust* (עפר) and *being* (נפש) in these lines (v. 30a–b) recall the state of the afflicted one, whose *being* needed rescue (v. 21a) and who was laid in the *dust* of death (v. 16c). Just as in Psalms 16, 17, and 23, we see the theme here of the one, suffering and afflicted, even to the point of death, who will be delivered and brought to new life. Psalm 22 adds to the story that this rescue affects all of humanity.

Part 3 and the entire psalm end with a climactic declaration that future generations will serve Yhwh and will continue to declare what he has done to generations to come (vv. 31–32). This section is added to the end of the two *aba'* sections and so stands out for emphasis as the psalm's climax. This section along with verses 23–24 frames unit D with the words *recount* (ספר) and *offspring* (זרע). Here, not only will the psalmist *recount* Yhwh's rescue of the afflicted to the *offspring* of Israel (vv. 23–24), but *offspring* will serve Yhwh as a result (v. 31a), and then they will also *recount* Yhwh's rescue to the next generation (v. 31b). The two lines that follow continue this sequence of declaring what Yhwh has done to the next generation, a people who will be born (v. 32b). Psalm 22 ends in a completely different place than it began—with people everywhere and from every time praising and feasting, all because of what Yhwh has done in rescuing the afflicted one.

REUSE AND DEVELOPMENT IN PSALM 22

I previously concluded that Psalms 17 and 22 are most closely connected with one another in terms of their shared distinctive elements, and that their strength of cohesion is significantly high. Psalms 17 and 22 are the only two psalms in the collection that can be classified as proper laments. As such, they have many structural correspondences, although we will see that the structure of Psalm 22 goes beyond Psalm 17 in significant ways. The two psalms are also closely connected in terms of their distinctive themes, lexemes, and phrases. All of their major themes are shared with one another and distinctive within the collection: distress, trust in Yhwh, beast-like enemies, deliverance, and satisfaction/feasting. The two psalms also share thirty-two lexemes, twenty-eight of which are distinctive: *lion* (ארי), *encompass* (נקף), *tear* (טרף), *sword* (חרב), *destroy* (שדד), *surround* (סבב), *mouth* (פה), *trust* (בטן), *satisfy* (שבע), *dwell* (ישב), *humanity* (אדם), *inherit* (חלק), *lip* (שפה), *being* (נפש), *bow* (כרע), *answer/afflict* (ענה), *deliver* (פלט), *hide* (סתר), *face* (פנה), *listen* (שמע), *call* (קרא), *night* (לילה), *earth* (ארץ), *speak* (דבר), *hand* (יד), *live* (חיה), *righteousness* (צדק), and *heart* (לבב). This is a large number compared to other psalms in the collection.[15] The first five of these lexemes are very rare, used only in these two psalms within the collection. These two psalms also share the highest number of distinctive phrases (three), which are combinations of the following lexemes: *sword* (חרב) and *my soul* (נפשי), *lion* (אריה) and *tear* (טרף), and *God* (אל), *call* (קרא), and *answer* (ענה).[16] Though their morphological cohesion is not as strong as when paired with other psalms, Psalms 17 and 22 still share distinctive forms of the following lexemes: *answer, hand, heart, satisfy,* and *night.* In what follows, I will explore the correspondences and development in structure between the two psalms and then various intensifications from Psalm 17 to 22.

STRUCTURAL SIMILARITIES AND INTENSIFICATIONS

According to modern form-critical categories, both Psalms 17 and 22 are best categorized as individual complaints or laments. As laments, the two psalms exhibit similar structures, each containing the following typical elements: a cry to Yhwh, the lament proper, motivation for Yhwh to intervene, petition, and statement of confidence and/or a vow.[17]

If you compare figures 7 and 9 earlier in this chapter, you'll notice that both psalms contain three parts, each part beginning with a petition. As laments, both of these psalms stand out by repeating the petition three times, which creates a close cohesion between them. Other structural similarities include the progression from motivation in part

---

15. The only psalms that share more distinctive lexemes when paired together are Pss 17 and 18 with thirty-one lexemes and Pss 18 and 22 with twenty-nine lexemes. Pss 18 and 19 also share twenty-eight lexemes. It is no coincidence that each of these include Ps 18, since it has a whopping fifty-one verses and therefore more opportunity for repeated words. It is significant, then, that Pss 17 and 22 share such a high amount of distinctive lexemes, with fifteen and thirty-two verses respectively.

16. Pss 18 and 20, 18 and 21, and 15 and 24 also share three distinctive phrases.

17. See Gunkel, *Introduction to the Psalms,* 121–98.

1 to distress in part 2 to confidence in part 3. The concluding section of confidence in both psalms uses the distinctive corresponding lexemes *righteousness* (צדק), *presence* (פנה), *satisfy* (שבע), and *live* (חיה), further strengthening the cohesion (Pss 17:14c–15; 22:27–32).

The structures of the two psalms also show intensification and progression from Psalm 17 to 22. At the most basic level, all three sections of motivation, distress, and confidence are expanded in Psalm 22. Specifically, Psalm 22 seems to intensify the themes of Psalm 17 through its feature of doubling—words, phrases, sections, or images repeated to enhance their effect.[18] Many of these doubled elements intensify the distress in Psalm 22. Doubling occurs on the larger structural levels down to the level of the line. For example, the psalm opens with the double petition, *my God, my God,* and the petition *do not be far* exists verbatim in verses 12 and 20. The following patterns of structural doubling indicate an intensification of distress in Psalm 22: (1) The description of distress occurs in two parts in Psalm 22, as compared to one in Psalm 17 (Pss 17:10–12; 22:7–9; 13–19). (2) There is doubling of the motivation (each beginning with *you* [אתה]) for God to answer the psalmist in Psalm 22, which frames the distress in verses 7–9 so that it stands out structurally for emphasis. (3) A section describing the animals as enemies (termed "outer distress") is doubled to frame the inner physiological distress of the psalmist, so that his torment stands out for emphasis. (4) The third petition in Psalm 22 heightens the distress of the psalm by its repetition of specific lexemes from the previous unit of distress, rather than only using typical language of petition from verses 2–3 and 12.[19]

Doubling also intensifies the theme of praise in Psalm 22. Doubling is a strong feature within the large section of praise that concludes the psalm (vv. 23–32). In Psalm 22, parts 1 and 2 each contain an *aba'* structure that focuses on distress; but part 3 contains *two consecutive aba'* structures to express confidence and fulfillment (vv. 23–32). The reason for praise is repeated at each of the two centers (*b* of each *aba'* structure). There is also verbal and lexical doubling on the level of the line that occurs at the beginning of various sections. A significant example of this occurs in the first reason for praise (subunit *b*) in verse 25a, where there is a verbal doubling followed by the doubling of the lexeme *afflict*: "He

---

18. See Schaefer, *Psalms*, 52; Futato, *The Book of Psalms*, 98.
19. These lexemes include the following: *Yhwh* (יהוה) in Ps 22:9, 20; *rescue* (נחל; Hiphil) in Ps 22:9, 21; *hand* (יד) in Ps 22:17, 21; *dog* (כלב) in Ps 22:17, 21; and *mouth of the lion* (פה אריה) in Ps 22:14, 22. See Auffret, "Les Psaumes 15 à 24," 419–20.

has not *despised* [בזה] and he has not *detested* [שׁקץ] the *affliction* [ענות] of the *afflicted* [עני]." The repetition makes this verse stand out for emphasis. Each of the opening lines in the final *aba'* structure (vv. 27a, 28a, and 30a) begins with doubling of the same verb form; this also occurs in the final verse of the psalm (v. 32a). The following additional elements are repeated twice within the section of praise: a vow to praise Yhwh (vv. 23, 26); the reference to those who *fear* (ירא) Yhwh (vv. 24, 26); imagery of a feast using the lexeme *eat* (אכל); those of the *earth* (ארץ) bowing *before* God (לפניו/לפניך; vv. 28, 30); and the blessing of *life* (חיה; vv. 27, 30).

In addition to the structural feature of doubling, the shift in structure in Psalm 22 is also a development from its parallel psalm, 17. While both Psalms 17 and 22 conclude with a section of confidence and fulfillment, the shift from lament to praise in Psalm 22 is one of the most dramatic in the Hebrew Psalter. Although lament psalms typically do conclude with a verse or two expressing confidence,[20] Psalm 22 shifts its focus to praise for the *final ten verses* of the psalm. The shift in structure is so dramatic that many posit that verses 1–22 and verses 23–32 were originally separate psalms.[21] I am inclined to think that verses 23–32 are integrally connected because of the reuse of various lexemes and the resulting reversal of circumstances that they indicate.[22] In its present form, the effect of this shift intensifies the praise and carries the narrative thread forward toward fulfillment.

The structural similarities and differences between Psalms 17 and 22 show how the themes of distress and praise are intensified in Psalm 22. There are additional elements—lexemes, morphologies, and phrases—that also show the intensification of these and other themes, including enemies as predatorial animals, trust in Yhwh, deliverance, and

---

20. Ps 88 is the exception. See D. M. Howard Jr., "Psalm 88 and the Rhetoric of Lament," in *My Words are Lovely: Studies in the Rhetoric of the Psalms*, ed. R. L. Foster and Howard, LHB/OTS 467 (New York: T&T Clark, 2008), 141–42.

21. See B. Duhm, *Psalmen* (Leipzig and Tübingen: Mohr, 1899), 68–74; Lipiński, "L'hymne à Yahwé Roi en Psaume 22,28–32," *Biblica* 50 (1969): 153–68; C. Krahmalkov, "Psalm 22,28–32," *Biblica* 50 (1969): 389–92; O. Keel-Leu, "Nochmals Psalm 22,28–32," *Biblica* 51 (1970): 405–13; P. Wiemar, "Psalm 22, Beobachtungen zur Komposition und Entstehungsgeschichte," in *Freude an der Weisung des Herrn, Beiträge zur Theologie der Psalmen, Festschrift für Heinrich Gross*, ed. E. Haag and F.-L. Hossfeld (Stuttgart: Verlag Katholisches Bibelwerk, 1986), 471–94.

22. Lexemes in vv. 23–32 that also occur in vv. 1–22 include the following: *recount* (ספר), *in the midst* (בתוך), *praise* (הלל), Yhwh (יהוה), *Israel* (ישראל), *despise* (בזה), *answer/afflict* (ענה), *heart* (לבב), *dust* (עפר), *being* (נפשׁ), and *people* (עם).

satisfaction/feasting. These themes and their corresponding elements will be addressed in turn.

INTENSIFIED DISTRESS

The theme of distress, especially with regard to the psalmist's enemies, creates a strong cohesion between Psalms 17 and 22, along with its related lexemes, morphologies, and phrases. In both psalms, the psalmist's *being* (נפש) is in danger, indicated by the distinctive phrases "deliver my *being* [נפש] ... by your *sword* [חרב]" (Ps 17:13) and "rescue my *being* [נפש] from the *sword* [חרב]" (Ps 22:21). Both psalms depict the enemies of the psalmist as arrogant, overwhelming, deadly animals (Pss 17:9–12; 22:8, 13–19, 21–22). The description of the enemy as *a tearing lion* (a corresponding phrase constructed from the lexemes טרף and ארי) and the highly distinctive lexemes *encompass* (נקף) and *sword* (חרב) occur only in Psalms 17 and 22 within the entire collection of Psalms 15–24, uniting them closely together.[23]

Both psalms depict the psalmist's petition for vindication from within the midst of deep distress, sharing pleas for Yhwh to *hear* (שמע), *answer* (ענה), *protect* (שמר), and *deliver* (פלט) the psalmist from his enemies (Pss 17:1–2, 6–9; 22:2–3, 12, 20–22). Yet the distress of Psalm 22 is systematically intensified from Psalm 17, so that within the storyline of Psalms 15–24, it is beyond any distress previously imagined. The distinctive phrase describing *calling* (קרא) to God (אל) for him to *answer* (ענה) exemplifies the distress of both psalms and is only used within these two psalms in the collection. Both phrases use the highly distinctive morphological form of ענה as *you answer*, which also only occurs here in the collection.[24] Whereas in Psalm 17, the psalmist *calls* (קרא) because he is confident that Yhwh will *answer* (ענה), in Psalm 22, the psalmist *calls* (קרא) repetitively—daily and nightly—but Yhwh does *not answer* (לא ענה; Pss 17:6; 22:3). This phrasal and morphological link creates a direct contrast between Yhwh's nearness in Psalm 17 and his farness in Psalm 22, increasing the distress in the latter.[25]

---

23. All four occurrences of ארי in the collection occur in Pss 17 and 22 (Pss 17:12; 22:14, 17, 22). These uses account for two-thirds of the uses in Book I (see Pss 7:3 and 10:9). טרף occurs in Pss 17:12; 22:14; נקף in Pss 17:9; 22:17; and חרב in Pss 17:13; 22:21.
24. ענה occurs in both psalms as a *Qal* imperfect second-person masculine singular verb.
25. אלהי אקרא יומם ולא תענה (Ps 22:3); אני קראתיך כי תענני אל (Ps 17:6). This phrase occurs in only one other place in Book I: Ps 3:5, making it exceedingly rare.

The contrast between the nearness of Yhwh in Psalm 17 and his far-ness in Psalm 22 is also evidenced by the reuse of the lexemes *speak/words* (דבר) and *night* (לילה). In Psalm 17, the psalmist is close to the *words* (דבר) of Yhwh, in contrast to the enemies who *speak* (דבר) arrogantly (vv. 4, 10); in Psalm 22, Yhwh is far from the psalmist's *words* (דבר) of groaning (v. 2). In Psalm 17, Yhwh visits the psalmist at *night* (לילה; v. 3); in Psalm 22, the psalmist calls out all *night* (לילה), but Yhwh does not answer (v. 3).

In Psalm 22, distinctive lexemes from Psalm 17 are used in contrastive ways, and the result is deeper distress. For example, whereas *deliver* (פלט) occurs as a petition in Psalm 17, it occurs in Psalm 22 to emphasize that he has not been delivered (Pss 17:13; 22:5, 9). *Lips* (שׂפה), once used to describe the righteousness of the psalmist, now describe the enemies' gaping and mocking mouths (Pss 17:1, 4; 22:8). The *mouth* (פה) of the enemy that spoke with arrogance in Psalm 17 now waits to devour the psalmist in Psalm 22 (Pss 17:10; 22:14). In Psalm 17, the *heart* (לבב), once searched and secure, is now melting like wax in fear (Ps 17:3; 22:15). The reuse of the lexemes *sword* (חרב) and *hand* (יד) also show a movement from Yhwh's power to the enemies' power, amplifying distress: in Psalm 17, Yhwh wields the *sword* against the enemies, but in Psalm 22, the enemies wield the *sword* against the psalmist (Pss 17:13; 22:21); the *hand* (or power) in Psalm 17:14 is Yhwh's, but in Psalm 22, the psalmist's *hands* are encircled and the *hand* of the dogs is against him (vv. 17, 21).

In addition, many of the lexemes used positively in Psalm 17:3–5 to describe the psalmist's righteousness are used negatively in Psalm 22; the result is a more dire portrayal of the psalmist's situation.[26] The strophe describing the psalmist's righteousness in Psalm 17 (vv. 3–5) is altogether absent in Psalm 22, which also indicates that the distress has increased to the point where the psalmist's sole focus is on the enemies as the motivation for God to answer, rather than trust in Yhwh's faithfulness to respond to righteousness.

BEAST-LIKE ENEMIES

In both Psalms 17 and 22, the enemies of the psalmist *surround/encompass* (סבב) him and are compared to a *lion* (ארי). However, in Psalm 22,

---

26. The lexemes *heart* (לב; Pss 17:3; 22:15), *night* (לילה; Pss 17:3; 22:3), *mouth* (פה; Pss 17:3, 10; 22:14, 22), and *humankind* (אדם; Pss 17:4; 22:7) are all used positively in Ps 17 to express the psalmist's righteousness, but in Ps 22, these are used to express his anguish.

the distress is intensified by repetition of this imagery in three places, in comparison with one occurrence in Psalm 17 (Pss 17:11; 22:13–14, 17,
21–22). The phrasal link made up of *lion* (ארי) and *tear* (טרף) closely binds
these psalms. In Psalm 17, this *lion* sits in hiding, waiting to *tear*, and in
Psalm 22, the *lion* is portrayed with mouth wide open in the act of *tearing* (Pss 17:12; 22:14, 22). Psalm 22 also goes beyond Psalm 17 in describing
the enemies not only as lions but as other beasts—dogs and bulls. The
biblical theme of humans becoming like beasts as they turn away from
God is front and center in Psalm 22.

In Psalm 22, the description of the psalmist's enemies as animals
(Ps 22:13–14, 17, 21–22) also alternates with the physiological experience
of the psalmist's body wasting away and the sheer terror he feels (Ps
22:15–16, 18–19), enhancing the distress of the psalm. In the sections describing this physiological terror, the progression is toward death, with
the first section indicating that the psalmist is dying and the second section declaring that the psalmist is as good as dead and that this is recognized by the beast-like onlookers who divide up his clothing.[27] It's worth
noting that whereas Psalm 17 portrayed the enemies as unjustly having
an *portion* (חלק), in Psalm 22 this becomes more threatening as it's the
psalmist's own clothing they *apportion* (חלק; Pss 17:14; 22:19).

FAILED EXPECTATIONS: TRUST IN PSALM 22

The theme of trust exists in both Psalms 17 and 22. The way the theme
of trust is used in Psalm 22 deepens the theme of distress, both by con-
tradictions between trust and suffering within the psalm itself and also
in comparison with Psalm 17. Within Psalm 22, there is a contradiction
between what the psalmist knows to be true about God and his reality, which creates a very strong sense of distress. This contradiction is
expressed from the very beginning of the psalm in the dire question
My God, my God, why have you forsaken me? where *my God* indicates hope
and covenant relationship, yet *forsaken* indicates broken covenant. The
construction *you have forsaken me* (עזבתני) is used in the perfect to indicate a sense of completed and final action. The psalmist expresses the

---

27. That the psalmist is dying is indicated by the phrase "you lay me in the dust of
death" (v. 16). Casting lots for one's clothing indicates that the psalmist is as good as
dead (v. 19). For example, in the Midrash, the people of Susa do that to Esther. *The
Midrash on Psalms*, trans. W. G. Braude, vol. 1 (New Haven, CT: Yale University Press,
1954), 304–5, 321. Likewise, in *ANET*, provision is given for dividing belongings upon
death. *ANET*, 183; see also Sir. 14:15.

contradiction between what he knows to be true—that God delivers those who trust in him—and what he experiences to be true—that God has abandoned him.

The abandonment the psalmist feels runs through verse 11 of the psalm and expresses itself in a negative comparison between himself and his ancestors, who trusted God. The psalmist recalls how past trust led to deliverance for his ancestors and sustained him as a baby, which creates a contrast with the present distress of the psalmist. In the first of these sections, the lexeme *trust* (בטח) is used three times emphatically to affirm that trust has always resulted in deliverance. The contrast continues in the following verse, where the psalmist's self-identification as a worm indicates that although he is more desperate than his ancestors, Yhwh still does not answer. By identifying himself as a worm and a reproach among humanity, he isolates himself from the community. The enemies mock the psalmist's trust in verse 9, and the psalmist expresses his despair at the contradiction between his own experience of trust from birth onward and the present moment of distress.

The complexity of trust in Psalm 22 stands in contrast to the use of the theme in Psalm 17. Whereas the theme is used in positive ways in Psalm 17 to express confidence in Yhwh's vindication, in Psalm 22 the theme is not used positively, creating disequilibrium.[28] In Psalm 17, the psalmist perceives himself as upright in regard to the works of *humans* (אדם; Ps 17:4); but here, he says he is not even a *human*, but a worm (Ps 22:7). Whereas in Psalm 17 the psalmist confidently pleads for God's *deliverance* (פלט; v. 13-14), in Psalm 22 he dissociates himself from the fathers who were *delivered* and is mocked for his commitment to God when he is not *delivered* (vv. 5, 9). The radical shift in the usage of the theme of trust and the lexeme בטח indicates a deepening distress centered on Yhwh's perceived abandonment of the psalmist.

The theme of trust in Psalms 17 and 22 also deepens our understanding of what the word righteousness means throughout the collection—that it involves trust in Yhwh. So far through this study, we

---

28. The psalmist especially expresses confidence in Yhwh's vindication in Ps 17:1, 15. The psalmist trusts that Yhwh will respond to the faithfulness of the psalmist with deliverance, based on the promise of Ps 15 and his covenant relationship with Yhwh (see Ps 17:3-5, where v. 5 uses the same phrase from Ps 15:5). This covenant relationship is implied by use of imagery from Deut 32, where Yhwh keeps Israel as the "apple of his eye" and spreads out his "wings" over her (Deut 32:11; Ps 17:8). The theme of trust occurs in Ps 22 in vv. 4-6, 10-11.

have seen how righteousness allows a person to enter the presence of Yhwh or serves as a motivation for Yhwh to deliver. Psalms 15 and 24:2–5 provide a great example of this, where the one who is righteous in deeds, speech, and heart is able to enter the presence of Yhwh. In Psalm 17, the psalmist uses both the language of *righteousness* and *trust* as leading to deliverance, connecting the two ideas semantically. He describes his righteousness as part of the motivation for Yhwh to answer him, saying things like *hear my righteous plea ... made without lips of treachery* (v. 1) and reminding God that there is no evil way in him (v. 3–4). Yet he also uses the language of *trust* as an impetus for God to deliver, when he prays that God would enact his *loyal love* (חסד) and deliver those who *take refuge* (חסה), or trust, in him (v. 7). Psalm 22 takes the theme further: rather than using any typical language of righteousness leading to deliverance, it's trust that the psalmist connects to deliverance. He does this through the negative comparison of how his ancestors trusted and were delivered (in contrast to himself). The connection is also evident, though more covertly, in his own pain and confusion caused when Yhwh *his God*, whom he trusts, does not deliver him. The enemies' mockery of the psalmist's trust—*commit to Yhwh, let him deliver him*—also shows that the assumed pattern is that trust leads to deliverance (v. 9). This parallel between both righteousness and trust leading to deliverance helps us further define righteousness as a relational term involving trust, lest we assume it is strictly adherence to an abstract moral code.

Failed Expectations: Secondary Connections with Psalm 18 and 20

The distress of the psalmist in Psalm 22 is further highlighted by its high cohesion with Psalms 18 and 20, as displayed in table 10 at the beginning of this chapter.[29] Although the subject of this chapter is the relationship between Psalms 17 and 22, because Psalm 22 also has high morphological cohesion with Psalms 18 and 20, it is important to explore the impact of that relationship.

Psalm 18 is a thanksgiving psalm for Yhwh's deliverance of the king, and Psalm 20 is a confident prayer for the king based on this past deliverance.[30] Both psalms express certainty that Yhwh will defend and deliver his Davidic king. On the heels of these two victorious psalms, the

---

29. See appendix 2 for further data.
30. I develop this idea further in the next chapter.

immense distress and abandonment of Psalm 22 stands in stark contrast. Shared morphological forms between these psalms also contrast the lack of deliverance in Psalm 22 with the confidence and deliverance of Psalms 20 and 18. The petitions of Psalm 22 use various distinctive forms of words shared with these previous two psalms. For example, the construction *my God* (אלי) is used only in Psalms 18 and 22 in the collection. When the psalmist cries out *my God* in Psalm 22:2, this recalls the praise of *my God* as refuge, shield, and salvation in Psalm 18:3. Psalm 18:51 concludes with the declaration that God gives great *salvation* (ישועה) to his king, and in Psalm 20, the people shout for joy at the king's *salvation* (v. 5). But in Psalm 22, the psalmist cries out that his *salvation* is far (v. 2).[31] In Psalm 20, the community confidently prays that Yhwh would *answer* (ענה) the king in his day of *trouble* (צרה), sending *help* (עזר; vv. 1, 3), and the fulfillment of this prayer is sure (vv. 7–10). But in Psalm 22, the same morphological form of *trouble* is used to express that trouble is near, but there is no *help* (v. 12).

The distress of Psalm 22 is also described with distinctive words and phrases shared with Psalm 18, and the result is a contrast. The most persuasive example of this is a phrase using the same morphological form of חפץ to mean *he delights in me/him*. In Psalm 18:20, this phrase occurs on the lips of the psalmist as *he rescued me because he delighted in me* (יחלצני כי חפץ בי). In Psalm 22:9, the phrase occurs on the lips of the mocking enemies as *let him deliver him, because he delights in him* (יצילהו כי חפץ בו).[32] In addition, the constructions *my hands* (ידי) and *my feet* (רגלי) are used in opposite ways between the psalms, resulting in increased distress. Whereas the psalmist uses these words in Psalm 18 to express God's provision for him in making his *feet* secure and training his *hands* for war, in Psalm 22, the psalmist's *hands* and *feet* are encircled by the enemies, reversing the security of Psalm 18 (Pss 18:35; 22:17). The result is a great contrast between the expectation of deliverance and the actuality of suffering, which further deepens the tone of distress in Psalm 22.[33]

---

31. Pss 20 and 22 use the same morphological form of ישועה as a common feminine singular construct noun. Ps 18:51 uses the same noun form but in the plural.

32. The verbs in these phrases differ but are phonologically similar, both beginning with י and containing ב, ל, and ה/ח. The elements כי חפץ ב are common to both phrases. See appendix 2 for data.

33. The morphological forms אקרא (Pss 18:4, 7; 22:3), רבים (Pss 18:17; 22:13), and מים (Pss 18:12; 22:14) are also used contrastively between these two psalms to create expectation and deepen distress.

INTENSIFICATION OF PRAISE

The heightening of distress in Psalm 22 creates a situation that is more dire than previously imagined, wherein the psalmist is utterly forsaken by "his God." However, the story does not end here. The despair is matched in strength with praise. We have already noted how the structure of Psalm 22, with its final ten verses of confident fulfillment, highlights the praise in the psalm. In addition, Psalm 22's lexical correlations with Psalm 17 and additional themes intensify praise in the psalm.

In Psalm 22, the deliverance that was hoped for in Psalm 17 is actualized. Psalm 22 uses lexemes shared with Psalm 17 and the result is a reversal of circumstances. For example, the lexemes *answer* (ענה), *listen* (שמע), *hide* (סתר), and *face* (פנה) are used in petitions in Psalm 17, but in proclamations of fulfillment in Psalm 22.[34] Yhwh fulfills or answers the psalmist's petitions in Psalm 22 by rescuing the afflicted. The experience of God's *righteousness* (צדק), defined throughout both psalms as his just deliverance of the afflicted, is also actualized in Psalm 22. In Psalm 17, the psalmist expresses confidence that upon waking, the psalmist will see God's *righteousness* (v. 15). In Psalm 22, God has demonstrated his righteousness in the act of delivering the afflicted, and generation after generation will declare this *righteousness* in an ongoing fashion (v. 32). In Psalm 17, the word *life* (חיה) expresses a temporary experience—the psalmist says that his enemies have pleasure in this life, in contrast to himself, who will awake in the presence of Yhwh (v. 14). But in Psalm 22, *life* is enduring: the psalmist prays that the people's hearts may *live* forever (v. 27), and declares that even the one who cannot preserve his own life will be safe and secure (v. 30).

This last correlation mentioned—*life* (חיה)—hints at an important development from Psalm 17 to 22: the deliverance that is realized in Psalm 22 leads to praise, not only for the psalmist but the entire community. The introduction of the communal implications in Psalm 22 is a development, and one that is consistent with previous developments explored from Psalms 15 and 16 to Psalms 23 and 24. This development contributes to the magnitude of praise in Psalm 22 and also is part of a larger theme introduced in that psalm, the theme of Yhwh's universal kingdom.

---

34. ענה is used in Pss 17:6; 22:22; שמע is used in Pss 17:1, 6; 22:25; סתר is used in Pss 17:8; 22:25; פנה is used in Pss 17:2, 9, 13, 15; 22:25, 28, 30.

A New Theme: Yhwh's Universal Kingdom

Perhaps the most profound development from Psalm 17 to 22 is the introduction of the theme of Yhwh's *kingdom* (מלוכה) and his *rule* (משל) extending to the ends of the earth in verses 27–32. This theme resolves all previous distress and continues to heighten the theme of praise. This new theme is indicated by use of shared of lexemes and themes in new ways and the widening in scope of various elements. Psalm 22 also reveals what event in the plotline initiates this expansion and development toward the kingdom.

EXPANSION TO ALL PEOPLE, PLACES, AND TIMES IN PSALM 22

The theme of praise in Psalm 22 progresses into a strong statement of confidence in verses 27–32, where the new theme of the global kingdom is introduced. When compared with Psalm 17, this prophetic section reverses the power of the enemies in Psalm 17:13–14 and expands the effect of the deliverance of the afflicted one to *all people*.

Through its use of shared lexemes and phrases with Psalm 17, the final ten verses of Psalm 22 show an expansion from the individual to the community and specifically contrast the power of the human enemy with the benefits received by the community of Yhwh. For example, in Psalm 17, the psalmist petitions that God would confront the enemies' *faces* (פנה) and *bring them down* (כרע), but in Psalm 22, these words occur in a declaration of praise that all who are in distress shall *bow before* (כרע) Yhwh's *presence* (פנה; Pss 17:13; 22:28, 30). In Psalm 17, the enemies are intent on bending the psalmist to *the earth* (ארץ), but in Psalm 22, all of *the earth* will turn to Yhwh. In Psalm 17, the wicked are *satisfied* (שבע) and have *life* (חיה), while in Psalm 22, the afflicted ones will be *satisfied* and have *life*.[35] Thematically, the *offspring* (זרע) of the wicked are satisfied in Psalm 17, but in Psalm 22, future *offspring* will proclaim the work of Yhwh

---

35. I am persuaded that Ps 17:14 refers to the positive inheritance of the enemies to express the psalmist's displeasure, rather than either a negative inheritance for the enemies or the inheritance of the treasured ones of Yhwh. First, there is no textual evidence for amending ממתים (*mortals*) in the MT to מות. Second, "their" in v. 14b most naturally corresponds to the enemies of v. 13, rather than a new subject. Third, the word "treasure" in v. 14c is singular, so it does not likely correspond with the plural "their" in v. 14b–c. Fourth, *with the living* (בחיים) here most naturally indicates the good blessing of life, rather than something in contrast with the better blessing of the afterlife, since the plural noun חיים is used most often to indicate being alive or to express more explicitly that life is a good gift or blessing.

in delivering the righteous (Pss 17:14; 22:31-32). This positive reuse of lexemes and themes depicts God's good kingdom as consuming wickedness.

The extension of God's good kingdom to all of the earth is further indicated by various expansions that take place within Psalm 22 itself, especially in verses 27-32. When compared with Psalm 17, the expansions
in Psalm 22 indicate that the deliverance of the afflicted affects *all people*.
Within Psalm 22 itself, the singular *afflicted* (עָנִי) is pluralized to *afflicted
ones* (עָנִים) to show that any and all who identify with the afflicted one
will participate in feasting and worship (vv. 25, 27). In other words, it is
because Yhwh has not despised the *affliction* (עֱנוּת) of the *afflicted one*
that *[all] the afflicted ones* who seek Yhwh will feast and worship. These
afflicted ones are defined in the next verse as not only those of the community of Israel but also those of the global community—the *nations*
(גּוֹיִם). The nations are not in view in Psalm 17 at all, and certainly not
for blessing. However, in Psalm 22, the expansion of blessing includes
not only the community of Israel but the nations as well. The actions
of the nations in worshiping Yhwh are described by the characteristi-
cally Israelite lexemes *remember* (זכר) and *turn* (שׁוּב) to indicate that the
nations are included with Israel in her worship of Yhwh as a result of
his deliverance. Various merisms also indicate that all people who seek
Yhwh (v. 27) will join in feasting and worshiping him: the fat and poor
(vv. 27, 30);[36] the living and the dying (vv. 27, 30); Israel and the nations
(vv. 24, 28-29). The final verses of the psalm indicate that *all people* does
not just include the present population, since *posterity* (זֶרַע), *future generations* (דּוֹר יָבֹאוּ), and *a people yet unborn* (עַם נוֹלָד) are said to worship
Yhwh because of his deliverance.[37] The inclusion of all people from all
places and all time in the worship of Yhwh indicates that verses 27-32
have in mind the theme of the kingdom of Yhwh.

Psalm 22:28 also includes spatial expansion, indicated by the phras-
es *all the ends of the earth* (כָּל אַפְסֵי אֶרֶץ) and *all families* (כָּל מִשְׁפְּחוֹת), the
former of which is used throughout the Hebrew Bible in expectation of

---

36. Because of the contextual similarities, I find it best to understand *fat* (דָּשֵׁן) and
poor (עָנִי) in relation to one another as forming a merism, rather than emending דָּשֵׁנִי
to a form of דָּשֵׁן as some have suggested, e.g., M. Dahood, *Psalms I*, AB 16 (Garden City,
NY: Doubleday, 1965), 143-44.

37. In v. 32, Yhwh's *righteousness* (צֶדֶק) is in parallel structure with the proclamation
"he has done it," indicating that the telling of Yhwh's righteousness can be defined
as a specific work. Contextually, this work is the deliverance of the afflicted, which
provides the source of praise in v. 25. Righteousness can best be understood then
as "vindication."

the kingdom.[38] When paired with *remember* (זכר) and *return* (שׁוב), these images recall the scattering of Genesis 11 and the promise of Genesis 12:3 that *all families of the earth* (כל משׁפחת האדמה) would be blessed. This theme of the kingdom of God in Psalm 22 is a significant expansion from Psalm 17, where no such theme is present.

THE KINGDOM AS THE EFFECT OF DELIVERANCE IN PSALM 22

Some have argued that the expansion of blessing to the community occurs on account of either the democratization of the Davidic identity to the Israelite community or the function of the afflicted one as a role model whose experience can be attributed to anyone who is going through suffering. For example, Hossfeld and Zenger argue that Psalms 15 through 24 reflect the process of constituting a collective identity in response to the shock of the exile by democratizing the Davidic identity or applying it to the community of the marginalized poor in Israel.[39] Miller likewise contends that because the king is a model for and equal to the people, kingship in these psalms is democratized, and the people are royalized.[40]

It is true that this psalm-group so far shows an extension to referents other than the Davidic king and that by their nature as psalms on the lips of the community, the community is meant to associate with the experiences and identity of the Davidic king. There are also signs in this psalm group, as Hossfeld and Zenger suggest, of what they call "group consciousness" (*Gruppenbewußtsein*; e.g., Pss 20:5, 8; 21:13; 22:25–31). However, signs of group consciousness and communal language do not *necessitate* that all qualities and interactions of the afflicted individual be attributed to all of Israel or the broader community. Rather, it is possible that the deliverance of the afflicted one here in Psalm 22 is redemptive; in other words, deliverance *affects* the people rather than *describes* the people.[41]

Certainly, the afflicted one does serve as a role model for all people, but he is not *solely* a role model. For example, the psalm does not depict it as a necessity for the community as a whole to experience the same deliverance as the afflicted one in order to receive blessing. Rather, the

---

38. Deut 33:17; 1 Sam 2:10; Pss 2:8; 67:7; 72:8; 98:3; Isa 45:22; 52:10; Jer 16:19; Zech 9:10; Prov 30:4.
39. Hossfeld and Zenger, "Wer darf hinaufziehn zum Berg JHWHs?," 167–68; see also Hossfeld and Zenger, "Komposition von Ps 24," in *Die Psalmen I*, 177.
40. Miller, "Kingship," 129–30.
41. See Sumpter, "Coherence," 203.

community is *told* of Yhwh's great work and serves Yhwh in response (Ps 22:31–32). And it is not only the poor who are uniquely in view in Psalm 22. *Poor* exists as part of a merism with *fat*, as do *the alive* and *the dying* and *Israel* and *the nations*, in order to demonstrate that *all people* are invited into Yhwh's kingdom. In other words, the poor do not stand out as the only ones receiving blessing from Yhwh in Psalm 22.

I find it best to conclude that the individual afflicted in Psalm 22 functions both as one to identify with and as the one *through* whom redemption comes. The community is meant to follow his example and trust in God's deliverance in the midst of suffering, but they also benefit from Yhwh's deliverance of the afflicted one. That the people worship Yhwh for his work on behalf of this individual makes sense if this one is the king, as many (including Hossfeld, Zenger, and Miller) understand him to be. Throughout the Hebrew Bible, the king functions as the representative of God's people. The people do not *become* the king, but they do benefit from the success and righteousness of the king. While the community does participate and resonate with the king, full democratization of the afflicted one in Psalm 22 would neglect this one's redemptive function. I find it more precise to view the afflicted one here as both a representative and example, and also the one through whom redemption comes. Specifically, Yhwh's kingdom is inaugurated by his deliverance.

SUMMARY

Psalms 17 and 22 are highly cohesive and therefore continue the pattern of parallel psalms further toward the center of the collection. As the only laments in the collection, both psalms express the deep distress of the psalmist. Yet Psalm 22 goes beyond 17 in the depth of its distress and the height of its praise. The developments from Psalm 17 to 22 also show consistency with the other psalm pairs in that Psalm 22 intensifies the experiences of Psalm 17; shows spatial, temporal, and communal expansion; and introduces the theme of Yhwh as the king. The deliverance of the afflicted one in Psalm 22 initiates the section of praise in the psalm, which involves the return of all humanity to Yhwh to worship, praise, feast, live, and be satisfied. In other words, the rescue of the afflicted one is the act that inaugurates Yhwh's kingdom on earth.

Within the broader context of the collection, Psalm 17 carries forth the confidence of Psalms 15 and 16 into the on-the-ground experience of suffering. Psalm 22's placement after Psalms 18 and 20 shows that even though Yhwh has promised deliverance for his anointed, the anointed one will also undergo great suffering. It makes sense that after the deliverance and cosmic effect of that deliverance in Psalm 22, Psalm 23 is a psalm of security and renewed trust in Yhwh. The placement of Psalm 22 before Psalm 24 clarifies that Yhwh's kingdom and arrival as king (depicted in Ps 24) come about as a result of his deliverance of the afflicted one.

The overall development as the collection moves inward toward Psalms 17 and 22 is from the ideal vision of God's kingdom to the on-the-ground experience of suffering (Pss 17 and 22). Psalm 22 ties these themes together: it is through that suffering that the ideal vision of the kingdom is ultimately realized. Reading forward from Psalm 22, Psalm 23 continues the theme of praise and feasting in light of suffering and deliverance and moves toward the arrival of God as king on earth in Psalm 24. It remains to be seen what Psalms 18, 20, and 21 add to this developing storyline. As the investigation continues inward to these three psalms, the driving question is whether these psalms confirm the chiastic pattern, especially in light of the fact that there are three psalms rather than two. I will also explore whether they exhibit the same developments toward the kingdom and expansions to the community as occurs in other psalm pairs.

6

The Hinge: The King's Deliverance in Psalms 18, 20, and 21

Psalms 18, 20, and 21 surround Psalm 19 at the center of the psalm group, the latter of which functions as part of the frame of the collection. From the first half of the collection to the second, we have observed a consistent development toward the kingdom of Yhwh, through revelation of his identity as king and communal and spatial expansions. In this chapter, I will explore the unique relationship among Psalms 18, 20, and 21, how these psalms contribute to the structure of the collection, and also their role in developing the storyline of the collection in their position at the center.

COHESION AMONG PSALMS 18, 20, AND 21

The connections between each of Psalms 18, 20, and 21 and every other psalm within the collection are visually presented in tables 11–13. These tables suggest that these three psalms are mutually and closely connected to one another.

Table 11. Psalm 18: Strengths of Cohesion

Psalm Pair	Lexemes	Themes	Structures	Phrases	Morphologies	Superscripts	TOTAL
18 and 15	0.33	0.00	0.00	0.00	0.14	0.00	0.47
18 and 16	0.55	0.04	0.00	0.00	0.07	0.00	0.66
18 and 17	0.88	0.05	0.00	0.00	0.64	0.00	1.57
18 and 19	0.82	0.13	0.00	0.00	0.77	0.30	2.02
18 and 20	0.63	0.24	0.00	0.29	0.59	0.30	2.05
18 and 21	0.80	0.27	0.00	0.28	0.56	0.30	2.20
18 and 22	0.83	0.00	0.00	0.07	0.87	0.30	2.06
18 and 23	0.24	0.10	0.00	0.00	0.27	0.00	0.60
18 and 24	0.53	0.07	0.00	0.10	0.31	0.00	1.16

Table 11 displays the distinctive lexical, thematic, structural, phrasal, morphological, and superscript links between Psalm 18 and every other psalm within the collection.[1]

The table shows that Psalm 18 is most closely connected to Psalm 21, especially due to shared themes, phrases, and superscripts; the two psalms also have strong lexical cohesion. Overall, Psalm 18 shows strong cohesion with the four psalms that follow it, Psalms 19–22: these each share distinctive superscript elements; Psalms 18 and 19 are closely connected by morphologies and lexemes, as we have seen with other neighboring psalms; Psalms 18 and 20, like 18 and 21, are closely connected in terms of themes and phrases; and Psalms 18 and 22 are lexically and morphologically cohesive. Before drawing conclusions about these relationships, let's examine the connections between each of Psalms 20 and 21 and the other psalms in the collection.

The strengths of cohesion between Psalm 20 and every other psalm within the collection are displayed in table 12:

Table 12. Psalm 20: **Strengths of Cohesion**

Psalm Pair	Lexemes	Themes	Structures	Phrases	Morphologies	Superscripts	TOTAL
20 and 15	0.26	0.06	0.00	0.00	0.32	0.21	0.86
20 and 16	0.72	0.12	0.00	0.00	0.11	0.00	0.95
20 and 17	0.59	0.21	0.00	0.00	0.00	0.00	0.80
20 and 18	0.63	0.24	0.00	0.29	0.59	0.30	2.05
20 and 19	0.54	0.10	0.00	0.00	0.14	1.00	1.78
20 and 21	0.54	0.96	0.00	0.26	0.42	1.00	3.17
20 and 22	0.59	0.16	0.00	0.00	1.00	0.51	2.26
20 and 23	0.51	0.14	0.00	0.00	0.13	0.21	1.00
20 and 24	0.61	0.23	0.00	0.00	0.52	0.21	1.57

Table 12 shows that Psalm 20 shares the strongest connection with Psalm 21, with an overall strength of cohesion of 3.17 and high levels of thematic and superscript cohesion. They also share phrasal cohesion. In addition to its strong cohesion with Psalm 21, Psalm 20 is also closely connected to Psalms 18 and 22. Psalm 20 is closely connected with Psalm 18 in terms of lexemes, themes, phrases, and morphologies, and like Psalm 18, it shares distinctive lexemes and morphologies with Psalm 22. Tertiarily, Psalm 20 is connected to Psalm 19 at the center.

This final table displays the strengths of cohesion between Psalm 21 and every other psalm within the collection:

---

1. See appendix 2 for further data related to tables 11, 12, and 13.

Table 13. Psalm 21: Strengths of Cohesion

Psalm Pair	Lexemes	Themes	Structures	Phrases	Morphologies	Superscripts	TOTAL
21 and 15	0.40	0.07	0.00	0.15	0.20	0.21	1.03
21 and 16	0.98	0.23	0.00	0.12	0.36	0.00	1.69
21 and 17	0.95	0.15	0.00	0.12	0.36	0.00	1.59
21 and 18	0.80	0.27	0.00	0.28	0.56	0.30	2.20
21 and 19	0.58	0.05	0.00	0.00	0.32	1.00	1.95
21 and 20	0.54	0.96	0.00	0.26	0.42	1.00	3.17
21 and 22	0.48	0.18	0.00	0.00	0.47	0.51	1.64
21 and 23	0.57	0.41	0.00	0.29	0.35	0.21	1.83
21 and 24	0.66	0.21	0.00	0.00	0.00	0.21	1.08

Table 13 reveals that Psalm 21 reciprocates the high level of cohesion with Psalm 20: the two psalms are most closely connected to one another. They have exceedingly strong thematic and superscript cohesion and also share distinctive phrases and morphologies. The table also shows that Psalm 21 is connected to Psalm 18, sharing the strongest morphological cohesion and also sharing phrases and lexemes. Psalm 21 also shows a tertiary connection with Psalm 19.

Now that all of the data have been presented for these three psalms, we can draw conclusions about their relationships. Psalms 20 and 21 are mutually most closely connected to one another. Because Psalms 20 and 21 are neighboring psalms, rather than parallel psalms across the collection, I will refer to them as "twin psalms," following the apt designation of W. Zimmerli.[2] Psalm 18's closest connection is Psalm 21, which reciprocates that connection, second only to its connection with Psalm 20. Psalms 18 and 20 also share strong cohesion. These relationships suggest that Psalms 20 and 21, when paired together, function as the chiastic counterpart to Psalm 18. Moreover, I will show later in this chapter how the overarching structures of Psalm 18 and Psalms 20-21 (when paired together) reflect each other with striking correspondence. (This correspondence is not accounted for on the above tables because the structure emerges only when Psalms 20 and 21 are treated together, while the tables treat them as discrete texts.) Each of Psalms 18, 20, and 21 shows secondary connections with Psalm 19

---

2. "Twin psalms" (*Zwillingspsalmen*) is a term used by Zimmerli to describe psalms that are closely related by key word links (*Stichwörter*) and themes. He lists the following as some examples of twin psalms: Pss 1-2; 3-4; 9-10; 14 and 53; 30-31; 31-32; 32-33; 38-39; 39-40; 40-41; 42-43; 43-44; 69-70; 73-74; 74-75; 77-78; 79-80; 80-81; and 127-128. Zimmerli, "Zwillingspsalmen," 106-11.

at the center. This is an important relationship, which I will explore in the following chapter.[3] Psalms 18 and 20 also show some cohesion with Psalm 22, but since Psalm 22 is so closely bound to Psalm 17, it does not seem to function as a chiastic counterpart to either Psalms 18 or 20. I will explore the connections between these psalms and Psalm 22 in the following chapter, where I draw conclusions about a linear reading of the psalm-group.

The close relationship between Psalms 18, 20, and 21 confirms that the shape of Psalms 15–24 is chiastic, as depicted in figure 10:

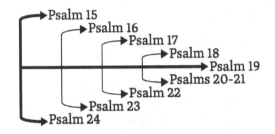

Figure 10. The Chiastic Shape of Psalms 15-24

This chiastic shape of Psalms 15–24 strongly suggests that these psalms form a distinctive collection. I will synthesize the overall message of this collection in the following chapter. It remains here to examine the message of and relationships between each of Psalms 18, 20, and 21.

THE SHAPE OF PSALM 18

Psalm 18 begins with a title that is both connected to its surrounding psalms and also unique. *For the director* (למנצח) links Psalm 18 with the four psalms that follow it, and yet each of these following psalms includes *of David* (לדוד). In contrast, Psalm 18 has *of the servant of Yhwh* (לאבד יהוה), linking this psalm closely with the next, Psalm 19, which speaks of David as the servant. The title is also one of a handful of historical superscripts in the Psalter, which places the psalm in the historical context of the rescue of David from Saul, and literarily, within the narrative of 2 Samuel 22, where this psalm is substantially re-presented. This elaborate title does not seem to stand apart from the structure of the psalm, since it contains various verbal links with the psalm itself. For that reason, I include it as a vital part of the structure of the psalm.

---

3. See "The Threefold Structure of Psalm 15–24" in ch. 7.

Structure 9

Psalm 18

Part					

1　**A**　　*1a For the director,*
1b of the servant of Yhwh,
1c who spoke to Yhwh the words of this song,
1d in the day Yhwh rescued him,
1e from the palm of all his enemies,
1f and from the hand of Saul.

2a And he said,
2b I love you, Yhwh, my strength;

3a Yhwh, my crag, and my stronghold, and the deliverer of me;
3b My God, my rock, I take refuge in him;
3c My shield, and my horn of salvation, my secure height.

　　　B　**a**　4a The one to be praised, I called on—Yhwh;
4b And from my enemy, I am saved.

　　　　　b　5a They encompassed me, the cords of death;
5b And the torrents of worthlessness terrified me.
6a The cords of Sheol surrounded me;
6b They confronted me, the snares of death.

　　　a'　7a In my distress, I called to Yhwh;
7b And to my God, I cried for help.
7c He heard from his temple my voice;
7d And my cry for help before him came into his ears.

　　　　　C　**1**　**a**　8a And it shook and it quaked, the earth;
8b And the foundations of the mountains trembled;
8c And they tossed to and fro, because he burned with anger.

9a It went up, smoke from his nostrils;
9b And fire from his mouth consumed;
9b Burning coals burned from him.

　　　　　　b　10a He bent the skies and came down;
10b And a heavy cloud was beneath his feet.
11a And he mounted upon a cherub and he flew;
11b And he flew swiftly upon the wings of the wind.

　　　　　a'　12a He made darkness his hiding place;
12b Surrounding him was his thicket,
12c —darkness of waters;
12d —dark clouds of fine mist.

13a From brightness before him, his dark clouds advanced,
13b —hail and burning coals of fire.
14a And he thundered from the skies, Yhwh;
14b And the Most High uttered his voice,
14c —hail and burning coals of fire.

　　　　　2　**a**　15a He sent his arrows and scattered them;
15b Great lightning bolts and confused them.

　　　　　　b　16a And they appeared, the channels of the waters;
16b And they exposed themselves, the foundations of the world,
16c from your rebuke, Yhwh,
16d from the blow of the breath of your nostrils.

　　　　　a'　17a He sent from high;
17b He took me;
17c He drew me out from great waters.

　　　　　3　**a**　18a He rescued me from my strong enemy;
18b and from those who hate me, because they were mightier than me.

　　　　　　b　19a They confronted me in the day of my calamity;
19b But Yhwh was my support.

　　　　　a'　20a He brought me out to a spacious place;
20b He delivered me because he delighted in me.

2   D 1 a 21a Yhwh rewarded me according to my righteousness;
21b According to the cleanness of my hands, he has recompensed me.

b   22a For I kept the ways of Yhwh;
22b And I have not been wicked from my God.

c   23a For all his judgments are before me;
23b And his statutes I do not take away from me.

b'   24a And I was blameless with him;
24b And I kept myself from iniquity.

a   25a And Yhwh recompensed me according to my righteousness;
25b According to the cleanness of my hands before his eyes.

2   26a With the loyally loving, you show yourself loyally loving;
26b With the blameless man, you show yourself blameless;
27a With the pure, you show yourself pure;
27b But with the crooked, you show yourself twisted.

28a For you, an afflicted people you save;
28b But the eyes of the high ones you make low.
29a For you, you cause to shine my lamp;
29b Yhwh my God illuminates my darkness.
30a For with you, I can run against a troop;
30b And with my God I can leap over a wall.

3   31a God—blameless is his way;
31b The speech of Yhwh is refined;
31c —A shield is he for all those who seek refuge in him.

3   C 1 32a For who is God besides Yhwh?
32b And who is a rock except our God?

2 a 33a God—the one who girds me with strength;
33b And he makes blamelessness my way.

b   34a The one who sets my feet like a doe.
34b And upon my high places he causes me to stand.
35a The one who trains my hands for battle,
35b So a bronze bow will bend [by] my arms.

a' 36a And you give me the shield of your salvation;
36b And your right hand supports me;
36c And your humility makes me great.

3   37a You widen my steps beneath me;
37b And they do not waver, my ankles.

38a I pursued my enemies and I overtook them;
38b And I did not turn back until their end.
39a I shattered them and they were not able to rise;
39b They fell beneath my feet.
40a And you have girded me with strength for battle;
40b You make bow those who rise, beneath me.

B a 41a And my enemies, you give me [their] neck;
41b And those who hate me, I annihilated them.

42a They cried for help, but there was no savior;
42b —Upon Yhwh, but he did not answer them.

b   43a And I made them as fine as dust upon the surface of the wind;
43b Like mud in the streets, I poured them out.

a' 44a You have delivered me from the strife of the people;
44b You have set me as the head of nations.

44c People I did not know serve me;
45a At the hearing of the ear, they obey me;
45b Foreigners cringe before me;
46a Foreigners wither;
46b And they tremble from their fortresses.

A 47a Alive is Yhwh!
47b And blessed is my rock!
47c And exalted is the God of my salvation!

48a God—the one who gives vengeance to me;
48b And he leads peoples beneath me;
49a —The deliverer of me from my enemies.
49b Surely from those who rise up, you exalt me;
49c From the man of violence, you rescue me.

50a Therefore, I will praise you among the nations, Yhwh;
50b And to your name, I will sing praises;
51a —The one who makes great the salvation of his king,
51b —And the one who shows loyal love to his anointed one,
51c —to David, and to his offspring, forever.

Psalm 18, like the others we have explored so far, has three main parts
(vv. 1–20, 21–31, and 32–51). The first and third parts mirror one another
broadly in their descriptions of Yhwh's deliverance of the king from his
enemies, while the central part (vv. 21–31) pauses the narrative movement to focus on the blameless character of and loyal relationship between Yhwh and the servant. Part 1 consists of three units (vv. 1–3, 4–7,
and 8–20), narrating the servant's cry to Yhwh in the midst of his distress and Yhwh's response of coming down and rescuing the psalmist.
Part 2 in the middle consists of one unit, focused on the reciprocal relationship between Yhwh and the servant. Part 3 then builds back out in
reverse order from part 1; it consists of three units (vv. 32–40, 41–46, and
47–51), together narrating the salvific empowerment of Yhwh against
enemies, whose cries to Yhwh are ineffectual. The repeated words and
ideas between parallel units within the psalm create the following seven-part chiastic structure:

Structure 10

A Introduction: The servant loves and praises Yhwh for his protection and salvation (vv. 1–3)
  B The servant cries out in his distress and Yhwh hears (vv. 4–7)
    C Yhwh rescues the servant from enemies (vv. 8–20)
      D Yhwh reciprocates loyal love and blamelessness (vv. 21–31)
    C' Yhwh empowers the psalmist in victory over enemies (vv. 32–40)
  B' Enemies cry out but Yhwh does not hear; rather they hear and obey the servant (vv. 41–46)
A' Summary: The king praises Yhwh for his salvation, exaltation, and love for the king and his seed
    (vv. 47–51)

Let us now explore the shape and message of Psalm 18 in more detail by
giving attention to the message of each unit and the relationships between corresponding units. Unit A consists of three subunits (vv. 1, 2, 3).
The first subunit identifies the speaker as the servant and introduces the
main plot of the psalm: Yhwh has rescued the servant from all his enemies. The second subunit (v. 2) begins with *and he said* (ויאמר), introducing the speech of the servant, which governs the rest of the psalm. This
is a unique opening to a psalm, because presumably every psalm is the
speech of the psalmist. This may be a feature of the historical superscript,
which functions as a narrative introduction. The word also creates a literary connection with verse 31, where the only other use of this lexeme
in the psalm occurs (as אמרת), there describing the speech of Yhwh. The
effect is a relationship between the psalmist's words and Yhwh's words.
This is a small hint at one of the main themes of the psalm: the reciprocal
relationship between Yhwh and the servant. There is another oddity in
this verse, and that is the declaration that the psalmist loves Yhwh (v. 2).
The lexeme for *love* here is רחם, which is typically employed by a superior

or one in authority over another.[4] It is a word that carries a nurturing and compassionate connotation. At first it appears odd that the psalmist would use this word toward Yhwh, but the relationship between this unit (A) and unit A' offers insight: In A', Yhwh shows *loyal love* (חסד) to his king. חסד and רחם are often paired throughout the Hebrew Bible to describe the character and covenant relationship between God and his human partners.[5] In that sense, they are parallel ideas. Here, as occurs elsewhere between parallel texts, these two related lexemes have been strategically placed to indicate a relationship to one another. The effect in the psalm is the portrayal of a reciprocal relationship of loving faithfulness between the servant and Yhwh.

The third subunit (v. 3) of unit A consists of three lines, each with three descriptions of Yhwh's character as a protective, saving God. These lines are united in sound by the first-person singular suffixes and in content as describing Yhwh as the psalmist's safe place. *I take refuge* (אחסה; v. 3b) stands out for emphasis as a verb among nouns, and as the final element of the middle line; notably, it will come up again as the final element of the third part of the central unit (v. 31c). Many of the words of verse 3 are repeated as key words throughout the psalm and occur at structurally significant locations (*deliver* [פלט], *My God* [אלי], *rock* [צור], *take refuge* [חסה], *shield* [מגן], and *save* [ישׁע]). Its description of the plot of the psalm (v. 1) and introduction of keywords (v. 3) reinforce the idea that unit A functions as an introduction to the psalm.

Unit B (vv. 4–7) is joined to unit A at the seam by the repetition of the lexeme *save* (ישׁע; vv. 3c, 4b). This is a common way that repeated words join units of text together. Like unit A, unit B consists of three subunits, this time in an *aba'* structure (vv. 4, 5–6, 7). The first and third subunits are joined by the phrase *I called to Yhwh* (אקרא יהוה). Both outer subunits also show a movement from the call (vv. 4a, 7a–b) to Yhwh saving the psalmist (vv. 4b; 7c–d), with the latter verses expanding on the former by doubling in length. The central subunit (vv. 5–6) describes the distress of the servant in terms of being surrounded. It consists of four lines, tightly bound together by overlapping parallel structures: there are two sets of inverted parallel lines (*aa'bb'*); repetition in the first and third line in the phrase *cords* (חבלי) *of death* and *cords* (חבלי) *of Sheol* and the sound play between *encompassed me* (אפפוני) and *surrounded me*

---

4. Some examples include Deut 30:2–3; 1 Kgs 3:26; Isa 49:15–6; 63:15; Jer 31:20; Pss 51:1; 78:38; 103:13; 106:46; Dan 1:9; 9:9; 2 Chr 30:9; Neh 1:11; 9:27–8.
5. E.g., Exod 34:6; Joel 2:13; Ps 103:8–9; Neh 9:17, 31; 2 Chr 30:9.

(סבבוני; *aba'b'*); and an outer frame of *death* (מות; *abb'a'*). The overarching *aba'* structure of unit B maps the ideas of enemy and death onto one another as confronting the psalmist. This correspondence is also a result of the wordplay between *Sheol* and *Saul*, which use the same letters in Hebrew (שאול, vv. 1f, 6a). As a whole, unit B introduces the storyline of the psalm by recounting the servant's cry and distress.

Unit C continues to move the plotline forward by focusing on Yhwh's response. The unit break is indicated by a shift in subject (from the psalmist to Yhwh) and in imagery. Unit C is expanded in length from previous units and consists of three subunits, each made up of three smaller sections. The effect of this expanded structure is to place emphasis on this significant moment of Yhwh's coming down to rescue the psalmist. The first subunit (vv. 8–14), is itself made up of three sections, the first describing the anger of Yhwh and quaking of earth (vv. 8–9), the second describing the action of Yhwh coming down (vv. 10–11), and the third describing the darkness and fire surrounding him (vv. 12–14). These three sections form an *aba'* structure, with the first and third united by their repetition of the words *fire* (אש) and *burning coals* (גחלים בערו), and their language of creation—*earth* (ארץ), *foundations* (מוסד), *waters* (מים), and *skies* (שמים). Verses 8 and 9 each consist of three lines. Verse 8 is unified by the sound play of words describing shaking: ותגעש, ותרעש, ירגזו, and ויתגעשו. The verse ends with the reason for the trembling—Yhwh's anger. Verse 9 expands on this anger through three parallel lines each moving deeper into the person of Yhwh, progressing from smoke going up to fire in the mouth to burning coals deep within him. This anger results in action, which is the focus of the central section (vv. 10–11) of this subunit. There Yhwh *comes down* (ירד), a word used in other defining moments when Yhwh chooses to enter humanity's world to bring about de-creation and re-creation, notably at Babel, Sodom, the deliverance from Egypt, and at Sinai (Gen 11:5, 7; 18:21; Exod 3:8; 19:18). In this psalm, as at Babel and in Egypt, Yhwh hears the people's cry and responds by coming down (Ps 18:7; Gen 18:20; Exod 2:23). Lexemes recalling Yhwh's descent at Sinai are employed throughout all three sections: *dark cloud* (עב), *skies* (שמים), *burning* (בער), *fire* (אש), *heavy cloud* (ערפל), and *mountain* (הר; cf. Deut 4:11). The third section (vv. 12–14) closes the subunit by describing Yhwh wrapped in darkness, radiating brightness, and thundering from the heavens. The creation imagery (*earth, skies, wind, waters*) and the Sinai imagery together depict Yhwh as responding to the cry of his servant in an active and personal way to bring about de-creation and re-creation.

The storyline continues in sequential fashion in the next subunit (vv. 15–17). This subunit also has an *aba'* structure (vv. 15, 16, 17). Sections *a* and *a'* are united by the lexemes *sent* (שׁלח) and *great* (רב) to describe how Yhwh acts on behalf of the psalmist against enemies. Section *b* at the center depicts the parting of the waters by the *wind/breath* (רוח) of Yhwh's *nostrils* (אף), an image that echoes the original act of creating a space for life by dividing the waters, and then especially the parting of the Red Sea by the *wind* of Yhwh's *nostrils* (Exod 14:21; 15:8), depicting this rescue in the form of the deliverance of Moses and Israel. The third section of this subunit (v. 17) solidifies the depiction of this servant as a Moses figure in its description of Yhwh *drawing out* (משׁה) the servant from *the waters* (מים). The lexeme *draw out* is extremely rare, used only in this psalm (and its re-presentation in 2 Sam 22) and in the description of Pharaoh's daughter *drawing out* Moses from *the waters* and naming him accordingly (Exod 2:10). The effect is a uniting of this servant figure with the figure of Moses, the leader of and intercessor for Israel.

The final subunit of unit C (vv. 18–20) summarizes the psalm thus far, as is evident by its use of repeated words that recall units A and B (*rescue* [נצל], *day*[יום], *enemy*[איב], and *confront* [קדם]) and also in terms of its content, which summarily states that Yhwh rescued the servant. Like the previous subunits, this subunit can also be understood as an *aba'* structure (vv. 18, 19, 20), with the outer sections united by Yhwh as the subject of their matching verb forms and by paronomasia of those verbs: יצילני and ויוציאני. Part 1 as a whole is delineated by an inclusio, using the words *in the day* (ביום), *Yhwh* (יהוה), *rescued* (נצל), and *enemy* (איב; vv. 1, 18–19). The final verse of part 1 (v. 20), seems to stand out in two ways. First, it is the first verse that does not contain any lexemes that have already been used. Second, new content is introduced: Yhwh's deliverance is a result of his *delight* (חפץ) in the servant. These two features give verse 20 a transitional function: they look forward to the next unit, which focuses on the servant's character and Yhwh's recompense.

Right at the center of the seven-part structure of the psalm are verses 21–31, part 2 of the psalm (also called unit D), framed by the lexemes *blameless* (תמם), *keep* (שׁמר), and *Yhwh* (יהוה; vv. 21–22, 24, 31). These verses dramatically shift the focus of the psalm away from the sequential plot we saw in part 1 to more general principles about how Yhwh engages with the righteous. The dramatic shift is evident in content, tone, and in its use of almost entirely new lexemes. It is notable that save (ישע; v. 28a), shield (מגן; v. 31c), and take refuge (חסה; v. 31c) are three lexemes of five lexemes that are also used in part 1, and that these words occur in the introduction to describe the character of God (v. 3). The character of God as reciprocating loyal love and blamelessness is the focus of this central part of the psalm.

Part 2 can be broken up into three subunits (vv. 21–25, 26–30, 31). The first consists of a five-part chiastic structure in the form of ab-cb'a': Verses 21 and 25 correspond almost verbatim in their language of Yhwh (יהוה) recompensing (שוב) the servant according to his righteousness (כצדקי) and the cleanness of his hands (כבר ידי), and in their inverted parallel structure. Verses 22 and 24 are united by language about keeping (שמר) the ways of Yhwh and by contrastive parallelism. At the center is verse 23, which alone consists of echoing parallelism and focuses on the instruction of Yhwh. The chiasm focuses attention on how Yhwh's instruction (c) undergirds the psalmist's blamelessness (b and b'), which leads to recompense (a and a'). The neat chiastic structure itself portrays God's instruction as ordered and wise.

The second subunit (vv. 26–30) further elaborates on the reciprocal character between Yhwh and the faithful. The subunit has three sections, the first consisting of another tightly structured set of echoing lines (vv. 26–27) that elaborate the general principle or reciprocal relationship. Yhwh is said to reciprocate loyal love (חסד), a term that is often used of Yhwh's relationship with his covenant partner. He is also said to reciprocate blamelessness (תמם)—a word which threads all three subunits of part 2 together (vv. 24a, 26b, 31a). The verses of the second section (vv. 28–19) are united as two sets of echoing lines (aa'bb') and also in an aba'b' echoing structure through repetition of for you (כי אתה) in verses 28a and 29a. This second section gets more specific about the recompense that God is said to provide: it involves saving the afflicted and making low the high (vv. 28–29). Notice how that key word from the introduction, save (ישע), comes up again here in this center section of the center subunit of the center part of the psalm; its structurally significant position confirms how central this idea of Yhwh's saving is. By the reuse of the words illuminate (נגה) and darkness (חשך; v. 29b) from the section of Yhwh's coming down in darkness (חשך) and brightness (נגה; vv. 12–13a), the idea of rescue here becomes closely associated with Yhwh's coming down. The third section of the subunit gets even more specific about the result of Yhwh's saving activity by introducing military imagery of running against a troop and leaping over a wall (v. 30), imagery that will further play out in the following unit (C').

The final subunit of part 2 (v. 31) functions in content as a summary, just as we saw at the end of part 1 (vv. 18–20). Its summary nature is further indicated by the high repetition of lexemes from within part 2 (God [אל], blameless [תמם], way [דרך], and Yhwh [יהוה]) and also from the introduction of part 1 (shield [מגן], speak [אמר], seek refuge [חסה]; vv. 2–3). As a whole, part 2 clarifies that Yhwh's instruction and his commitment to respond with loyal love are the foundation for the rescue that the servant recounts in the psalm.

The final part of the psalm, part 3, is made up of three units (C': vv. 32–41; B': vv. 41–46; and A': vv. 47–51), themselves each made up of three subunits. Unit C' picks up the storyline from part 1 and focuses on how Yhwh empowers the servant and exalts him over his enemies forever. It is similar to its parallel unit (C) in its description of Yhwh's engagement with the servant and also in its use of the repeated words my feet (רגלי), beneath (תחת), great (רבה), and enemies (איבי), but differs by describing the result of Yhwh's engagement as the servant's success in battle, rather than the general hearing of the cry. In that sense, it is more concrete and specific. The first subunit of unit C' consists of a double question about God's identity, calling him a rock (צור; v. 32), which echoes the introduction once again. The second subunit (vv. 33–36) can be viewed as an aba' structure that provides the answer to verse 32. The outer sections a and a' use the lexeme give (נתן) and describe how Yhwh supports the servant (vv. 33, 36). The central section, b, consists of four lines that share imagery of the feet and hands of the servant (vv. 34–35). The third subunit of unit C' (vv. 37–40) is united by its use of beneath me/my feet in each of its three sections (vv. 37, 38–39, 40). It provides the result of the empowering: the servant overtakes his enemies. Like the second subunit, this one too uses the word my feet at the center and concludes with a phrasal repetition of the opening line of that subunit, you have girded me with strength (אזר חיל; vv. 33a, 40a). It is worth noting that the question-answer-result structure of unit C' bears similarities (in structure, not content) to that of an entrance liturgy, which we find in Psalms 15 and 24 in the broader literary context.

Unit B' (vv. 41–46) continues the narrative thread from unit C' by focusing on the servant's defeat of his enemies, linking the two units together with the words enemies (איבי) and you give me (נתנה לי). Simultaneously, unit B' provides a contrast to its parallel unit, B' (vv. 4–7), through its use of the repeated words *cry for help* (שוע), *enemies* (איבי), *save* (ישע), *hear/ obey* (שמע), and *ear* (אזן; vv. 4, 7, 41–42, 45). Whereas in unit B, the servant *cries for help* and is *saved* from his *enemies*, in unit B' the *enemies cry for help* but there is no *savior*. In unit B, God *hears* the servant's cry with his *ears*; in B', the enemies *obey* (שמע) as soon as they *hear* (שמע) with their *ear*. This reuse of lexemes has the effect of contrasting God's response to the servant with his response to the enemies, in alignment with the general principles expounded in part 2 (see especially v. 28). The reuse of lexemes also indicates an ironic reversal where the *enemies* of the *servant* (עבד) *of* Yhwh (v. 1) now *serve* (עבד) the servant (v. 44c).

Structurally, unit B' consists of three subunits that can be viewed as an *aba'* structure (vv. 41–42, 43, 44–46). The first subunit is made up of two sets of parallel lines focused on Yhwh's giving over of the enemies to the servant. The second subunit (v. 43) is interesting in that it reuses two lexemes from the initial descent of Yhwh—*fire* (שחק) and *wind* (רוח; vv. 11b, 12b)—to describe what the servant does to the enemies. Perhaps the effect is a uniting of Yhwh's action in rescuing the psalmist with the action of the psalmist against his enemies: this one is a representative of Yhwh and acts in alignment with him. The third subunit returns to the theme of the first (vv. 41–42): Yhwh delivers the servant from the enemies, here described as the *people* (עם) and *nations* (גוי), two words picked up in the final unit, A'. The subunit has two sections, the first consisting of a set of lines describing Yhwh's deliverance and exaltation and the second using five lines to expand on the idea of the exaltation over other nations: as the earth trembled before Yhwh, now the peoples tremble before the servant (v. 46b). The depiction echoes Psalm 2, where, although the *nations* conspire against Yhwh's anointed, Yhwh installs him as king over the nations, who are warned to take refuge in him. The servant has not to this point in the psalm been identified as the king, but this association with Psalm 2 depicts him as such.

Now we come to the final unit, A', which closes part 3 of the psalm with praise (vv. 47–51). Just as parts 1 and 2 closed with a summary, so also does part 3, indicated by its abundant use of lexemes that occur at various points throughout the psalm: Yhwh (יהוה), *rock* (צור), *exalt* (רום), God (אל), *salvation* (ישע), *give* (נתן), *lead/speak* (דבר), *people* (עם), *beneath* (תחת), *deliver* (פלט), *enemy* (איב), *rise up* (קום), *rescue* (נצל), *nations* (גוי), and *loyal love* (חסד). Unit A' also calls back to unit A to frame the entire psalm with praise for Yhwh as his *rock*, *salvation*, and *rescue*, key words used at significant junctures throughout the psalm. Structurally, like each previous unit, unit A' consists of three subunits (vv. 47, 48–49, 50–51). The first consists of three parallel lines praising Yhwh's characteristics, much like the three lines of praise that began the psalm in verse 3. The second subunit describes the actions of God in rescuing and exalting the servant. Just as God is exalted by the servant (v. 47c), the servant is exalted by God (v. 49b).

The third subunit of unit A' (vv. 50–51) is perhaps the most significant of the entire psalm. It begins with a commitment to praise Yhwh among the nations (a slightly more positive portrayal than the description of their submission in the previous unit). What follows is the identification of the servant as the *king* (מלך)—and not just David, but also *his offspring* (זרעו)—*forever* (עד עולם). God's character is such that he will show *loyal love* (חסד)—in this psalm expressed as engaged action to deliver the suffering king—to his anointed king forever. The effect is that the deliverance described in this psalm is a promised pattern of the deliverance that God will continue to enact for his future faithful king(s). This promise has the potential to provide hope in a future faithful king whom God will deliver. We can see this storyline fleshed out in subsequent psalms in the group, especially Psalms 20–22.

THE SHAPE OF PSALM 20

Structure 11

Psalm 20

Part			
			¹ *Of the director. A psalm of David.*
1	A	a	²ᵃ May he answer you, Yhwh, in the day of distress; ²ᵇ May he set you high, the name of the God of Jacob. ³ᵃ May he send you help from the holy place; ³ᵇ And from Zion, may he support you.
		b	⁴ᵃ May he remember all your gift-offerings; ⁴ᵇ And your going-up-offerings, may he find fat. *Selah.*
		'a	⁵ᵃ May he give to you according to your heart; ⁵ᵇ And all your counsel, may he fulfill.
2	B		⁶ᵃ May we shout with joy at your salvation; ⁶ᵇ And in the name of our God may we lift the banner. ⁶ᶜ May he fulfill, Yhwh, all your requests.
3	A	1	⁷ᵃ Now I know that Yhwh saves his anointed one; ⁷ᵇ He answers from the skies of his holiness, ⁷ᶜ with the might of salvation of his right hand.
		2	⁸ᵃ These, in chariotry, and these, in horses; ⁸ᵇ But we, in the name of Yhwh our God, we boast. ⁹ᵃ They, they will bow and they will fall; ⁹ᵇ But we, we will stand and we will be restored.
		3	¹⁰ᵃ Yhwh, save the king! ¹⁰ᵇ May he answer us in the day of our calling.

Psalms 20 and 21 are each discrete literary units, and yet they are closely linked together, even structurally. I will first explore the shape of each individual psalm and then treat them together briefly before looking at how they correspond to Psalm 18.

Psalm 20 as a whole is framed by an inclusio, consisting of the words Yhwh (יהוה), answer (ענה), in the day (ביום), and David/the king (דוד/מלך; vv. 1–2a, 10). These lines reveal the main idea of the psalm: it is a communal plea that Yhwh answer or save the king in the day of distress. In the first instance, the people pray that Yhwh would answer the king, and in the second, they pray that Yhwh would answer them by saving the king. These close correspondences and yet difference reveal a close relationship between the king and the people: his fate affects theirs, and so to speak of answering him is to speak of answering them.

Following the title, the psalm can be divided into three parts (vv. 2–5, 6, 7–10). The first and third parts mirror each other in their tripartite structure; verse 6 stands at the center of the psalm, emphasizing the anticipated joy of the community at Yhwh's salvation of the king.

The first part of the psalm, verses 2–5, are joined by their repetitive use of the second-person suffix ך, the use of imperfect verbs in every line, and echoing parallelism. The three units form an aba' structure, with the motivation for Yhwh's rescue standing at the center (v. 4). The final line of each of the three units (v. 3b, 4b, 5b) is inverted in structure. Verses 2–3 form the first unit. Each line contains the same verb form and suffix to express prayer for the king. The first two lines move from general to specific in their shift from a plea to answer to a plea to set high (v. 2). The second set of parallel lines also moves from general to specific, from sending help to the specific kind of help: support (v. 3). Together, these two sets of lines move from time to place, from in the day of distress to the holy place and Zion.

Verse 4 forms the second unit. It continues the imperfect verb forms from the previous verse but differs so that the suffix your (ך) is connected to nouns rather than verbs—your gift-offerings (מנחתך) and your going-up-offerings (עולתך). The placement of that suffix at the end of the first line (v. 4a) creates continuity with the end of the previous unit (v. 3b). This unit consists of one set of echoing lines about Yhwh finding the king's offerings pleasing. In other words, the king's faithfulness to Yhwh serves as a motivation for Yhwh to deliver him, just as we saw in the center of Psalm 18.[6] There is a movement from general (remembering offerings) to

---

6. Jacobson points out that a מנחה (Ps 20:4) is a way to express loyalty to a god (see 1 Kgs 18:29, 36). See deClaissé-Walford, Jacobson, and Tanner, The Book of Psalms, 217.

specific (*finding fat*). Verse 4 ends with *selah* (סלה), perhaps signaling its structural significance as part *b* of the *aba'* structure of vv. 2–5.

In verse 5, the idea of giving creates continuity with verse 4, but this time, it is Yhwh who gives to the king, elaborating on the idea of Yhwh's reciprocation of the king's faithfulness. The sound play of the suffixes for *your* (ך), this time attached to both nouns and verbs, brings together the structures of both previous units. *Heart* (לבב) and *counsel* (עצה) connote the ideas of will and plans, so the prayer is that Yhwh would make the king successful and victorious in his endeavors. The parallel lines show an intensification from Yhwh *giving* (נתן) to *fulfilling* (מלא) *all* (כל) of the desires of the king.

Verse 6 stands out at the center of the psalm. Its focus shifts from prayer for the king to the result of his salvation for the people: joy and victorious celebration. Its first two echoing lines focus on the result of the people, while the third line functions as a summary of the request expressed so far (vv. 2–5), repeating the verb *may he fulfill* (ימלא) from the line just before (v. 5b) as well as recalling the first line of the psalm in *the name of God* (שם אלהים; cf. v. 2b). This latter repetition shows the shift in focus to the people by the use of the first-person plural suffix. This central verse shows both how the king and the people are closely united in their fates and yet also how there is a distinction between the king and people: his deliverance affects them. This is an important nuance of the ideas of unity and the democratization of the Davidic identity in this psalm group: the king remains a distinct figure, but his fate and the people's are unified.

Verses 7 begins the third and final part, made up of three parts (vv. 7, 8–9, 10). Verse 7 breaks from what comes before in various ways: it begins with the particle *now* (עתה) and shifts to the first-person singular *I* and the perfect verb form *I know* (ידעתי). In content, it functions successively from the plea of the previous verses by expressing confident knowledge that Yhwh does *answer* (ענה) and *save* (ישע), recalling the first and last lines of what comes before (vv. 2a, 6a). The expression of confidence defines the tone of the psalm as expectant hope rather than that of a lament, which also includes a plea. Verse 7 shows internal cohesion in the sound play between *saves* (הושיע) and *his anointed* (משיחו; v. 7a) and between the endings of each line: *his anointed* (משיחו), *from his holy skies* (משמי קדשו), and *salvation of his right hand* (ישע ימינו). The lexeme *save* frames the verse. It is likely that the individual of verse 7 is a community member rather than the king because the king is still spoken of in the third person, and the psalm quickly returns to the first-person plural *we* in verse 8 for the remainder. A possible explanation of the change to first person in verse 7 is that it functions as an example of the *shout for joy* prayed for in the previous verse.

Verses 8–9 form the second unit of part 3, contrasting the people with those who don't trust in Yhwh in an *aba'b'* structure (vv. 8a, 8b, 9a, 9b). Verse 8 focuses on trust in military means versus trust in Yhwh. Verse 9 consists of two parallel lines contrasting the result of those who don't trust with those who do, each using two verbs that unite the lines through both structure and sound play: *they will bow* (כרעו) and *we will stand* (קמנו) are paired in sound, as are *they will fall* (ונפלו) and *we will be restored* (ונתעדד), each starting with נו. The two pairs of lines are closely united through their sets of contrasts and in the use of *but we* (ואנחנו) in verses 8b and 9b.

Verse 10 closes the psalm by recalling the first lines, as already mentioned. It reiterates the communal plea and finally identifies the referent of the poem explicitly as the king. The parallelism between these final lines to *save the king* and *answer us* combines the fate of the two.

THE SHAPE OF PSALM 21

Structure 12

Psalm 21

Part			
			¹ᵃ *Of the director. A psalm of David.*
1	1		²ᵃ Yhwh, in your strength the king is glad; ²ᵇ And in your salvation how he rejoices greatly.
	2		³ᵃ The desire of his heart you have given him; ³ᵇ And the request of his lips you have not withheld. *Selah.*
	3	*a*	⁴ᵃ For you meet him with blessings of goodness; ⁴ᵇ And you place on his head a crown of gold.
		b	⁵ᵃ Life he asked of you; ⁵ᶜ You gave to him length of days, forever and ever. ⁶ᵃ Great is his glory because of your salvation; ⁶ᵇ Majesty and honor you set upon him.
		a'	⁷ᵃ For you place on him blessings for ever; ⁷ᵇ You make him joyful with gladness in your presence.
2			⁸ᵃ For the king trusts in Yhwh; ⁸ᵇ And because of the loyal love of the Most High, he will not be shaken.
3	1	*a*	⁹ᵃ It will find, your hand, all your enemies; ⁹ᵇ Your right hand will find those who hate you. ¹⁰ᵃ You make them like an oven of fire at the time of your presence; ¹⁰ᵇ Yhwh in his anger will swallow them; ¹⁰ᶜ It will consume them, fire.
	2	*b*	¹¹ᵃ Their fruit from the earth you will destroy; ¹¹ᵇ And their offspring from the sons of humanity. ¹²ᵃ Though they intend against you evil, ¹²ᵇ and they devise a plot, ¹²ᶜ they will not prevail.
	3	*a'*	¹³ᵃ For you will make them turn the shoulder, ¹³ᵇ when your bow-strings you aim at their faces. ¹⁴ᵃ Be exalted, Yhwh, in your strength! ¹⁴ᵇ We will sing and praise your might.

Psalm 21, like Psalm 20, can be viewed as three parts (vv. 2-7, 8, 9-14). Even more specifically, like Psalm 20, the first and third parts of Psalm 21 mirror one another in their tripartite structures (vv. 2, 3, 4-7; vv. 9, 10-13, 14), with the central part consisting of only one verse (v. 8). The psalm is framed by an inclusio of the words *praise* (זמר), *Yhwh* (יהוה), and *in your strength* (בעזך; vv. 1a-2a, 14), which reveal the main idea of the psalm: it is praise for Yhwh for his strength. His strength is defined throughout the parts of the psalm as his blessing of the king in various ways (part 1) and his destruction of his enemies (part 3). The central part (part 2) focuses on the reciprocal relationship of trust and loyal love between Yhwh and the king.

Part 1 of the psalm is made up of three units, with the third being an expanded unit (vv. 2, 3, 4-7). Verses 2-7 as a whole are closely bound by their frame of *gladness* (שׂמח) and internal repetitions of *you gave to him* (נתנה לו), *in your salvation* (בישועתך), *blessings* (ברכה), *you place* (תשׁית), and *ever* (עד). The focus of part 1 is on the joy of the king over the blessings Yhwh has given him. Again, as in Psalm 20, the speaker is someone other than the king—presumably the community—praising Yhwh for his salvation of the king.

The first unit of part 1 (v. 2) focuses on the joy of the king. It consists of one set of echoing lines, united in content and by the ב-prepositions and suffixes *your* (ך). The verse introduces the themes of the whole and is packed with words used throughout the psalm: *praise* (זמר), *Yhwh* (יהוה), *in your strength* (בעזך), *king* (מלך), *be glad* (שׂמח), and *in your salvation* (בישועתך). The second unit of part 1 (v. 3) is also made up of a set of parallel lines, moving forward from the last set by expressing the reason for rejoicing: Yhwh has given the king everything he desired. Notice that *selah* (סלה) is in the same position here as it was in Psalm 20—in the middle of the tripartite first unit—furthering the structural parallels between the two psalms.

The third unit of part 1 is expanded, consisting of four sets of parallel lines, which correspond to their verse numbers (vv. 4-7). This unit moves from the more general tone of the last unit (v. 3) to specific, elaborating on the things Yhwh has given. The unit can be viewed as an *aba'* structure, with verses 4 and 7 framing the inner verses as sets of parallel lines with the corresponding lexemes *for* (כי), *blessings* (ברכות), and *you place* (תשׁית). The middle lines, verses 5-6 consist of two sets of parallel lines, further specifying the blessings given: *life//length of days* (v. 5), *glory//majesty* and *honor* (v. 6). Each set of parallel lines is united by sound play—verse 5 in the repetition of מ and i-class vowel sounds (ממך, חיים, and ימים), and verse 6 in the repetition of ד and o-class vowels (גדול כבודו and הוד והדר) and the correspondence between ישועתך and תשוה.

Part 2 of the psalm consists of just one verse at the center (v. 8), much like Psalm 20. Part 2 moves the poem from the king's gladness (part 1) to the reciprocal relationship between the king and Yhwh: *the king trusts in Yhwh*, and Yhwh shows *loyal love* to the king, which results in him *not being shaken* (a phrase first introduced in Psalm 15:5c as a promise to the one who would follow Yhwh's way). Verse 8 shows cohesion with what comes before by its repetition of the lexeme *king* (מלך; cf. v. 2) and by opening with a כי-clause (cf. vv. 4, 7). Yet it differs in content, centering on Yhwh's faithful love for his king and the enduring nature of that love. It also stands out from what has come before in that it does not consist of a tight echoing structure, but rather of developing, or progressing parallelism.[7]

Part 3 moves from Yhwh's treatment of the king in parts 1 and 2 to Yhwh's treatment of the enemies. Part 3, like part 1, consists of three units (vv. 9, 10-13, 14). The first unit is made up of two parallel lines, closely bound through repetition and synonyms, where the community declares that "you" will find your enemies. While it is unclear at first whether "you" refers to Yhwh or the king, it seems better to interpret these words as addressed to Yhwh because of internal consistency and similarity with its parallel psalm, 18: in Psalm 21, "you" clearly refers to Yhwh in part 1 (vv. 2-7) and the final unit of part 3 (v. 14); *right hand* (ימין; v. 9) is used most often in the collection to refer to Yhwh[8]; the ambiguous *you make them like … fire* (אש; v. 10a) is clarified through parallelism to be Yhwh's *fire* (//Yhwh's anger; vv. 10b-c); *fire* is also Yhwh's in Psalm 18:9, 13, and 14; the bow and arrow is Yhwh's in Psalm 18:14; and *your presence* (פנך; v. 10a) often refers to Yhwh.

The second unit of part 3 is made up of four verses, which can be viewed as an *aba'b'* alternation of sets of three (vv. 10, 12) and two parallel lines (vv. 11, 13), and also as an *aba'* structure with verses 10 and 13 framing the unit with *you make them* (תשיתמו) and *presence/face* (פנה). The latter is parallel in structure to what we saw in part 1, unit 3 of the psalm (vv. 4-7), even using the same word, *you place/make* (תשית) to frame the unit. Moreover, both *presence* and *you place/make* conclude the units (vv. 7, 13), creating a contrast between Yhwh's treatment of

---

7. This is sometimes called "synthetic" parallelism.
8. See Pss 16:11; 17:7; 18:36; and 20:7. ימין is only used of the king in Ps 16:8.

the king and his treatment of the enemies: Yhwh *places* blessing and gives his *face* to the king, while he *makes* the enemies turn and threatens their *faces*. Together, the four verses of unit two move from abstract (vv. 10–11) to concrete (vv. 12–13). The first two verses focus on the image of fire consuming the enemies (v. 10) and on the result, that their offspring are destroyed (v. 11). The second two verses both begin with *for* (כי) and move to the concrete description of the enemy's plans not succeeding (v. 12) because Yhwh threatens them with his bow (v. 13).

Part 3 concludes the entire psalm with parallel lines praising Yhwh for his strength and might (v. 14). It functions as a summary, recalling the first line of the psalm and unifying the praise of the king (v. 2a) and the praise of the people (v. 14b).

PSALMS 20 AND 21 AS TWIN PSALMS

As I mentioned above, Psalms 20 and 21 are closely related through corresponding elements. The unique relationship between the two psalms can be described in terms of request and fulfillment.[9] In Psalm 20, the community petitions Yhwh for his salvation of the king, and in Psalm 21, the community rejoices in this fulfilled petition. The correspondences between the two psalms are primarily thematic, structural, and lexical. In fact, Psalms 20 and 21 share fourteen lexemes, and every single one of them is distinctive, or occurs at a higher rate in the psalm pair than in the collection overall.[10]

According to modern form-critical genre categories, Psalms 20 and 21 are both royal psalms of the community.[11] Some propose that Psalm 20 is best termed an intercessory petition and hypothesize that it was used before entering into battle or a military alliance.[12] While Psalm 20 can be called an intercessory petition, it is distinct from a lament, since it expresses no complaint about God, the situation, or the enemy. In

---

9. Various scholars identify Pss 20 and 21 as joined by the idea of fulfillment, e.g., M. Dahood, *Psalms I*, 131; Kuntz, "King Triumphant," 173; Westermann, *The Living Psalms* (Grand Rapids: Eerdmans, 1989), 57; McCann, "The Book of Psalms," 757; Craigie, *Psalms 1–50*, 186; Schaefer, *Psalms*, 50; Wilson, *Psalms*, 397; Futato, *The Book of Psalms*, 96; Ross, *Commentary on the Psalms*, 510. See appendix 2 for further data.

10. These are שאל, עוד, יום, זמר, ימין, גבר, נצח, נתן, ישע, מלך, כל, לבב, דוד, and יהוה.

11. Gunkel, *Introduction to the Psalms*, 99.

12. See, e.g., Mowinckel, *The Psalms in Israel's Worship*, 245; Craigie, *Psalms 1–50*, 185; Futato, *The Book of Psalms*, 83; Ross, *Commentary on the Psalms*, 491; deClaissé-Walford, Jacobson, and Tanner, *The Book of Psalms*, 215–17.

corresponding terms, Psalm 21 can be called a psalm of intercessory praise.[13] Some view Psalm 21 as a thanksgiving after a battle for the royal victory prayed for in the preceding psalm, which would link Psalm 21 even more closely with Psalm 18 (also a royal thanksgiving).[14] However, while Psalm 21 does contain a joyful proclamation of Yhwh's deliverance and blessing, it does not contain many of the other elements that are typical of the thanksgiving psalm.[15] Still others understand Psalm 21 to function within the setting of coronation, especially because of the reference to crowning the king in verse 4.[16]

While the original setting ultimately remains unknown, what can be concluded is that Psalms 20 and 21 correspond in their identification as royal psalms of the community. While the genre designations "royal" and "community" are thematically descriptive rather than structurally descriptive, Psalms 20 and 21 also exhibit corresponding structures. We have already seen how both psalms consist of three parts, with the first and third parts each consisting of three units and a central part consisting of one verse. When Psalms 20 and 21 are paired together, a new structure emerges as a result of correspondences in lexemes and themes between the two psalms. First, it may be helpful to notice the striking correspondences at the so-called "seam" of the two psalms. Psalm 20 ends with "Yhwh [יהוה], save [ישע] the king [מלך]," and Psalm 21 begins with the same lexemes: "Yhwh [יהוה], in your strength, the king [מלך] is glad, and in your salvation [ישע], how he greatly rejoices." The tight repetition functions like Velcro at the seam between the two psalms, inviting us to explore further structural similarities.

When reading through the two psalms together, perhaps the most striking correspondence is in these words of the people: "May he give to you according to your heart, and all your counsel, may he fulfill" in Psalm 20 (v. 5), and in Psalm 21, "The desire of his heart you have given him, and the request of his lips, you have not withheld" (v. 3). Both

---

13. Jacobson uses this term in deClaissé-Walford, Jacobson, and Tanner, *The Book of Psalms*, 223.

14. E.g., Dahood, *Psalms I*, 131; Hossfeld and Zenger, *Die Psalmen I*, 139.

15. E.g., narration of trouble, narration of calling upon God, narration of deliverance, or a thank offering. See Gunkel, *Introduction to the Psalms*, 22–40, 199–221.

16. E.g., Anderson, *Psalms 1-72*, 179; Craigie, *Psalms 1-50*, 190; Gerstenberger, *Psalms: Part 1*, 107; A. Weiser, *The Psalms* (Philadelphia: Westminster, 1962), 210; K. Seybold, *Die Psalmen*, HAT I, vol. 15 (Tübingen: J. C. B. Mohr, 1996), 92. Mowinckel, however, understands Ps 21 to function as a blessing before battle. Mowinckel, *The Psalms in Israel's Worship*, 69.

verses use the distinctive lexemes *give* (נתן) and *heart* (לבב) to speak of Yhwh fulfilling the king's desires. If we begin by noticing this distinctive corresponding phrase (in units C and C' below) and work both outward and inward from there, a chiastic structure emerges:

A   **Petition**: Help the king in the day of distress (20:1-3)
 B   **Petition**: Remember the faithfulness of the king (20:4)
  C   **Petition**: Give according to the king's heart, which results in joy (20:5-6)
   D   **Trust**: The people trust in Yhwh; Yhwh surely saves the king (20:7-21:2)
  C'   **Fulfillment (expanded)**: Yhwh gives the king his heart's desire, resulting in joy (21:3-7)
 B'   **Fulfillment**: The faithfulness of king is reciprocated by God (21:8)
A'   **Fulfillment (expanded)**: Yhwh eliminates the king's distress (21:9-14)

Figure 11. The Chiastic Relation of Psalms 20 and 21

Figure 11 shows how each of the petitions of units A, B, and C in Psalm 20 are fulfilled in reverse order in C', B', and A' in Psalm 21. When Psalms 20 and 21 are read together, unit D, where the two psalms overlap (Ps 20:7-21:2), stands at the center, expressing the people's trust in Yhwh to save the king. The majority of the center (unit D) consists of the final part of Psalm 20 (vv. 7-10), which is the climax of that poem, so it is no surprise that it stands at the center of the chiastic structure when the psalms are paired together. Psalm 21 then systematically and elaborately fulfills the petitions of Psalm 20 in reverse order. I will briefly treat each of the corresponding units in what follows.

Unit A includes the title of Psalm 20 and the petition for help and support for the king (v. 1). The petition of unit A is fulfilled with an extended statement of confidence in unit A' that Yhwh resolves the distress of the king by defeating his enemies. While the initial petition is more abstract in its reference to a *day of distress*, the fulfillment is concrete and specific in describing Yhwh's defeat of the enemies. The time reference *in the day of distress* (Ps 20:2a) in unit A is matched by the time reference *at the time of your presence* in A' (Ps 21:10a). Both units involve a downward movement: the initial petition focuses on Yhwh coming down from on high (from Zion and the holy place), and the fulfillment continues the downward movement with the enemies being eliminated from the earth and swallowed. Both units use the name of Yhwh and the distinctive lexeme זמר: unit A opens with the title, *a psalm* (מזמור) *of David*, and unit A' closes with a final *praise* (זמר) to Yhwh. The A and A' frame is also connected to the center unit, D. Those correspondences will be explored shortly.

Units B and B' are united by the theme of the king's faithfulness, and each consists only of two simple lines (Pss 20:4; 21:8). In both psalms,

each of these verses stands out as the center of an *aba'* structure: In
Psalm 20, verse 4 stands out because of its emphasis on the faithfulness
of the king to Yhwh to motivate Yhwh's action on his behalf (vv. 2–3, 4,
5). Likewise, in Psalm 21, verse 8 stands out as the central element of
the tripartite psalm and again focuses on the trust of the king. Units B
and B' also indicate a pattern of request and fulfillment. Whereas Psalm
20:4 functions as a petition that Yhwh would remember the faithfulness
of the king, Psalm 21:8 not only states the trust of the king but also indicates that Yhwh indeed reciprocates that faithfulness with loyal love.
The correlation also clarifies that righteousness is defined not as adherence to a moral standard, but as trust, or loving commitment, to the person of Yhwh. This definition of righteousness is consistent with what
we have seen in other psalms so far[17] and is significant for the message
of the whole collection, which begins and ends with an emphasis on the
psalmist's righteousness as a prerequisite for accessing Yhwh's presence. Psalm 21 is linked to these prior mentions of righteousness by the
phrase *not shake* (בל מוט/לא), which also occurs in Psalms 15:5, 16:8, and
17:5. Psalm 21 clarifies that the nature of righteousness is trust, to which
Yhwh responds with the faithful act of delivering and drawing near.

Units C and C' likewise demonstrate that Psalm 21 functions as a fulfillment of Psalm 20. In unit C, the community prays that Yhwh would
give the king the desires of his heart and fulfill his plans, and unit C'
rejoices that Yhwh has done so. Units C and C' are closely united by the
distinctive lexemes *give* (נתן), *heart* (לבב), *Yhwh* (יהוה), *request/ask* (שאל),
and *in your salvation* (בישועתך). Each unit begins with the corresponding
phrase composed of *give* and *heart*. In Psalm 20, the phrase functions as
a petition that Yhwh would *give* to the king according to his *heart* (v. 5),
and in Psalm 21, as a fulfillment: Yhwh *has given* the desire of the king's
heart (v. 3). Unit C' of Psalm 21 expands on this statement by describing what it is Yhwh has given: *blessings of goodness, a crown of gold, long
life, glory, salvation, majesty,* and *honor.* The effect of the expansion is
that God's fulfillment of the people's request is far greater than imagined. The list ends with *joy* and *gladness* in Yhwh's presence (v. 7), which
matches the second petition of unit C in Psalm 20: *May we shout with joy*
(רנן) *at your salvation* (v. 6a). In other words, the two units are closely
related structurally by their opening phrases and their conclusions of

---

17. See "Failed Expectations: Trust in Psalm 22" in ch. 5. McCann also draws attention to the close relationship between trust and *loyal love* (הסד) in "The Book of
Psalms," 758.

joy. Notice how the petition in Psalm 20 is focused on the people's joy in Yhwh's salvation of the king, while the fulfillment describes the king's joy. The correlation between the two units unites these ideas into one: the people's joy and the king's joy are inseparable, and they are both tied to Yhwh's rescue of the king.

Unit D, the chiastic center (Ps 20:7–21:2), may at first seem like an odd combination of verses, since it stretches across the two psalms. Yet in their present arrangement, these verses are highly structured. I will re-present the verses here with their distinctive repetitions:

Structure 13

20:7a Now I know that *Yhwh* (יהוה) *saves* (הושיע) his anointed one.
20:7b He answers from the skies of his holiness,
20:7c with the might of *salvation* (ישׁע) of his right hand,

> 20:8a These, in chariotry, and these, in horses,
> 20:8b But we in the name of *Yhwh* (יהוה) our God, we boast.
> 20:9a They, they will bow and they will fall,
> 20:9c But we, we will stand and we will be restored.

20:10a *Yhwh* (יהוה), *save* (הושיע) the *king* (מלך)!
20:10b May he answer us in the day of our calling.

21:1a Of the director, a psalm of David.
21:2a *Yhwh* (יהוה), in your strength the *king* (מלך) is glad.
21:2b And in your *salvation* (ישׁע) how he rejoices greatly.

Notice first how closely the two psalms are connected at their seam (Pss 20:10–21:2): they each use the distinctive lexemes *Yhwh* (יהוה, as a vocative), *save* (as הושיע and ישׁע) and *king* (מלך). Psalm 21:2 functions as a direct fulfillment of the petition of Psalm 20:10. Now, notice how these verses also correspond to Psalm 20:7, which uses both forms of the lexeme ישׁע that envelop the final section: הושיע (20:10a) and ישׁע (21:2b), as well as יהוה. While Psalm 20:7 does not use the lexeme *king*, it uses the synonym *anointed one* (משׁיח). Because of these correspondences, I view this unit as an *aba'* structure, where subunit *a'* actualizes the confidence of subunit *a* as an "on-the-ground" petition based on that confidence. Right at the center, as subunit *b*, are verses 8 and 9 of Psalm 20, which focus on how the people trust in Yhwh as their God and because of that are restored, in contrast to those who do not trust. The people's trust in Yhwh's salvation of the king stands as the central focus of these two psalms when read together.

There is one more fascinating structural connection worth noting when Psalms 20 and 21 are paired, and that is the connection between the structural center, unit D, and the outer edges of units A and A' (Pss 20:1; 21:14). Just as the outer subunits of the center, *a* and *a'* of part D, are closely connected to one another through the repetition of Yhwh, save, and king//anointed (Pss 20:7; 20:10–21:2), so these subunits are also connected to the outer verses of the entire chiasm through lexical repetitions and synonyms:

```
 ┌─A   Psalm (זמר) David (דוד; 20:1)
 │         ...
 │      D ┌─a  Yhwh (יהוה), anointed one, might (גבורה; 20:7)
 │        │    ...
 │        └─a' Yhwh (יהוה; 2x), king (מלך; 2x), Psalm (זמר), David (דוד), strength (עוז; 20:10–21:2)
 │         ...
 └─A'  Praise (זמר), Yhwh (יהוה), strength (עוז), might (גבורה; 21:14)
```

Figure 12. Psalms 20–21: Connections between the Frame and Center

The lexeme for psalm/praise (זמר/מזמור) unites the outer units with the center (A, A', and a'). David (דוד) and its synonyms, anointed one (משיח) and king (מלך), link the opening line with both outer subunits of the center (A, and a and a'). Likewise, might (גבורה) and strength (עוז) of the final line link it to both outer subunits of the central unit (a and a'). The complexity of connections strengthens the overall chiastic structure proposed, where Psalms 20:7–21:2 form the central unit. It also structurally highlights Yhwh's mighty salvation on behalf of his king.

The various connections between Psalms 20 and 21 indicate their unique relationship as "twin psalms." Their correspondences demonstrate that while they are both royal psalms of the community, Psalm 20 is a communal intercession for the king, and Psalm 21 expresses the fulfillment of that intercession with communal praise over the king's success.

REUSE AND DEVELOPMENT FROM PSALM 18 TO PSALMS 20–21

While Psalms 20 and 21 are closely connected to one another, each psalm also exhibits a strong cohesion with Psalm 18, as shown on tables 11–13 at the beginning of this chapter. Almost a third of the lexemes in Psalm 20 are rare lexemes used in Psalm 18: send (שלח), set high (שגב), ride (רכב), support (סעד), anoint (משח), ask (שאל), skies (שמים), call (קרא), answer (ענה), rise (קום), bow (כרע), fall (נפל), distress (צרר), Yhwh (יהוה), know (ידע), save (ישע), day (יום), give (נתן), God (אל), direct (נצח), and name (שם). The last seven of these are also morphologically distinctive.[18] The two psalms are also closely connected by distinctive phrases—save the king (ישע מלך), Yhwh our/my God (יהוה אלהי/נו), and save ... his anointed (ישע משיחו)—and

---

18. In Ps 20 there are sixty-three non-incidental lexemes, twenty-seven of which also occur in Ps 18. See appendix 2.

the themes of distress, deliverance, Yhwh as mighty warrior, the human king, the human warrior, and Yhwh's support and strength in battle. Psalms 18 and 21 are closely connected by their sheer number of lexical *dis legomena*, or lexemes whose only occurrences in the collection are in these two psalms—*exalt* (רום), *fire* (אש), *nostril* (אף), *hate* (שׂנא), *great* (גדל), *able* (יכל), *sing* (שׁיר), as well as the morphological forms of *praise* (זמר), *head* (ראשׁ), *give* (נתן), and *son* (בן). In addition, within the collections of Psalms 15–24, only these two psalms refer to Yhwh as the *Most High* (עליון; Pss 18:14 and 21:8). The two psalms also share the distinctive lexemes *enemy* (איב), *place* (שׁית), *give* (נתן), *confront* (קדם), *strength* (עוז), *hand* (יד), *show loyal love* (חסד), *bless* (ברך), *ask* (שׁאל), *consume* (אכל), *stretch* (נטה), *seed* (זרע), and *forever* (עולם), and the morphological forms of *seed* (זרע) and *director* (נצח). Psalms 18 and 21 are further connected by the three rare phrases *all enemies* (כל איב), *fire consumes* (אשׁ אכל), and *forever and ever* (עד עולם), as well as by the distinctive themes of distress, deliverance, Yhwh as mighty warrior, fire/anger, the human king, Yhwh giving support and strength in battle, and covenant love/promise.

Regarding structure/genre, while the matching designation of "royal psalm" indicates thematic correspondence rather than structural, Psalms 18, 20, and 21 exhibit strikingly similar parallel structures. Not only is each psalm made of three parts, but when Psalms 20 and 21 are read together, they, like Psalm 18, form a seven-unit chiastic structure, with a center unit (D) made up of three subunits. This striking correspondence is unlikely to be coincidental.

Because of the strong cohesion between Psalms 18, 20, and 21, I view the latter two as the chiastic counterpart to the former. It remains to explore the correlations between these three psalms and how, in their present arrangement, Psalms 20 and 21 develop the ideas of Psalm 18.

PSALMS 20–21 ARE PATTERNED AFTER THE DELIVERANCE OF PSALM 18

You'll recall from earlier in this chapter that Psalms 20 and 21 are communal psalms of petition and praise respectively and that Psalm 18 is a thanksgiving psalm describing the deliverance of king David. By their location in the collection and through the reuse of various distinctive elements, Psalms 20–21 look back on Psalm 18 as the pattern for which they express their confident petition and hope in Yhwh's deliverance of future Davidic kings.

The very first lines of Psalm 20 strongly echo the deliverance of Psalm 18. Psalm 20:2 says, "May he answer you, Yhwh, in the day of distress; may he set you high, the name of the God of Jacob." Every single lexeme except for *Jacob* (יעקב) is found also in Psalm 18.[19] Patterned on the servant saying to Yhwh that he is his *high place* (משגב) in Psalm 18, the prayer of Psalm 20 is that Yhwh would *set high* (שׂגב) the king—an action attributed to Yhwh in only these two places. The phrase *in the day of distress* (ביום צרה) recalls the setting from the superscript of Psalm 18, "*on the day* [ביום] David was rescued from Saul," and "*on the day of my distress* [ביום־אידי]" (v. 19).

The next line of Psalm 20 (v. 3) picks up on the language of Yhwh empowering the king in battle in Psalm 18. In Psalm 20, the people pray that Yhwh would *send* (שלח) help from the holy place, just as Yhwh had *sent* from on high to rescue David (Ps 18:17), and that Yhwh would *support* (סעד) the king, just as he *supported* him in battle in Psalm 18 (v. 36). The distinctive language from Psalm 18 of Yhwh empowering against enemies permeates Psalm 20, including the people *calling* (קרא) on the *name* (שם) of *Yhwh our God* (יהוה אלהינו) to *answer* (ענה) from the *skies* (שמים) and *save* (ישׁע), *protect* (שׂגב), and *give* (נתן) to the king (מלך). The thanksgiving of Psalm 21 also reflects Yhwh's empowerment in recalling how he defeats *all enemies* (כל איב) and *those who hate* (שׂנא) him (Pss 18:18//21:9); how they are not *able* (יכל; Pss 18:39//21:12); and in the celebration of Yhwh's *strength* (עז; Pss 18:18//21:2, 14). Yhwh also raises up the king in Psalm 21, just as he does in Psalm 18: in Psalm 18, the king is exalted as the *head* (ראשׁ) over foreigners (v. 44); in Psalm 21, Yhwh places a crown upon the king's *head* (v. 4). Yhwh also *gives* (נתן) abundantly to the king in both psalms (Pss 18:33, 36, 41; 21:3, 5). His various gifts in both psalms include *life* (חי), *greatness* (גלל), [honor because of] *salvation* (ישׁע), and *loyal love* (חסד) *forever* (עד עולם; Pss 18:26–28, 36, 47, 51; 21:2, 4–6, 8).

In the center of the chiasm formed by Psalms 20–21, we find a strong statement of trust in Yhwh that echoes Psalm 18, further showing that Psalms 20–21 base their confidence on the prior deliverance of the Davidic king. Just as the enemies of Psalm 18—those who would *rise up* (קום) against the king—were caused to *bow* (כרע) and *fall* (נפל), now the community is confident that Yhwh will cause their enemies to *bow* and *fall*, while they will *rise* (Pss 18:39–40//20:9). This central section also contrasts the people who trust in Yhwh with those who trust in *chariots* (רכב), a rare lexeme used only elsewhere in this collection in Psalm 18 to

---

19. *Jacob* (יעקב) likely points forward to Ps 24, where the community called *Jacob* gathers at the arrival of Yhwh (Ps 24:6).

depict with vivid imagery Yhwh *mounting* (רכב) a cherub to come down on the wind to rescue his king (Pss 18:11//20:8).

Psalms 20 and 21 also echo Psalm 18 in their depiction of Yhwh's descent. A large unit within Psalm 18 (vv. 8–20) vividly depicted Yhwh's theophanic appearance and rescue of the servant. In addition to the mention of *chariots* (רכב) just noted, various other lexemes in Psalms 20–21 echo that scene. In Psalm 20:7, Yhwh is said to answer from the *skies* (שמים), just as he did in Psalm 18:10. Psalm 21:9–13 recalls God's brilliant descent from heaven with fire as a warrior by its clustered use of the distinctive lexemes *fire* (אש), *anger* (אף), *make* (עשׂה), *hate* (שׂנא), *be able* (יכל), *put* (שׁית), *enemy* (איב), and *hand* (יד). Two distinctive phrases also occur in these verses that closely tie God's appearing as a warrior on behalf of the king in Psalm 21 with that of Psalm 18. The first is constructed from the lexemes *fire* (אש) and *consumes* (אכל) and describes God's actions toward the enemies. This phrase is highly distinctive and occurs only in Psalms 18:9 and 21:10 in all of Book I. The second phrase includes the lexeme *all* (כל), the same morphological form *enemies* (איבי), and *hand* as כף or יד (Pss 18:1 and 21:9). The reuse of theophanic language and imagery indicates that Yhwh the warrior continues to act in dynamic ways to deliver his king, just as he did in the past.

PSALMS 20–21 ECHO THE DAVIDIC PROMISE

The confidence of the community in Psalms 20–21 is based not only on the example of Yhwh's past deliverance of David in Psalm 18, but also on Yhwh's promise to David and his offspring articulated there. Psalm 18:50–51 includes a vow to praise the name of Yhwh as the one who saves his king and shows loyal love to his anointed, to David and his offspring, forever. This is the well-known promise of 2 Samuel 7 that Yhwh would establish David's house and kingdom forever, linked with that passage by the following corresponding lexemes: *seed* (זרע), *king/kingdom* (מלך/ממלכה), *loyal love* (חסד), *David* (דוד), as well as the lexemes עד and עולם together as a phrase indicating *forever* (2 Sam 7:8, 12–13, 15–16).

Psalms 20 and 21 echo this enduring promise to David. If we return once more to the center of the chiastic structure of Psalms 20–21, we find that the statement of trust (Ps 20:8–9) is surrounded by a matching frame expressing confidence in Yhwh's *saving* (ישׁע) of the *king*// *anointed one* (משׁיח//מלך; Pss 20:7, 10; 21:1–2), which is closely linked with Psalm 18:51's *praise* (זמר) of Yhwh for the *salvation* of his *king//anointed one*. Psalm 21:5 echoes Psalm 18:51 by its use of the distinctive phrase constructed from עד and עולם (*forever and ever*) to describe Yhwh's blessing of the king. Psalm 21:8 again reiterates the Davidic promise that Yhwh will show *loyal love* (חסד) to the *king* (מלך) forever (Ps 18:51) by proclaiming that the *king* trusts in Yhwh, and in the *loyal love* of the Most High he shall not be moved. In fact, both the first and last verses of Psalm 21 echo Psalm 18:50–51: Psalm 21 begins with joy in Yhwh's *salvation* of the *king* (Ps 21:2) and ends with *praise* (Ps 21:14), which seems to indicate that the whole of Psalm 21 has Yhwh's promise to the king in mind. Furthermore, the final verse of Psalm 21 echoes not only the last verses of Psalm 18, but also its first, by the promise to *sing* (שיר) of Yhwh's strength.[20] In other words, Psalm 21 as a whole echoes the promise of Psalm 18:51, and the final verse of Psalm 21 recalls the whole of Psalm 18. The connections between Psalms 20–21 and the promise of Psalm 18:50–51 show that the community who speaks in Psalms 20–21 bases its confidence on Yhwh's promise to maintain faithfulness to future Davidic kings.

CLARIFICATIONS REGARDING FAITHFULNESS, DELIVERANCE, AND PRESENCE

Reading Psalms 18, 20, and 21 together further clarifies both the definition of faithfulness and the relationship between Yhwh's presence and his deliverance. Regarding faithfulness, we had seen in previous psalms how righteousness and trust are connected terms, so that righteousness involves not just performing right actions but relational dependence and connection to Yhwh.[21] Psalms 18, 20, and 21 confirm the relational element and clarify that faithfulness is reciprocal. In Psalm 18, Yhwh's faithful relationship with his human king was revealed to be one of mutual faithfulness, not only in deed but also in terms of affection. The first and last lines of the psalm expressed the *love* (רחם) of the king toward Yhwh and the *love* (חסד) of Yhwh toward the king. In the center this relational reciprocity is the focus (vv. 21–31). So also in Psalms 20–21, the king and people are shown to express faithfulness to Yhwh, in the form of offerings (20:4), but also trust, which is connected to Psalm 18 by the distinctive phrase *Yhwh our/my God* (יהוה אלוהי[נו]), in whose *name* (שם) the people depend (Pss 18:29; 20:8). Psalm 21:8 also declares *trust* (בטח) on the part of the king and the response of *loyal love* (חסד) from Yhwh.

---

20. שיר occurs only in these two places within the collection, making it a case of *dis legomena*.

21. See especially "Failed Expectations: Trust in Psalm 22" in ch. 5.

In other words, it is not just obedient actions but obedience from the heart that Yhwh desires.

Psalm 18 also clearly connected Yhwh's faithfulness to the king to his acts of deliverance on behalf of the king. Psalms 20 and 21 further clarify that Yhwh's deliverance leads to the ultimate reward of Yhwh's presence: the final gift given to the king is blessing and gladness in Yhwh's presence forever (Ps 21:7). Deliverance initiates this blessing of presence, a development also visible in the narrative movement from deliverance in Psalm 22 to presence in Psalm 23 to the full realization of this presence in Psalm 24 at Yhwh's arrival. Yhwh's presence as the ultimate reward is also indicated in Psalms 15 and 24, which frame the collection with the goal of entering his presence. At first, this pattern seems to contrast with Psalm 22, which seems to suggest that Yhwh's presence *is equivalent to* his deliverance. However, taken together, we can conclude that Yhwh's presence is both in some way equivalent to his deliverance and is also the ultimate goal or result *following* deliverance. The relationship between faithfulness, deliverance, and presence can be represented as follows:

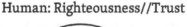

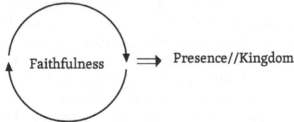

Figure 13. Faithfulness, Deliverance, Presence, and Kingdom

The figure shows that faithfulness involves a reciprocal relationship where the human draws near with trust (equivalent with righteousness) and Yhwh draws near with his presence, which is sometimes equivalent with deliverance (e.g., in some places in Pss 18, 20, and 22). Yhwh's deliverance and presence initiate the fuller realization of his presence (e.g., in Pss 21, 23, and 24). Psalm 22:23–32 narrates how Yhwh's deliverance initiates his kingdom, and Psalm 24 depicts Yhwh's kingdom as the full realization of his presence among his people.

EXPANSIONS FROM PSALM 18 TO PSALMS 20 AND 21

In previous psalm pairs, we have observed various intensifications and expansions from the first psalm to its counterpart. Psalm 18 paints such a vivid and powerful picture of Yhwh the warrior rescuing his king that at first glance it seems that the pattern of intensification cannot hold true for the royal psalms. However, there are two significant extensions or expansions from Psalm 18 to Psalms 20–21. The first is related to fulfillment and extension of the Davidic promise into the future, and the second is an expansion to the community.

We have noted already how Psalms 20 and 21, by their location following Psalm 18, are patterned after the deliverance found there and base their confident prayer and praise on the promise of Yhwh to David and his descendants. The placement of these psalms and their repeated lexemes not only expresses a movement toward the continued fulfillment of Yhwh's promise to deliver his human king, but also extends this promise to future kings. It seems that Psalms 20–21 are speaking of future king(s) in the line of David for a few reasons: First, they show a strong dependence on the promise of Psalm 18:50–51 about Yhwh's faithfulness to David's *offspring* (זֶרַע) *forever* (עוֹלָם), suggesting that this futuristic promise is a theme of the two psalms. Second, Psalm 18 begins with a superscript about how Yhwh delivered David from *all his enemies and from the hand of Saul.* This depicts a completion of Yhwh's deliverance on David's behalf and also places Psalm 18 at the end of David's life as a model for kings to come. Third, within the narrative of 2 Samuel 22, where Psalm 18 is substantially re-presented, we find David at the end of his life, speaking his last words (cf. 2 Sam 23:1). For these reasons, when we reach Psalms 20–21, it seems we find a community who is confident in Yhwh's promise to David, praising Yhwh and praying that he will continue to show faithfulness in those same ways to any (unnamed) Davidic king. These psalms then provide a good example of when the superscript title of *David* (לְדָוִד) seems to mean something like *about the Davidic king.*

The second expansion, expansion to the community, is the central and prevailing shift from Psalm 18 to Psalms 20 and 21. This development is also consistent with those identified between other parallel psalm pairs, especially from Psalms 15 to 24 and 17 to 22. In this development toward communal inclusion, Psalms 20 and 21 go beyond any other psalm by depicting the speaking subjects of these psalms as the community.

Genres, themes, lexemes, and phrases in Psalms 20 and 21 indicate this prevailing development of communal inclusion. The genres of

Psalms 20 and 21 are the first indication of community inclusion, since both psalms are communal intercessions (either petition or praise) on behalf of the king. Psalms 20 and 21 are not only psalms of the community, but they reuse lexemes and phrases that describe the individual in Psalm 18 and apply them to the community. For example, in Psalm 18, the king's enemies *rise* (קום) against him, *fall* (נפל), and *are brought to their knees* (כרע), while the king is exalted; Psalm 20 reapplies this pattern to the community, who are confident that their enemies will *be brought to their knees* and *fall*, while they will *rise* (Pss 18:39, 40, 49; 20:9). In addition, the highly distinctive phrase *Yhwh my God* (יהוה אלהי) is spoken by the king in Psalm 18 but is appropriated by the community as *Yhwh our God* (יהוה אלוהינו) in Psalm 20 (Pss 18:29; 20:8). This phrase occurs only in these two psalms within the collection, increasing the likelihood of intentional connection. The theme of the king's trust in Yhwh in Psalm 18 is also expanded to the community in Psalm 20 (vv. 9-10). Finally, in Psalm 21, the lexemes *sing* (שיר) and *praise* (זמר), which were used to describe the human king's activity in Psalm 18, are reused by the community (Pss 18:1, 50; 21:14).

THE COMMUNITY'S RELATIONSHIP TO THE KING

Within the storyline of the collection, Psalms 20 and 21 are the first psalms that introduce the community. Others who have analyzed Psalms 15-24 as a subunit within the Psalter have noted the voice of the community in Psalms 20 and 21 as well as the inclusion of the community throughout the entire collection.[22] Hossfeld, Zenger, and Miller have termed this expansion *democratization*, whereby the Davidic identity is applied to the people. However, the correspondences between Psalms 18, 20, and 21 indicate that the relationship between the deliverance of the king and the blessing of the community is not only one of *identification* or *democratization*, but also of *cause and effect*. I have made this same observation previously in my exploration of Psalm 22.[23]

I infer this cause-and-effect relationship from the distinction between the king and the people. Within Psalm 20, there is narratival development from the people's prayer for Yhwh to provide success for the

---

22. See, e.g., Hossfeld and Zenger, "Wer darf hinaufziehn zum Berg JHWHs?," 168; Miller, "Kingship," 130; Brown, "Psalms as Collections," 88–89; Sumpter, "Coherence," 204.

23. See "The Kingdom as the Effect of Deliverance in Psalm 22" in ch. 5.

king (vv. 1–5) to the result of communal joy in [his] salvation (v. 6). Psalm 21 also expresses the joy of the people because of the king's salvation (v. 14). It is because of Yhwh's salvation of the king that the people will have joy. The salvation of the king affects them. In the words of R. A. Jacobson, he is the "channel through which God blesses the people."[24] It's important to note that the king is sometimes depicted as a warrior (Ps 18:38–43) and at other times as the one being saved by Yhwh (Pss 18:18, 44; 20:2, 3, 7; 21:2–7, 9–13)—the redeemer and the one redeemed. Together, Psalms 18, 20, and 21 depict both Yhwh and the king participating in the salvation of the king and, by effect, the people.

In addition to being affected by the king's salvation, the community of Psalms 20 and 21 identifies with its king and so is included in his salvation. This identification is evidenced through the use of various distinctive lexemes and themes that first describe the king and then describe the people. The reuse of these elements includes internal recurrence (Pss 20–21) and recurrence from Psalm 18. For example, in Psalm 20, the people proclaim their trust in Yhwh, just as the king is said to trust him in Psalms 18 and 21.[25] This indicates that the people are not merely affected by the deliverance of the king but must also exhibit the same trust in Yhwh as their king does in order to be identified with him. That the people must exhibit trust in Yhwh is also supported by the description of them in Psalms 22:7 and 24:6, which describe the community as seekers of Yhwh. In addition, the people's trust has an identical result as that of the king: just as the enemies of the king fall (נפל), are brought to their knees (כרע), and cannot rise (קום), so also the enemies of the people (Pss 18:39, 40, 49; 20:9). Whereas the people pray for Yhwh to answer you (עניך; i.e., the king) at the beginning of the psalm, by the end, they pray that Yhwh would answer us (יעננו). As Jacobson notes, by the end of Psalm 20, "The you has become us and the day of distress has become the day of our calling."[26] Likewise, just as the king rejoices in Yhwh's strength (עז) at the beginning of Psalm 21, so also the people sing and praise Yhwh's strength at the end.[27]

---

24. deClaissé-Walford, Jacobson, and Tanner, The Book of Psalms, 226.

25. See especially Ps 21:8; see also Ps 18:2–4, 21–25, 31.

26. deClaissé-Walford, Jacobson, and Tanner, The Book of Psalms, 219. Both phrases use the distinctive construction ביום.

27. Both verses use the same morphological form of עז, which itself occurs only in these two places in this psalm. The phrase is בעוזך meaning "in your strength."

In sum, the community is both *affected* by the salvation of the king, and *identifies* with him in attitude toward Yhwh and in his benefits. The people are both in solidarity with the king and separate from him. He remains as their representative, and his fate affects their own.

SUMMARY

Psalms 20 and 21 demonstrate a special relationship of petition and fulfillment. As adjacent psalms with a strong cohesion, these "twin psalms" together look back on Psalm 18 as the established pattern of God's salvation of the Davidic king. They especially focus on the promise in Psalm 18:51 of Yhwh's enduring faithfulness to future Davidic kings. Because of the close relationship between Psalms 20-21 with Psalm 18, I have concluded that Psalms 20-21 function together as the chiastic counterpart to Psalm 18. Such a conclusion along with the existence of well-defined boundaries around these psalms buttresses the view that Psalms 15-24 form a distinctive chiastic collection.

The placement of these royal psalms at the center of the collection is meaningful for the storyline of Psalms 15-24. The centrality of the royal psalms identifies the human king as the central character of the collection (along with Yhwh) and his deliverance as the central act. Yhwh's deliverance of the king in the royal psalms highlights his enduring faithfulness to the king and the people, especially as demonstrated in Psalms 18:51 and 21:8, which each express Yhwh's commitment to show *loyal love* (חסד) to his Davidic king.

In their position at the center of the collection, the royal psalms provide an explanation for the shifts that take place in Psalms 22-24. They fill in the plotline by signifying further that the deliverance of the human king is what initiates this development toward the kingdom. The king's deliverance functions as the hinge point for the development toward inclusion of the wider community in the second half of the chiasm. To this point, I have argued that there is a consistent development from the individual to the community from the first half of the chiasm to the second. This development can best be explained by the act of deliverance of the king in Psalms 18, 20, and 21 and how this deliverance benefits the wider community both by *effect* and *identification.*

The deliverance of the king at the center also provides another facet of the answer to the opening question of the collection, *Who may ascend the mountain of Yhwh?* The question was already partially answered by the description of the righteous—any who seek him (Ps 24:6)—in the frame of the collection. The opening question, "Who may ascend?" is radically reframed by the royal psalms as not only "who" but also "how." The question of "how" is answered in terms of God's faithful actions on behalf of his faithful king. It is through God's deliverance of his faithful king that all those who seek him will be invited into his presence.

7

The Message of Psalms 15-24

I have analyzed the meaning of each set of parallel psalms in depth, yet the question remains: In light of the relationships between parallel psalms and the chiastic shape they form, what is the message of the collection overall? I will answer this question in two ways: First, I will summarize the consistent developments between parallel psalms that contribute to a progression in the storyline. Second, I will explore the effect of reading this collection in order in light of the connections between psalms—especially parallel psalms, but also neighboring psalms and other connections where appropriate.

CONSISTENT DEVELOPMENTS BETWEEN PARALLEL PSALMS

My methodology is based on an understanding that Hebrew parallelism can exist on the level of the psalm and also that parallel texts, including psalms, do not merely involve repetition but also development: the second psalm corresponds to the first and yet develops the message through dynamic reuse of literary elements. Because the structure of the collection is chiastic, I consider those developments that *consistently* occur between the various psalm pairs to be most helpful for understanding the message of the collection.

From the first half of the chiasm to the second, the parallel psalms exhibit a general pattern of intensification and fulfillment: Psalm 15 introduces the question of who may enter Yhwh's presence; in Psalm 24, that entering is fulfilled in the depiction of Yhwh's arrival. The themes of joy and trust in Psalm 16 are intensified in Psalm 23. Likewise, the distress and praise of Psalm 17 are heightened in Psalm 22, and the psalmist's confidence in Yhwh's provision of *satisfaction* (שׂבע) in his *presence* (פנה) is fulfilled. Psalms 20 and 21 confirm the promise of Psalm 18:51 that Yhwh will indeed be faithful to deliver the Davidic king. In addition to this general pattern of intensification and fulfillment, there are several specific developments that consistently occur between the parallel psalms in the collection. These can help us understand the overarching message when these psalms are read together. These consistent developments include the intensification or realization of Yhwh's presence; the revelation of Yhwh's identity as king; and communal, spatial, and temporal expansions. Taken together, these developments progress the storyline of the collection forward toward the full arrival of Yhwh's kingdom.

Yhwh's Presence Intensified

The theme of Yhwh's presence is prominent within the collection. Between psalm pairs, there is not only correspondence regarding this theme, but intensification, showing that it plays an important role in the storyline.

Psalms 15, 19, and 24 frame the collection with the goal of entering Yhwh's presence. In Psalm 15, the question is raised of who may enter Yhwh's presence, depicted as sojourning in his tent and dwelling on his holy mountain (v. 1). The answer given is that only the fully righteous one may enter. Psalm 19 carries the theme of presence forward by showing that one may become righteous by aligning oneself with Yhwh's creation (vv. 2–7) and Torah (vv. 8–11) and also through the forgiveness of Yhwh from transgression (vv. 13–14). The psalm ends with a prayer that the psalmist's whole being would be favorable before Yhwh's *presence* (פנה; v. 15). In Psalm 24, we find the most dramatic intensification of Yhwh's presence throughout the collection: Yhwh's arrival as king. Those who seek Yhwh's *presence* are gathered together (v. 6), and Yhwh the king arrives to dwell among his people forever (vv. 7–10). This is the finale of the storyline. The identification of Yhwh as king at his arrival associates the fullness of his presence with the realization of his kingdom. He is the king (vv. 7–10) who reigns among all his people (v. 6) in his place, his cosmic temple (vv. 1–2, 7, 9).

The intervening psalms also show movement toward the fullness of Yhwh's presence. Psalm 23 exhibits intensification of the theme of Yhwh's presence from Psalm 16. While both psalms seek Yhwh's presence as the ultimate reward, Yhwh's presence stands at the structural center of Psalm 23 in the intimate statement *you are with me* (אתה עמדי; v. 4). In Psalm 23, Yhwh's presence is wholly satisfying, as evidenced by the language of feasting and the psalmist's *cup overflowing* (כוסי רויה; v. 5). Yhwh's presence provides the secure place amidst any distress; he is present even in the *darkest valley* (גיא צלמות; v. 4). In other words, even in the midst of suffering and distress, Yhwh's kingdom is partially realized through his presence *with* his people (v. 4).

The developments between Psalms 17 and 22 and among the royal psalms further elucidate the nature of God's presence. While Psalms 17 and 22 both express the theme of satisfaction in Yhwh's presence, the latter clarifies the nature of God's presence. In Psalm 22, the centrality of Yhwh's presence is emphasized, since the fact that Yhwh is *far* (רחק) is the central problem, and that he does not hide his *face* (פנה), the resolution. Psalm 22 goes beyond Psalm 17 in defining Yhwh's presence as active, involving deliverance. While Psalms 18 and 20 focus more on Yhwh's deliverance than his presence, Psalm 21 clarifies that Yhwh's eternal presence is the ultimate reward and that dwelling in his presence forever comes about as a result of his deliverance (v. 7).

YHWH IDENTIFIED AS KING

As the collection begins, we learn much about who Yhwh is. He is set apart as holy (Ps 15); *Lord* (אדון; Ps 16:2); provider and sustainer (Ps 16), glorious judge (Ps 17:2–5); savior (Ps 17:6–15); warrior, rock, and redeemer (Ps 18); creator (Ps 19:2–7), lawgiver (Ps 19:8–11); the one with the power to acquit (Ps 19:13–14); and the one with power to bring victory to the king (Pss 20–21). These are all certainly things a powerful deity who rules the cosmos does, yet the collection is not explicit about Yhwh's identification as the king until Psalm 22. There, the *kingship* belongs to Yhwh, and he is *ruler of the nations* (v. 29). The whole earth bows before him, into the future (vv. 30–31). This identification of Yhwh as the king of the earth comes as a result of his deliverance of the afflicted one (vv. 22, 32).

In Psalm 23, Yhwh is referred to as a shepherd, a motif that carries royal connotations.[1] The designation *my shepherd* (רעי) is a highly personal way of acknowledging that the psalmist lives under the kingship of Yhwh. Psalm 24 too goes far beyond its counterpart, Psalm 15, by repeatedly identifying Yhwh as *the glorious king* (מלך הכבוד) at the arrival of his presence as king in his cosmic temple (vv. 7–10). In addition, correspondences with the theme of creation in Psalm 19 carry the plotline forward in Psalm 24: in Psalm 19, the proclamation of Yhwh's glory goes out into all the earth, while Psalm 24 depicts the realization of Yhwh's dominion as the glorious king throughout all the earth. The storyline ends with a dramatic fulfillment of the theme of Yhwh's kingship.

---

1. See "Royal and Communal Dimensions in Psalm 23" in ch. 4.

Expansion to All People, Places, and Times

Perhaps the most dramatic shift from the first to the second half of the chiasm is a widening in scope related to people, places, and times. The consistency of these developments from each psalm to its parallel indicates that this is a significant component of the message of the collection. The widening in scope both imparts a quality of expansiveness to Yhwh's kingdom and also finality: all is fulfilled and completely under his dominion.

Psalms 15–19 have the individual faithful or royal figure as their primary referent. They begin with a description of the righteous one (Ps 15) and move through the experiences of trust (Ps 16), lament (Ps 17), rescue (Ps 18), and praise (Ps 19). Their titles all refer to David, and the experience of the king in Psalm 18 seems to confirm that the preceding psalms are about the royal individual.

Beginning in Psalm 20, however, there is a significant expansion to the community. Psalms 20 and 21 consist of communal prayer and praise, which include the community in Yhwh's blessing of the king. Recall how Psalms 20 and 21 use corresponding lexemes and phrases that describe the king in Psalm 18 and apply them to the community. Just as the king's enemies *rise* (קום), *fall* (נפל), and *are brought to their knees* (כרע) in Psalm 18, so the community is confident that *their enemies* will *be brought to their knees* and *fall*, while they will *rise* (Pss 18:39, 40, 49; 20:9); *Yhwh my God* (יהוה אלהי) of Psalm 18 becomes *Yhwh our God* (יהוה אלוהינו) in Psalm 20 (Pss 18:29; 20:8); the theme of trust is expanded to the community (Pss 18; 20:9–10), as is the *singing* (שיר) and *praise* (זמר; Pss 18:1, 40; 21:14). In Psalm 22, the rescue of the afflicted individual, presumably the Davidic king, brings about the flourishing of the community (Ps 22:20–32). The broadness of the community is made explicit in this psalm: it includes the rich and the poor (vv. 27, 30); the living and the dying (vv. 27, 30); and Israel and the nations (vv. 24, 28–29). Just as Yhwh rescued the *afflicted one* (עני), so now all *the afflicted ones* (עניים) who seek Yhwh will feast and worship (vv. 25, 27). Psalm 23 contains more subtle communal allusions in its imagery of the shepherd and its theme of the house of Yhwh. The collection ends in Psalm 24 with a striking communal expansion: the qualities of the righteous individual of Psalm 15 (who seems to be the royal figure if we read backwards from Ps 18) are used to describe the entire community (Ps 24:6). The result is that just as the righteous king is connected to Yhwh and may enter his presence, so also the righteous community. This community is depicted as present at his arrival as king of the cosmos.

Spatial widening also begins in the latter half of the collection. In Psalm 22, the phrases *all the ends of the earth* (כל אפסי ארץ) and *all families* (כל משפחות) depict Yhwh's kingdom as breaking all bounds and recall the Abrahamic promise that Yhwh's kingdom would reunite all peoples (Gen 12:3).[2] No such spatial scope was present in its parallel, Psalm 17. Psalm 23 also includes subtle spatial expansion by its development from the specific imagery of the land of Israel in Psalm 16 to the spatially broader terms of *green pastures* (נאות דשא), *water of restfulness* (מי מנחות), and *right paths* (מעגלי־צדק). Psalm 24 caps the collection with the entire cosmos as Yhwh's dominion of rule (vv. 1–2), in contrast to Psalm 15, where the locality is fixed at Jerusalem (הר קדשך; אהלך; v. 1).

Like spatial expansion, so also temporal expansion takes place in the second half of the collection. Psalms 20 and 21 focus heavily on the promise to David from Psalm 18:51, that Yhwh would show loyal love to future Davidic offspring, forever. Psalms 20–21 extend this promise into the future by depicting the deliverance described there after the pattern of Yhwh's deliverance of David in Psalm 18. Psalm 22 also includes temporal expansion in its reference to *posterity* (זרע), *future generations* (דור יבאו), and *a people yet unborn* (עם נולד), who will benefit from the deliverance of the afflicted. Psalm 24 continues the thread of future generations benefiting from the deliverance of a future king by using the term *generation* (דור) from Psalm 22:31 and depicting this faithful generation as participating in Yhwh's ultimate arrival. The preservation of this collection of psalms through a time when there was no king further creates a forward trajectory that envisions an ideal future king.

Together, the intensifications and expansions that take place through reuse and addition in the second half of the chiasm depict Yhwh as the king and the entire cosmos and all those who seek him as participating in his kingdom. His faithfulness to his human king is enduring, as is his rule over all as the king of the universe. These expansions function to progress the storyline toward its finale, the ultimate arrival and rule of Yhwh the king.

---

2. אפסי ארץ is used throughout the Hebrew Bible in expectation of the kingdom. See Deut 33:17; 1 Sam 2:10; Pss 2:8; 67:7; 72:8; 98:3; Isa 45:22; 52:10; Jer 16:19; Zech 9:10; Prov 30:4.

READING PSALMS 15–24 FROM BEGINNING TO END

I have thoroughly demonstrated that Psalms 15–24 form a chiastic collection. But readers or hearers of this psalm group most likely experience the collection in order, from beginning to end. What is the effect of experiencing it in this way? The ten psalms in this group are proximate enough that many of the echoes and correlations would enable the audience to recall previous uses to mind, so that they would intuit the movement toward fulfillment, expansiveness, and Yhwh's kingdom. Reading these psalms in order could both create associations between parallel psalms and also move the storyline forward sequentially toward the kingdom. It is that sequential storyline that I will now explore.

The Threefold Structure of Psalms 15–24

In addition to the chiastic structure of Psalms 15–24, this collection can be viewed as three overarching movements. In the previous chapter, we explored the close connections between Psalms 18, 20, and 21, at the center of the collection. You may recall that Psalm 19, at the very center, was connected not only to the frame of the collection (Pss 15 and 24), but also to its neighboring psalms, 18–21.[3] Likewise, Psalms 18, 20, and 21 reciprocate this connection with Psalm 19. Because of cohesion between Psalms 18–21, this group of four psalms can be seen as the central movement of the psalm group.

Working outwards, Psalms 15–17 can be grouped into a cohesive movement. If we refer back to table 3, we find that apart from its chiastic counterparts (Pss 19 and 24), Psalm 15 shares the highest phrasal cohesion with Psalm 16 and also some strong lexical cohesion with both Psalms 16 and 17.[4] Like Psalm 15, Psalm 16 also shows strong secondary cohesion with its neighboring psalms, sharing its highest phrasal cohesion with Psalm 15 and its highest morphological cohesion with Psalm 17. It also shares high lexical cohesion with Psalm 17, so that its overall cohesion with Psalm 17 is second only to Psalm 23, its chiastic counterpart. Psalm 17 follows this same pattern: second to its connection with Psalm 22, Psalm 17 is most closely connected to its neighboring psalm, 16, sharing high morphological and lexical cohesion and some phrasal

---

3. See table 5 in ch. 3.
4. While Ps 15 also shares some lexical and superscript cohesion with Ps 23, this is likely due to links between Pss 23 and 24 that by effect also correspond to Ps 15 as Ps 24's counterpart.

links. It is also connected to its other neighbor, Psalm 18, through lexical links, which serves to connect the two overarching movements (i.e., Pss 15–17 with Pss 18–21) at their seam.

When we look at the final three psalms, Psalms 22–24, we find more diverse connections. After its cohesion with Psalm 17, Psalm 22 does share its highest thematic connections with its neighboring psalms, Psalms 21 and 23, but also has close connections with Psalm 18 and 20 at the center.[5] Psalm 23 shares its strongest superscript cohesion with Psalm 24 and also strong lexical cohesion with Psalm 22, but after its cohesion with Psalm 16, it is most closely connected by overall cohesion with Psalm 21, due to lexical, thematic, phrasal, and morphological links. In addition to its connections to the frame (Pss 15 and 19), Psalm 24 shares its strongest superscript cohesion with Psalm 23 but is also connected lexically to Psalms 20 and 21.

My hypothesis about these connections is as follows: Psalms 22–24 show some cohesion with one another, but as the final movement of the collection, they also echo previous psalms to draw the entire storyline to a close. This is similar to what we have seen even on the level of the psalm. For example, the final unit of Psalm 18 (A′) reused various lexemes from the entire psalm, not just its corresponding chiastic unit (A). The high cohesion among Psalms 18–21 at the center and Psalms 15–17 at the beginning strongly imply that that Psalms 22–24 can be grouped together as movement 3 of the collection. The overarching shape of the collection can be displayed as follows in figure 14:

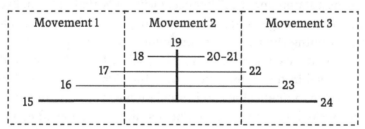

Figure 14. The Tripartite Chiastic Shape of Psalms 15–24

Psalms 15–17 form movement 1, Psalms 18–21 form movement 2, and movement 3 consists of Psalms 22–24. I will now explore the message of

---

5. Ps 22 has high lexical and morphological cohesion with Ps 18, high morphological cohesion with Ps 20, and high thematic cohesion with Pss 21 and 22. It is also connected by superscript to Pss 19–21.

the collection when experienced from beginning to end, in light of links between neighboring, parallel, and nearby psalms.

MOVEMENT 1: PSALMS 15–17

Psalm 15

Psalm 15 establishes the ideal of entrance to Yhwh's presence and presents this vision as the aim of the collection (v. 1). The tone is didactic and idealistic: there is no mention of suffering or enemies or rescue. Psalm 15 describes the one who may access Yhwh's presence in terms of whole-person righteousness: he does it, speaks it, in his heart, with his eyes, and with his possessions (vv. 2–5). The psalm ends with a promise that this righteous one *will not be shaken* (לא ימוט; v. 5), which in the context of the poem relates to the opportunity to enter Yhwh's presence. The promise is for enduring blessing: this one will not be shaken, *ever* (עולם).

Psalm 16

The tone of Psalm 16 is slightly less idealistic than that of Psalm 15 in that it begins with a prayer for God to *keep* (שמר) the psalmist, implying need for protection in the midst of distress. Psalm 16 is an expression of the psalmist's confidence in Yhwh, especially because he has followed in his way or is righteous. The most striking correspondence between the two psalms is the distinctive phrase *not shaken* (בל/לא מוט), used in Psalm 16 as a statement of confidence: *I will not be shaken* (v. 8). Because of the psalms' arrangement in the collection, the use in Psalm 16 has the effect of framing the psalmist's confidence there in light of the promise to the righteous one in Psalm 15. The psalmist's confidence in Psalm 16 is described in terms consistent with the righteous one of Psalm 15 (e.g., devotion to Yhwh alone and association with the righteous rather than the wicked; Pss 15:4; 16:2–4). The distinctive lexeme *lift up* (נשא) is used in both psalms to describe how the psalmist does *not* (בל/לא) *lift up* either reproach against a neighbor (Ps 15:3) or the names of other gods (Ps 16:4). In both, the psalmist's whole person participates, including the *heart* (לב; Pss 15:2; 16:9). Psalm 16 carries the theme of righteousness forward by imbuing it with the relational quality of trust in Yhwh (e.g., *I take refuge in you*; v. 1). The psalmist also expresses confidence that his body *will dwell* (שכן) securely, using the same lexeme introduced in the opening question, "Who may *dwell* on your holy mountain?" (Ps 15:1). As in Psalm 15, the ultimate reward in Psalm 16 is Yhwh's presence, which the psalmist is confident that that he will enjoy forever (v. 11). The effect of these correspondences is that, in the psalms' present arrangement, the figure of Psalm 16 relies on and declares that he is the righteous one of Psalm 15 and therefore is confident in Yhwh's promise to deliver him from any impending distress.

Psalm 17

That distress is quick in coming. In Psalm 17, the storyline takes a turn toward lament, as the psalmist petitions for Yhwh's rescue in the midst of his suffering. The correlation with Psalms 15 and 16 is present right from the superscript, *of David* (לדוד), but also shows a transition from *psalm* (מזמור; Ps 15) and *miktam* (מכתם; Ps 16) to *prayer* (תפלה) in Psalm 17, implying distress. In its location in the collection, Psalm 17 continues to rely on the promise stated in Psalm 15 and reiterated in Psalm 16 that the righteous one *will not be shaken* (בל/לא מוט). The psalmist uses the distinctive phrase to describe how his footsteps *do not totter* as he holds fast to the path of Yhwh (v. 5).

Psalm 17 uses various lexemes related to righteousness that are distinctive shared lexemes with Psalms 15 and 16 (especially Ps 16). The effect is that the figure of Psalm 17 is portrayed as the righteous one of Psalms 15 and 16. Psalm 17 opens and closes with *righteousness* (צדק) as a description of the psalmist, harkening back to the *doer of righteousness* (פעל צדק) in Psalm 15 (Pss 15:2; 17:1, 15). In fact, the word for *doer*, פעל, is the same root used in Psalm 17 to contrast the psalmist with the wicked through the phrase *the works* (פעלה) of humanity. Psalm 17 shares other distinctive corresponding lexemes with Psalm 15 that contrast the wicked with the righteous one: their *speech* (דבר), *eyes* (עין), and *hearts* (לבב) contrast with his own and also with the righteousness described in Psalm 15 (Pss 15:2, 4, 5; 17:10–12). Righteousness is whole-person righteousness, extending to the *heart* (לבב; Pss 15:2; 16:9; 17:3), *lips* (שפה; Pss 16:4; 17:1), and *word* (אמר; Pss 16:2; 17:6). In both Psalms 16 and 17, the psalmist follows the right *way* (דרך; Pss 16:11; 17:4) and is instructed by Yhwh at *night* (לילה; Pss 16:7; 17:3). The distinctive lexical correspondences between Psalms 16 and 17 also portray a reciprocal relationship between Yhwh and the righteous psalmist: as Yhwh *grasps* (תמך) the psalmist's lot, so the psalmist *holds fast* (תמך) to Yhwh's path (Pss 16:5; 17:5); as the psalmist shows *loyal love* (חסד), so Yhwh shows *loyal love* (Pss 16:10; 17:7); as Yhwh is at the psalmist's *right hand* (ימין; Ps 16:8), so Yhwh uses his *right hand* to rescue the psalmist (Ps 17:7); as Yhwh *keeps* (שמר) the psalmist (Ps 16:1), so the psalmist *keeps* from violent paths (Ps 17:4).

In Psalm 17, the psalmist's confidence in Yhwh's deliverance is expressed in terms that strongly echo Psalm 16: In both psalms, he prays to be *kept* (שמר) by Yhwh and *takes refuge* (חסה) in Yhwh (Pss 16:1; 17:7–8), and is sustained by his *right hand* (ימין; Pss 16:11; 17:7). The psalm ends by echoing the confident ending of Psalm 16. The psalmist prays that Yhwh would deliver *his being* (נפשו; Ps 17:13), echoing the declaration that Yhwh would not abandon *his being* (Ps 16:10). The psalmist then contrasts his own *satisfaction* (שבע) in Yhwh's presence with the *portion* (חלק) of the wicked in this *life* (חיים), who are *satisfied* for a short time (Ps 17:14–15), which echoes the promise that Yhwh provides *life* and *satisfaction* for the psalmist in his *presence* forever (Ps 16:10–11).

Together, Psalms 15–17 establish that entering Yhwh's presence is the ultimate aim, and that the means of such access is through righteous character. From Psalms 15–17, the plot moves from the idealistic vision (Ps 15) to confidence in that vision (Ps 16) to confidence in that vision in the midst of the realities of suffering and opposition (Ps 17). The storyline of movement 1 concludes in Psalm 17 with the confident expectation that the righteous will enter Yhwh's presence and experience everlasting joy there. At this point in the story, it is not clear *who* the righteous one is, whether individual, royal one, or community; *how* one becomes righteous; and *what if* this righteous perfection is not humanly attainable—in other words, whether the requirements preclude entrance to Yhwh's presence for the king or the people. The psalms of movement 2 provide some resolution to these questions.

Movement 2: Psalms 18–21

I have discussed the relationships between Psalms 18, 20, and 21 at length previously.[6] What remains is to survey the effect of experiencing Psalms 18–21 linearly, to address the connections between these royal psalms and Psalm 19 at the center of the collection and also to explore the function of Psalms 18–21 in the overarching plotline of the collection.

Psalm 18

Psalm 18 shifts the direction of the collection to focus on the king and deliverance, while also carrying forward the theme of righteousness from

---

6. See ch. 6.

the previous psalms. Psalm 18 begins with a historical superscript that sets the psalm within the narrative context of Yhwh's deliverance(s) of David specifically. The superscript as well as verse 51 frame the psalm as a royal psalm about the Davidic king. The shift in referent to the king (rather than the righteous individual) could be considered to be a clarification of the identity of the individual in Psalms 15–17 or could indicate that the king appropriates the ideals of righteousness prescribed in Psalms 15–17. In either case, it can be said that the focus of the collection shifts indefinitely to the king in Psalm 18.

Psalm 18 also develops the storyline by its shift in structure to a thanksgiving, which appropriately follows the answered lament of Psalm 17 and moves the storyline forward. Psalm 18's description of the call to Yhwh in distress in verses 4–7 is packed with lexemes that correspond to the petition of Psalm 17:6: *call* (קרא), *enemy* (איב), *God* (אל), *heard* (שמע), and *ear* (אזן). Yhwh's deliverance in Psalm 18 also follows the description of Yhwh in Psalm 17 as *savior* (מושיע; Pss 17:7; 18:42), *refuge* (חסה; Pss 17:7; 18:3, 31), *deliverer* (פלט; Pss 17:13; 18:3, 44, 49), and the one who shows *loyal love* (חסד; Pss 17:7; 18:26, 51). These correspondences unite the first two movements together at their seam and also portray David's thanksgiving in Psalm 18 as a response to Yhwh answering the lament of Psalm 17.

As a thanksgiving psalm, most of Psalm 18 describes the distress, deliverance, and praise of the psalmist. But the central unit, verses 21–31, pauses that narrative flow to focus on a description of the righteousness of the psalmist and how Yhwh responds to that righteousness. This section uses a new set of vocabulary, found in Psalms 15–17: *blameless* (תמם; Ps 15:2), *righteous* (צדק; Pss 15:2; 17:1, 15), and *keep* (שמר; Pss 16:1; 17:4, 8). The effect is that Yhwh's deliverance in Psalm 18 is congruent with his promise to sustain and rescue the righteous one of Psalms 15–17. In Psalm 18, the faithful relationship between the king and Yhwh is shown to be reciprocal (vv. 21–31) and is described in affectionate terms like *love* (רחם) and *loyal love* (חסד; vv. 2, 51). Taken together with Psalm 15–17, Psalm 18 shows that the result of righteousness is both entrance to Yhwh's presence and deliverance. The central section on righteousness in Psalm 18 also foreshadows the description of the Torah in Psalm 19.

Yhwh is depicted as a warrior in Psalm 18, a depiction that becomes a major theme in the rest of the collection.[7] Psalm 18 also establishes the

---

7. Yhwh's theophanic appearance both contributes to his warrior identity and also is linked to the psalmist's confidence in Ps 17:15 that he would see Yhwh's form.

promise that God will be faithful to deliver the Davidic king forever (v. 51), both focusing the collection on the king and foreshadowing the deliverance of future kings. In Psalm 18, the king experiences the deliverance and access to Yhwh's presence that has been the object of desire since Psalm 15 and provides hope in Yhwh's continued deliverance of his king.

Psalm 19

At the center of the chiasm, Psalm 19 slows the pace of the storyline for praise and reflection. The tone shifts from that of the previous three psalms, which were grounded in the human experiences of trust, lament, and thanksgiving, to reintroduce the more idealistic tone of Psalm 15. The connections we previously explored among the frame— Psalms 15, 19, and 24—revealed that the way to enter Yhwh's presence is through a righteousness that aligns with creation and Torah. When Psalm 19 is read within its linear literary context (i.e., within Pss 18-21), a new nuance emerges: entrance to Yhwh's presence comes about as a result of the deliverance of the Torah-obedient king.

Within the narrative progression, Psalm 19 functions as the king's praise to Yhwh because of his faithful deliverance in Psalm 18. In the final verses of Psalm 18, the king vows to praise Yhwh, whom he calls *my rock* (צורי), a lexeme unique to these two psalms in the collection. Psalms 18 and 19 are also the only two psalms that refer to the psalmist as the *servant* (עבד), linking the two psalms together as about the same individual. On the heels of the great theophanic deliverance of Psalm 18, Psalm 19 functions as praise to Yhwh the warrior god over all, who delivers his king. When Psalm 19:2-7 is read as a discrete literary unit, the speech of the heavens seems to declare the creative and sustaining power of God and his consistent and active character. When read in light of literary links with Psalm 18, the declaration of Yhwh's glory is more specifically about his deliverance. The psalm opens with two lexemes from Psalm 18: *skies* (שמים) and *works/do* (מעשה). In Psalm 19, the *skies* reveal God's glory (vv. 2, 7). These are the same *skies* that are torn open and burst with lightning and thunder as Yhwh descends in Psalm 18:10-14. In Psalm 19, the sky-dome also declares God's *work*, a distinctive lexeme used just one verse prior at the close of Psalm 18:51 to describe the saving loyal love that Yhwh shows to the anointed one. The *world* (תבל), whose foundations were laid bare at the descent of Yhwh in Psalm 18:16, also reveals God's glory in Psalm 19:5. The distinctive lexical links *do, skies,* and *world* suggest that the declaration of creation in Psalm 19 has to do with Yhwh's work as a deliverer. This is consistent with other verbal links we have seen between Psalm 19 and the framing psalms, 15 and 24. The *mighty* (גבור) sun, who dwells in a *tent* (אהל; Ps 19:6), is analogous to Yhwh, *mighty in battle* (גבור מלחמה; Ps 24:7–10), who dwells in a *tent* (Ps 15:1). These links indicate that the *glory* (כבד) declared by creation in Psalm 19 is the *glory* of Yhwh the warrior, who delivers his king (Ps 19:1; 24:7–10).

The placement of and links between Psalms 18 and 19 also function to unite the themes of the king and Torah to portray the king as Torah-obedient. Recall that Psalm 18 paused to focus on the righteousness of the king in verses 21–31. In Psalm 19, various lexemes from that section—*blameless* (תמם), *revive* (שוב), *pure* (בר), *enlighten* (נגה), and *judgment* (משפט)—are clustered together to describe the Torah. The effect is that, taken together, Psalms 18–19 depict a Torah-obedient king and connect the king's faithfulness closely with Yhwh's deliverance.

In Psalm 19, the storyline of the deliverance of the king, which is continued in Psalm 20, is suspended for praise. In pausing to praise Yhwh for his faithfulness, Psalm 19 functions to impart confidence in the sure reality that God is the faithful deliverer of his faithful king. By slowing the narrative progression, Psalm 19 also refocuses attention on living wisely until the fulfillment of Yhwh's kingdom (which is described in Ps 19's counterparts, 15 and 24). The silent yet comprehensible message of creation and the verbal message of Torah both function to reveal the person of Yhwh as righteous deliverer and forgiver. Wise living involves responding to Yhwh with whole-person Torah-faithfulness. Psalm 19 is about living faithfully until Yhwh arrives as king (Ps 24), with confident hope in Yhwh's faithful deliverance of his king.

Psalms 20–21
Psalms 20 and 21 return to the storyline of Yhwh's faithful deliverance of the king, but with increased confidence. The promise of Yhwh to show loyal love to his king has been made (Ps 18) and celebrated (Ps 19). Psalms 20–21 take the storyline further through links with Psalm 18, showing that Yhwh will continue to be faithful to his promise to future kings.[8]

Like Psalm 18's cohesion with Psalm 19, so also Psalms 20–21's cohesion with Psalm 19 unites the themes of the human king and Torah together to portray the king as Torah-obedient and Yhwh's deliverance of this king

8. See "Reuse and Development from Psalm 18 to Psalms 20–21" in ch. 6

as central. Psalms 19–21 are closely united by their superscripts—*Of the director* (למנצח); *A psalm of David* (מזמור לדוד)—as well as by various lexemes. In Psalms 20–21, Yhwh gives the king the desire of his *heart* (לבב), a distinctive lexeme used in Psalm 19, where it describes how Torah transforms the *heart* (Pss 19:9, 15; 20:5; 21:3). The portrayal of the king, therefore, is one whose heart is transformed by Torah, and Yhwh gives to him according to his heart's desire. In Psalm 21, there is also a cluster of distinctive lexemes from Psalm 19 that are used to describe the blessing of Yhwh on the king: *gladness* (שמח; Pss 19:9; 21:2); *glory* (כבד; Pss 19:2; 21:6); *forever* (עולם; Pss 19:10; 21:5, 7); *gold* (זהב//פז; Pss 19:11; 21:4); and *presence* (פנה; Pss 19:15; 21:7). In Psalm 19, these words describe Yhwh's and the Torah's character. The application of these lexemes to the king in Psalm 21 strengthens the relationship between the king and Torah. The joining of the themes of Torah and kingship at the center of the collection reflects the introduction to the Psalter (Pss 1–2) as well as the "kingship law" of Deuteronomy 17, which define the ideal king as the one faithful to Torah.[9] Distinctive lexemes between Psalms 19 and 20 also unite the two psalms in content as about the deliverance of the king: In Psalm 19, the *skies* (שמים) proclaimed the *knowledge* (ידע) of God, exemplified by the *mighty* (גבר) sun (vv. 2–3, 6). You may recall from connections with Psalm 18 that this seemed to be an analogy for the delivering work of Yhwh. Psalm 20 supports that idea in verse 7: Now I *know* that Yhwh saves his anointed … from the *skies* … with *might* (Ps 20:7).

Perhaps the most striking shift in plot in Psalms 20 and 21 is in the theme of communal inclusion. Psalm 20 is a communal petition for Yhwh to save the king based on the promise of Psalm 18:51 and the faithfulness of the king to Torah (Pss 19; 20:4). Psalm 21 functions as a fulfillment of Psalm 20, wherein Yhwh delivers the king, and the entire community rejoices (v. 14). Psalms 20–21 reuse lexemes from Psalm 18 to show that the people are united with the king in his trust of Yhwh and also benefit from his deliverance.[10] The answer to the initial question of

---

9. See, e.g., Allen, "David as Exemplar," 544–46; Mays, "The Place of the Torah-Psalms," 3–12; Miller, "Kingship," 127–42; Grant, *The King as Exemplar: The Function of Deuteronomy's Kingship Law in the Shaping of the Book of Psalms* (Atlanta: SBL, 2004), 71–119.

10. E.g., they describe the fate of their enemies in language that echoes the fate of the king's enemies (*rise* [קום], *fall* [נפל], *bow* [כרע]); they apply the distinctive phrase *Yhwh my God* (יהוה אלהי) to themselves as Yhwh *our God* (יהוה אלהינו); they display the same trust that the king displays; and they respond in the same way as the king with *song* (שור) and *praise* (זמר).

Psalm 15 about who may enter Yhwh's presence has unfolded in multiple layers. The *who* is the righteous king and all who identify with him. Psalms 18–21 have also provided an answer to the *how*: it is through God's faithful deliverance of his faithful king that all who seek Yhwh will be invited into his presence.

The placement of Psalms 18–21 at the center of the collection identifies the Torah-obedient king as the central character of the collection and his deliverance by Yhwh as the central act and also the means through which the community enters Yhwh's presence. At the very center, Psalm 19 functions to keep the ideal vision of the kingdom at the forefront, in the midst of the on-the-ground experiences of life in the surrounding psalms. The connections between Psalms 18–21 bind the themes of Torah and king together. Yhwh's deliverance of this king demonstrates his commitment to show *loyal love* (חסד) to the king (see esp. Pss 18:51 and 21:8), even into the future (Pss 18:51; 20–21). Together, these psalms function to impart hope in an ideal and faithful king through whom Yhwh's kingdom will come about. This hope in a future king provides hope for the audience in whatever circumstance they find themselves in. The third and final movement explores this hope through the darkest valley, when all seems lost.

MOVEMENT 3: PSALMS 22–24

Psalm 22

Because Psalm 22 follows two royal psalms, it is likely that the primary referent of Psalm 22 continues to be the Davidic king. On the heels of movement 2 and the great deliverance of the Torah-obedient king, Psalm 22 is shocking! Thus far, a pattern of petition and deliverance has been established (Pss 17–18; Pss 20–21), based on the promise of Psalm 15 that the righteous *will not be shaken* (לא ימוט; v. 5). In Psalm 22, however, there is a break in the plotline (a disjuncture that is also represented by a different superscript and change in tone to lament), and the Davidic king finds himself abandoned and forsaken. This state is contrary to the Davidic promise of Psalm 18:51 and the established pattern of petition and deliverance (especially within the closest literary context of the two previous psalms). Distinctive correlations between Psalm 22 and its surrounding psalms reveal in Psalm 22 the most immense distress and loss of hope, the most striking reversal and renewal of hope, and a shocking inclusiveness and revelation of Yhwh as king.

I have previously shown how the distinctive elements that Psalm 22 shares with Psalm 17 depict a distress deeper than previously imagined.[11] In Psalm 22, the description of enemies as surrounding animals and the shared phrases related to distress function to cue in the reader to the comparison being made between the two psalms.[12] The correlating distinctive phrase describing *crying* (קרא) to God (אל) for him *to answer* (ענה) is particularly striking because it is used as a petition in Psalm 17, but as a statement of the psalmist's despair that God does *not answer* his *cry* in Psalm 22, deepening the distress.

You may recall that in addition to the correlations between Psalms 17 and 22, Psalm 22 also has some strong correlations with the royal psalms, 18, 20, and 21.[13] Like its connections with Psalm 17, the connections between the royal psalms and Psalm 22 function to intensify the distress in the latter, especially because it follows directly after these psalms in its arrangement in the storyline. For example, the opening lines of Psalm 22 directly contrast with the royal psalms: *my God* (אלי) is a construction used only in Psalms 18 and 22. In Psalm 18, it sits alongside other designations for God that express the king's security in him—my crag, my stronghold, my rock, etc. (v. 3)—but in Psalm 22, it begins the cry of dereliction (v. 2). The cry that God is far from the psalmist's *salvation* (ישועה) in the same verse echoes the only other uses of the word as a noun in the royal psalms, where it describes God's promise to bring *salvation* to the king (Ps 18:51) and expresses confident petition and praise based on that promise (Pss 20:6; 21:2, 6). The following line, that the psalmist calls *daily* (יום) to his God (אלהים), who does not *answer* (ענה; v. 3) contrasts not only with Psalm 17 but also especially with Psalm 20, where God always *answers* in the *day* of distress.[14]

Various other correlations with the royal psalms create a strong contrast with the promise and pattern of deliverance there and what

---

11. See "Intensified Distress" in ch. 5

12. Recall that, alongside Pss 18 and 20, Pss 17 and 22 share the greatest number of distinctive phrases (three) in the collection: the petition to deliver the psalmist's *being* (נפש) by/from the *sword* (חרב; Pss 17:13; 22:21); the description of the enemy as a *tearing* (טרף) *lion* (ארי; Pss 17:12; 22:14); and the psalmist's *call* (קרא) for God (אל) to *answer* (ענה; Pss 17:6; 22:3).

13. See tables chs. 7 and 8.

14. In addition to its use in Ps 22:3, God as אלהים is used so far in the collection only in Pss 18 and 20 (Pss 18:7, 22, 29, 30, 32, 47; 20:2, 6, 8). God *answers* in Pss 18:42; 20:2, 7, 10. The lexeme *day* is used to describe the day of rescue (Pss 18:1, 19) and is sometimes even expressed as the *day* Yhwh *answers* (Pss 20:2, 10).

happens in Psalm 22. The lexeme *trust* (בטח) describes the reciprocal, faithful relationship between Yhwh and the king in Psalm 21:7, but is used as an expression of pain in Psalm 22, where the psalmist contrasts himself with the ancestors who *trusted* and were delivered. The words used for *deliver* in Psalm 22—פלט and נצל—are highly distinctive and recall and contrast with deliverance in the royal psalms.[15] The enemies' mockery of the psalmist in Psalm 22:9, *let him rescue him, for he delights in him* (יצילהו כי חפץ בו), strongly echoes the declaration the psalmist makes in Psalm 18:18-20, *he delivered me* (יצילני) ... *because he delighted in me* (כי חפץ בי). In Psalm 22:12, the psalmist describes his state as one of *distress* (צרר) with no *helper* (עזר), contrasting with the designation of Yhwh as bringing *help* in *distress* (Pss 18:7; 20:2-3). In Psalm 22:16, the psalmist describes himself as being laid in the *dust* (עפר) of death by Yhwh, a word used only elsewhere to describe the state of the enemies and the psalmist's victory over them in Psalm 18:43.

In addition to the enhanced distress created by lexical correlation with surrounding psalms, lexical correlation also creates the most striking reversal of this distress, so that Psalm 22 represents the turn in the plotline from crisis to resolution. The turning point of the psalm itself, expressed as *you have answered me* (עניתני; v. 22), not only echoes lexemes internal to Psalm 22 but also reaffirms the pattern of the royal psalms, that Yhwh indeed *answers* (ענה) his king (cf. Ps 20:2, 7). The next line immediately echoes the praise of Psalm 20, which emphasizes boasting in the *name* (שם) of Yhwh (Ps 20:2, 6, 8): the psalmist vows to praise Yhwh's *name* in the congregation, even calling the congregation by the same name as in Psalm 20, *Jacob* (יעקב), which is used only in these two psalms and at Yhwh's arrival as king among his community (Pss 20:2; 22:24; 24:6).

Yhwh's rescue of the psalmist in Psalm 22 not only reaffirms the promise and pattern of the royal psalms that Yhwh will rescue his king, but it adds to the plotline in various ways. First, the deliverance in the midst of the deepest distress functions to provide continued hope in Yhwh's faithfulness, even when the situation looks completely dire or even seems to contrast with the promises of Yhwh. Second, the psalmist is depicted as afflicted and suffering, rather than quickly rescued from distress or victorious as in previous psalms, 18-21. Taken together with the royal psalms, this adds a significant dimension to the character and

---

15. פלט is used in Pss 17:13; 18:3, 44, 49; 22:5, 9; נצל is used only in Pss 18:1, 49; 22:9, 21.

experience of the ideal king as one who suffers greatly. Third, it is notable that the righteousness of the psalmist is never set forth as a motivation for deliverance in Psalm 22, a pattern found in every other psalm
so far. Instead, the psalmist refers to himself as a worthless worm and
contrasts himself with his trusting ancestors. The absence of the theme
of righteousness portrays Yhwh as faithful to deliver his king because
of his own character and faithfulness to his promise, not simply as a response to righteousness. This move both deepens the portrayal of Yhwh
as relentlessly faithful and opens the door for perhaps the broader community—not just the ideal king of Psalms 18–21—to have the opportunity to enter Yhwh's presence. This is exactly the next move in the psalm.

The fourth and highly significant way Psalm 22 carries the plotline
forward is in its inclusion of all people in the blessing of Yhwh because
of his rescue of the afflicted king and the true kingship of Yhwh. The
spatial widening of the kingdom of Yhwh has been foreshadowed and
the communal widening was initiated in Psalms 20–21. I have previously
explored the expansion to the community that takes place within the
shape of Psalm 22 and also in comparison with its counterpart, Psalm 17.[16]
Literary links with the royal psalms add more nuance. Because of the rescue of the afflicted king by Yhwh the king, all afflicted ones will benefit.
Psalm 22:27 consists of a short blessing to the people that echoes significant lexemes from the blessing given to the king in Psalm 21:3–7: just
as Yhwh gave the king the desire of his *heart* (לבב) and *life* (חיה) *forever*
(עולם), so the blessing from the king to the people is "May your *hearts
live forever*" (Ps 22:27). Within Psalm 22 itself, the expansion of blessing
beyond the community of Israel to the nations is apparent. Shared distinctive lexemes from the royal psalms confirm that the nations participate in the same blessing: Whereas the lexeme *remember* (זכר) is used of
the faithful community in Psalm 20:8, it is used of the *ends of the earth*
(אפס ארץ) in Psalm 22:28. This description, along with *all the families*
(כל משפחה) of the nations in the next line, recalls the Abrahamic promise. What is of interest is the use of the word *nations* (גוי), since the lexeme is used to describe enemy nations in Psalm 18:44. While the psalmist
praises Yhwh *among the nations* in Psalm 18:50, it is unclear there whether these nations join in praise. Psalm 22 clarifies that indeed they will
worship in the presence of Yhwh (v. 27) because Yhwh is the king *of
the nations* (v. 29). This is a significant transformation of the character

---

16. See "Expansion to All People, Places, and Times in Psalm 22" in ch. 5.

of *the nations* in the storyline and also the first mention of Yhwh as the king. If the royal psalms were about how Yhwh empowers his anointed one, Psalm 22 is about how Yhwh is the true king, who rescues his human king and any who identify with him. Various other shared lexemes demonstrate inclusion. The word *dust* (עָפָר) had been used previously to describe how the enemies were smashed to *dust* (Ps 18:43) and how the psalmist was laid in the *dust* (Ps 22:16); now we find that *any* (כֹּל) who go down to the *dust*—presumably the king or his enemies—are invited to find life in Yhwh the true king (Ps 22:30). The psalm ends with a declaration that *offspring* (זֶרַע) will serve Yhwh—a lexeme previously used of both David's line (Ps 18:51) and the enemy's seed (Ps 21:11)—perhaps making the point that *all* are invited.

The psalm ends with a declaration that future generations will declare Yhwh's *righteousness* (צְדָקָה), that *he has done it* (עָשָׂה). The use of *righteousness* is the only use in the psalm, and it contrasts to previous uses, where it referred to a righteous human or king. The attribution to Yhwh alongside no mention of human righteousness again emphasizes that this psalm is about Yhwh and his faithfulness. His righteousness is defined by the words *he has done it*, referring to the deliverance of the anointed and expansion of his kingdom to include any and all who identify with him.

Psalm 23
The tone of Psalm 23 is one of confidence, the effect of which is that it functions as part of the resolution that continues from Psalm 22. Psalm 23 is a psalm of trust, like its chiastic counterpart, Psalm 16, but the confidence and joy expressed within is greater.[17] In its location in the collection, Psalm 23 functions as a continuation of the praise and feasting of Psalm 22. Within the storyline, the heightening of praise from its chiastic counterpart follows as a result of the deliverance from suffering and proclamation of the kingship of Yhwh in Psalm 22:23–32. The celebratory feasting in Psalm 23 is therefore set within the context of the worldwide feast of Psalm 22.

At the center of Psalm 23 in verse 4 is a statement of Yhwh's presence with the psalmist through the darkest valley. Taken within the context of the psalm, this statement is one of security in Yhwh's presence. But verbal links within the broader literary context connect this statement

---

17. See "Reuse and Development in Psalm 23" in ch. 4.

closely with the experience of immense suffering and ultimate deliverance found in Psalm 22: The reference to the *valley of death-shadow* likely reflects the lowest point of the collection so far, Psalm 22:16, when the psalmist is *set in the dust of death*. Its location after Psalm 22 makes clear that it is because of the deliverance of the afflicted there that the psalmist can declare that even in that darkest valley, he will not fear harm. The reason given is *for you are with me*, a statement of the nearness of God that reflects the problem (*farness* [רחק]) and resolution (*answering* [ענה]) of the previous psalm. Taken together, the result in Psalm 23 is that the statement *you are with me* brings confidence even when God seems to have forsaken his people, as in Psalm 22. The following line in Psalm 23, which mentions Yhwh's *rod*, implies his kingship and, in context, builds on the idea from the previous psalm that *the kingship belongs to Yhwh* (Ps 22:19). In other words, the peace of the psalmist in Psalm 23 is a result of Yhwh's presence in the midst of suffering, his faithfulness to deliver the afflicted king, and his kingship over all.

It is likely that Psalm 23 has the human king as its referent, both because of its literary context following Psalms 18–22, but also because of links between Psalms 23 and 21.[18] A distinctive word cluster that links the two psalms shows that the honor Yhwh bestows on his guest in Psalm 23 is royal honor. Psalm 23:5–6 describes the blessing of the psalmist in terms of Yhwh's blessing to the king after victory in Psalm 21:4–8: he brings *goodness* (טוב), *loyal love* (חסד), *days* (יום), *life* (חיה), blesses the *head* (ראש), and gives *length of days* (ארך ימים), a distinctive correlating phrase between both psalms. The links portray the figure in Psalm 23 as the human king. And although the first-person singular pronouns and suffixes in Psalm 23 express the personal nature of God's presence with the king, in its broader literary context, this is an experience that is available to those who identify with the king, as the expansions of the king's blessings to all in Psalms 20–22 have shown. The dining at the table in the presence of enemies (Ps 23:5) is also suggestive that these enemies have now come under the authority of Yhwh and his anointed king, feasting alongside all *those who seek him* (דרשיו; Ps 22:27).[19]

Placed just before the full arrival of Yhwh's kingdom in Psalm 24, Psalm 23 depicts a tension between the arrival of the kingdom and the present suffering by its expression of hope amidst distress and its

18. See "Increased Satisfaction in Psalm 23" in ch. 4.
19. See "The Shape of Psalm 23" in ch. 4.

language of journey. In Psalm 23, the presence of Yhwh is central, giving the impression that the awaited resolution of Psalm 15 has arrived.
While Yhwh's presence in Psalm 23 is certainly an expression of his
kingship, there are hints that Yhwh's kingdom is not present in its fullness, since distress and enemies are still mentioned (vv. 4-5). Likewise,
the last line *I will return to the house of Yhwh*, though it expresses unwav-
ering confidence, also expresses a state of not yet being in the house of
Yhwh, a theme that is fulfilled in the following psalm, 24. That Psalm 23
is moving toward this great arrival of the king is also indicated by the
language of journey or movement in the psalm, including its expansive
spatial imagery, lexemes associated with movement, and imagery of
shepherding.[20] This dynamic language in Psalm 23 depicts a pilgrimage
that ends at the house of Yhwh (v. 6). In its location before Psalm 24,
Psalm 23 depicts a confident progression toward the arrival of Yhwh's
kingdom, and yet that final experience of resting in his presence forever is still future. Psalm 23 indicates that trust in Yhwh's presence is the
space of refuge until his ultimate arrival.

Psalm 24

Psalm 24 depicts the full arrival of Yhwh's kingdom. It begins with a statement of all creation under Yhwh's dominion (vv. 1-2). The spatial expansion evident in the second half of the chiasm comes to its fulfillment here.

The question-answer-result structure of Psalm 24 mirrors Psalm
15, and yet at its position at the end of the collection, it carries additional nuance. The double question about who may enter essentially
reiterates that at the beginning, and the description of the righteous
one seems to echo the description of the righteous individual of Psalm
15—the one who is righteous in act, heart, and speech. However, by this
point and because of connections with Psalm 19, we now know that the
way one becomes a righteous person is through alignment with Yhwh's
creation and Torah and through Yhwh's own forgiveness (Ps 19).[21] We
have also seen through links between the royal psalms and Torah
psalm (Pss 18-21) that this description of the righteous individual gets
uniquely applied to the human king. The next verse of Psalm 24 seems
to key into this by declaring as a result that the righteous one *bears
blessing* and *justice* from Yhwh, acts that befit a ruler and will benefit

---

20. See "Increased Trust in Psalm 23" in ch. 4.
21. See "Reuse and Development in Psalm 19" and "The Righteous One May Enter" in
ch. 3.

his community (v. 5). We have also already seen in Psalms 20–22 how
the community not only benefits from the blessings of the king, but
identifies with and participates in his same blessing. The next verse
of Psalm 24 goes there, declaring, *this is the generation of the seekers of
him*, closely identifying the community with the righteous royal one,
so that the distinction becomes blurry. The designation *the generation
of the seekers of him* (דור דרשיו) recalls the *seekers of him* (דרשיו) and the
generation (דור) who will worship Yhwh in light of hearing of his great
work of deliverance in Psalm 22:27, 31. *Seekers of him* also recalls the
initial aim of the collection to enter Yhwh's presence (Ps 15), indicating that the answer has come. The identification of this community as
Jacob (יעקב) recalls the designation of the community in Psalm 22:24,
where inclusivity was the theme. In light of Psalm 22, *Jacob* no longer
means only the nation of Israel, but includes the ends of the earth, all
families, the nations, the rich and poor, the living and dying, present
and future generations (Ps 22:27–32).

With Yhwh's global, creation-wide community ready for his arrival, Yhwh enters his temple. Through analogy with all creation as
his sacred space in verses 1–2, Yhwh's temple is depicted as cosmic
in scope, not restricted to one place. In no uncertain terms, Yhwh is
identified as the glorious king. The designations *strong* (עז), *mighty in
battle* (גבור מלחמה), and *Yhwh of hosts* (יהוה צבאות) depict him as the
warrior king (vv. 7–10). If, when read as a discrete unit, the designations of Psalm 24 seemed like one-off ways to refer to Yhwh, we now
know that his identity as the warrior king is central to the storyline of
the collection. Psalms 18–21 depict Yhwh as the deliverer of his Torah-
obedient king. In Psalm 22, God's nearness to and deliverance of the
king initiates worldwide praise that characterizes the kingdom of God
in verses 23–32.[22] Psalm 23 depicts Yhwh as the king who is present
with and protecting the psalmist. Yhwh is the warrior king who saves
his anointed king and the community of that king—that is the proclamation at his arrival in Psalm 24.

At the end of the plotline, Psalm 24 answers the question of *who* may
enter Yhwh's presence as the faithful anointed king and his community,
and the *how* as through the faithfulness of this king and Yhwh's faithful
deliverance of him. Yhwh's kingdom—the fullness of his presence as
king on earth—is the final scene.

---

22. See "A New Theme: Yhwh's Universal Kingdom" in ch. 5.

TENSION BETWEEN SUFFERING AND HOPE

Psalm 24 closes the collection with an ideal vision of the kingdom. But when we read the collection as a whole, we find a tension between a present reality of suffering and the ideal kingdom, as well as language of journey that resonates with finding ourselves somewhere in between. The existence of the idealistic, didactic frame (Pss 15, 19, and 24) around the more existential psalms (those concerned with the on-the-ground experience of the psalmist) is the first indicator that there is a tension between the fullness of Yhwh's kingdom and the present reality. The frame has a more idealistic vision than the intervening psalms, as evidenced by comparison of their structures and themes with that of other psalms within the collection. In the frame, the ideal vision of Yhwh's kingdom (Pss 15 and 24) and a picture of perfect faithfulness (Ps 19) are set forth, whereas the intervening psalms express both painful and joyful experiences of humanity, despite faithfulness. Psalms 16 and 23 model the way of trust while living within the tension. These two psalms express confidence in the ideal vision of Yhwh's kingdom. In this way, they serve as a bridge between the idealistic outer psalms (Pss 15, 19, 24) and the existential psalms within (Pss 17-22). The theme of suffering in Psalms 17 and 22 and the theme of deliverance from suffering in Psalms 18, 20, and 21 imply that the realization of Yhwh's kingdom involves a journey through suffering. Psalms 17 and 22 create disequilibrium between the ideals and confidence of the outer psalms and the present and painful realities of suffering.

When read in consecutive order, we find not only a tension between the realities of the kingdom (Pss 15, 19, 24), hope (Pss 16 and 23), and suffering (Pss 17-18, 20-22), but also a deepening of trust as a result of suffering. Psalm 15 sets forth the ideal vision of entering Yhwh's presence, orienting the reader around the promise that the righteous one would not be shaken (Ps 15:5). Psalm 16 expresses confidence in the promise that Yhwh would indeed preserve the righteous one. Psalm 17 takes a turn toward disorientation, and yet within his petition, the psalmist still expresses confidence in Yhwh's promise; we learn that even within suffering, we can trust that Yhwh will be faithful. Psalm 18 adds another dimension to the storyline, depicting the suffering and deliverance of the anointed king, further affirming Yhwh's faithfulness to his promise in the midst of suffering. Psalm 19 pauses the storyline for praise, and to reorient the reader around the ideal vision of Yhwh's global dominion and beautiful instruction. Psalms 20-21 move forward with a renewed sense of confidence in Yhwh's continued deliverance of his king(s) into the future.

The collection could have ended here on a high note, but the storyline continues and the result is a more complex message. Psalm 22 plunges the reader into the depths of the king's despair. By the looks of it, all seems lost and God's promise, failed; he is nowhere to be found. The language of shame, suffering, defeat, and death dominate the psalm. If Psalm 17 was a psalm of disorientation, in retrospect it seems like nothing now. Then without warning, Psalm 22 takes a turn. Yhwh rescues the king, and as a result, the global community is invited into his blessing. The psalm ends by declaring that this moment is the one that will be told of into the future, that Yhwh has rescued the afflicted. In light of the rescue of the afflicted king, Psalm 23 reorients the reader to trust and rest in Yhwh, but this time a much deeper experience of it, one that finds confidence in the midst of the valley of death because Yhwh is present. The collection ends with a return to the ideal kingdom in Psalm 24, but now with unshakable confidence in the reality of it, Yhwh's faithfulness to deliver the faithful king, and the refuge of his presence in the midst of our suffering until he arrives as king.

SUMMARY

In this book, my aim has been to explore the shape and message of Psalms 15–24. I have done this by developing an editorial-critical method for identifying different types and strengths of links between psalms. Underlying my method is the idea that parallelism can exist between blocks of text, including entire psalms, both neighboring and distant. I have evaluated every possible psalm-pair combination in this collection in terms of distinctive lexical, structural, thematic, morphological, and superscript links.[23] From this statistical analysis of literary links between psalms, I have concluded that the following psalms exist in distinctive, or unique, relationships: Psalms 15, 19, and 24; Psalms 16 and 23; Psalms 17 and 22; and Psalms 18, 20 and 21, with these final two psalms forming a pair of "twin psalms." These sets of parallel psalms form an identifiable chiastic pattern.

Psalms 15, 19, and 24 form the frame of the collection and establish the goal of accessing Yhwh's presence through Torah faithfulness. Psalms 16 and 23 are connected to one another as psalms of trust and

---

23. See appendices 2 and 4.

express confidence in the realization of this goal. Psalm 17 and 22 reflect the experience of suffering, shifting the tone from joyful trust to deep distress and prayer for deliverance. The royal psalms, Psalms 18, 20, and 21, are joined together structurally and as psalms about the human king. Together, they emphasize Yhwh's enduring faithfulness to provide the Davidic king with deliverance and blessing.

From each psalm to its chiastic counterpart, I have observed a consistent broadening in time, space, and human referent; an intensification of Yhwh's presence; and the introduction of the new theme of Yhwh as the king. These dynamic shifts reveal a progression in the storyline toward the fullness of Yhwh's kingdom, which is depicted as his presence on earth among his diverse community. The position of Psalms 18–21 at the center of the collection depicts Yhwh's deliverance of his ideal king as the way that Yhwh's kingdom comes about. This message is significant because it defines the messianic expectation in terms of the suffering and deliverance of the Davidic king and expresses the result as the inclusion of all nations in the kingdom of Yhwh. Until Yhwh's kingdom is fully realized, life is portrayed as a journey of suffering, trust, and hope in a future and ideal king.

This study offers a contribution to the idea that the Psalter exhibits a unified shape by demonstrating cohesion and development within the Psalms from the micro-level upward. It is my hope that additional and similar studies of collections within the Psalter will provide continued support for the claim that the Psalter forms a unified whole and will further illuminate its shape.

Appendix 1

Equations

In this appendix, I provide the specific equations that I use to calculate levels of cohesion between elements. These calculations form the basis of understanding whether psalms are closely correlated.[1]

In order to identify the strength of cohesion between each possible psalm pair in Psalms 15–24,[2] I first identify every repeated lexeme, morphology, phrase, theme, structure, and superscript between every possible pair of psalms in Psalms 15–24. Then I assess how rare each specific repetition is. In this step, I seek to understand whether an element occurs at a higher rate in a psalm pair than its average in the collection, as well as how much higher its rate of occurrence is. (See appendix 3 for distinctive elements.)

I use equation 1 to calculate the distinctiveness of a shared lexeme or theme; equation 2 for a shared structure, phrase, or superscript; and equation 3 for a shared morphology. Each of these equations compares the rate of occurrence in a psalm pair with its average rate in the collection:

EQUATION 1: THE DISTINCTIVENESS OF A LEXEME, PHRASE, OR THEME IN A PSALM PAIR

$$\frac{Average\ rate\ in\ psalm\ pair}{Average\ rate\ in\ collection} = \frac{\dfrac{n_{e\ (ps\ pr)}}{n_{l\ (ps\ pr)}}}{\dfrac{n_{e\ (15-24)}}{n_{l\ (15-24)}}} = p$$

---

1. Refer to "Calculating the Strength of Cohesion Between Psalm Pairs" in ch. 3 for further description.
2. I.e., Pss 15 and 16; 15 and 17; ... 15 and 24; 16 and 17; ... 16 and 24; ... and 23 and 24.

EQUATION 2: THE DISTINCTIVENESS OF A STRUCTURE OR SUPERSCRIPT
IN A PSALM PAIR

$$\frac{Average\ rate\ in\ psalm\ pair}{Average\ rate\ in\ collection} = \frac{\dfrac{n_{e\ (ps\ pr)}}{2}}{\dfrac{n_{e\ (15-24)}}{10}} = p$$

EQUATION 3: THE DISTINCTIVENESS OF A MORPHOLOGY
IN A PSALM PAIR

$$\frac{Average\ rate\ in\ psalm\ pair}{Average\ rate\ in\ collection} = \frac{\dfrac{n_{e\ (ps\ pr)}}{n_{lex\ (ps\ pr)}}}{\dfrac{n_{e\ (15-24)}}{n_{lex\ (15-24)}}} = p$$

The key for the equations above is as follows:

- n_e is the number of occurrences of a particular repeated element, either in the psalm pair *(ps pr)* or in the collection (15-24).
- n_l is the number of non-incidental lexemes, either in the psalm pair *(ps pr)* or in the collection (15-24).
- n_{lex} is the number of occurrences of the particular lexeme.
- p is the strength of cohesion of the particular element.
- If $p > 1$, the particular element in the psalm pair is distinctive.
- If $p \leq 1$, the particular element in the psalm pair is not distinctive.

The difference between equations 1-3 is the way that the rate is calculated. In equation 1, the rate is a function of the number of occurrences of a lexeme, phrase, or theme (n_e) per total number of lexemes per psalm pair (n_l). In equation 2, the rate involves the number of occurrences of a structure or superscript (n_e) per number of psalms rather than per number of lexemes (either 2 or 10). This is because when these types of repeated elements occur in the collection, they typically occur at a rate of one per psalm. I use equation 3 to identify the number of occurrences of a lexeme in a particular morphology (n_e) per the number of times that particular lexeme is used (n_{lex}).

In the equations above, if the rate of occurrence of the particular element in the psalm pair is the same as its rate in the collection, p will equal one, in which case the element is not distinctive. If the rate of occurrence in the psalm pair is lower, p will be less than one, and the element is not distinctive. If the rate of occurrence in the psalm pair is higher, p

will be greater than one, and the element is distinctive. The strength of cohesion per each distinctive element is presented in appendix 2.

After calculating the strength of cohesion of each shared element per psalm pair, I add together the strengths of cohesion of the distinctive elements according to criteria type (e.g., lexical, morphological, etc.) to find the total *strength of cohesion per link type*. The strengths of cohesion per link type reveal which psalms have the strongest lexical, thematic, structural, phrasal, morphological, or superscript connections.

In order to assess the overall strength of cohesion between two psalms, I add together each of the strengths of cohesion per criteria type. Both the strengths of cohesion per link type and the overall strengths of cohesion are presented on the tables throughout chapters 3–6. Those psalms that exhibit higher strengths of cohesion when paired together than when paired with other psalms in the collection are called a *distinctive psalm pair* or *parallel psalms*.

Appendix 2

Distinctive Elements and Strengths of Cohesion

Tables A-F provide the data for each distinctive shared element per psalm pair, including lexemes, morphologies, phrases, themes, structures, and superscripts. Each of the tables below has some of the following columns: the designated psalm pair (Psalms); the shared element; the number of elements per psalm pair (*ne(ps pr)*); the number of elements in the collection (*ne(15-24)*); and the strength of cohesion per shared element (*p*). For corresponding morphologies (table B), both lexemes and their morphological must correspond, so both are listed. Therefore, table B includes not only the number of morphological repetitions per psalm pair, but also a column for the number of occurrences of the lexemes within which that morphology occurs (*nlex*), both within the psalm pair (*ps pr*) and the collection (15-24). The final two columns of each table include the total strength of cohesion between a psalm pair (Total), as well as that strength of cohesion adjusted to a decimal portion of the number one (Adjusted). I have adjusted these final numbers in light of the highest recorded total strength of cohesion, which I indicate on each table by an asterisk (*) in the total column. For example, on table A, the pair of Psalms 17 and 22 exhibits the highest total strength of lexical cohesion when compared with every other possible psalm pair—59.99. Therefore, I use this strength of cohesion to adjust all of the lexical strengths per each psalm pair to a decimal portion of the number one, by dividing by 59.99.

TABLE A. DISTINCTIVE LEXEMES AND STRENGTHS OF COHESION

Psalms	Lexeme	n_e (ps pr)	n_e (15-24)	p	Total	Adjusted
15 and 16	שכן	2	2	10.27	30.50	0.51
	מוט	2	4	5.14		
	קדש	2	6	3.42		
	נשא	2	8	2.57		
	נתן	2	10	2.05		
	לבב	2	10	2.05		
	כבד	2	10	2.05		
	דוד	2	11	1.87		
	יהוה	6	58	1.06		
15 and 17	כסף	2	2	7.34	30.54	0.51
	פעל	2	2	7.34		
	עין	4	7	4.19		
	מוט	2	4	3.67		
	דבר	3	8	2.75		
	צדק	3	9	2.45		
	לבב	2	10	1.47		
	דוד	2	11	1.33		
15 and 18	לקח	2	3	3.07	19.67	0.33
	רגל	4	5	2.46		
	תמם	6	8	2.30		
	הר	2	3	2.05		
	נתן	6	10	1.84		
	עשה	3	5	1.84		
	דבר	4	8	1.54		
	עין	3	7	1.32		
	עולם	2	5	1.23		
	צדק	3	9	1.02		
	יהוה	19	58	1.01		
15 and 19	אהל	2	2	7.39	43.89	0.73
	אמן	2	3	7.39		
	נקה	3	4	5.54		
	עשה	3	5	4.43		
	ירא	2	5	2.95		
	תמם	3	8	2.77		
	לבב	3	10	2.22		
	עין	2	7	2.11		
	דבר	2	8	1.85		
	צדק	2	9	1.64		
	זמר	2	9	1.64		
	כבד	2	10	1.48		
	דוד	2	11	1.34		
	יהוה	9	58	1.15		
15 and 20	קדש	3	6	5.38	15.33	0.26
	זמר	2	9	2.39		
	נתן	2	10	2.15		
	לבב	2	10	2.15		
	דוד	2	11	1.96		
	יהוה	7	58	1.30		
15 and 21	רעע	3	5	5.30	23.97	0.40
	מוט	2	4	4.41		

Psalms	Lexeme	n_e (ps pr)	n_e (15-24)	p	Total	Adjusted
15 and 21	עולם	2	5	3.53		
	זמר	3	9	2.94		
	נתן	3	10	2.65		
	לבב	2	10	1.77		
	כבד	2	10	1.77		
	דוד	2	11	1.61		
15 and 22	בזה	3	3	4.57	39.01	0.65
	לשון	2	2	4.57		
	קרב	2	2	4.57		
	גור	2	2	4.57		
	חרפה	2	2	4.57		
	עשה	3	5	2.74		
	רעע	3	5	2.74		
	ירא	3	5	2.74		
	רגל	2	5	1.83		
	קדש	2	6	1.52		
	לבב	3	10	1.37		
	דבר	2	8	1.14		
	צדק	2	9	1.02		
	זמר	2	9	1.02		
15 and 23	הלך	2	2	12.99	34.11	0.57
	רעע	3	5	7.79		
	ירא	2	5	5.20		
	צדק	2	9	2.89		
	זמר	2	9	2.89		
	דוד	2	11	2.36		
15 and 24	שבע	2	2	9.91	54.91	0.92
	נשא	7	8	8.67		
	הר	2	3	6.61		
	כבד	6	10	5.95		
	עולם	3	5	5.95		
	נקה	2	4	4.96		
	קדש	2	6	3.30		
	צדק	2	9	2.20		
	זמר	2	9	2.20		
	לבב	2	10	1.98		
	דוד	2	11	1.80		
	יהוה	8	58	1.37		
16 and 17	תמך	2	2	6.28	50.28	0.84
	חלק	2	3	4.19		
	ארח	2	3	4.19		
	שפה	3	5	3.77		
	ימין	3	6	3.14		
	שמר	3	6	3.14		
	שבע	2	4	3.14		
	חסה	2	4	3.14		
	מוט	2	4	3.14		
	לילה	2	5	2.51		
	נפש	3	8	2.35		
	פנה	5	16	1.96		
	חסד	2	7	1.79		
	אמר	2	7	1.79		
	חיה	2	7	1.79		

Psalms	Lexeme	$n_{e\,(ps\,pr)}$	$n_{e\,(15\text{-}24)}$	p	Total	Adjusted
16 and 17	ארץ	2	8	1.57		
	לבב	2	10	1.26		
	דוד	2	11	1.14		
16 and 18	חבל	3	3	2.87	32.96	0.55
	רבה	2	2	2.87		
	שאול	2	2	2.87		
	נחל	2	2	2.87		
	חסה	3	4	2.15		
	חפץ	2	3	1.91		
	שוה	2	3	1.91		
	נתן	6	10	1.72		
	חסד	4	7	1.64		
	אל	12	22	1.56		
	ימין	3	6	1.43		
	שמר	3	6	1.43		
	ידע	2	4	1.43		
	ראה	2	4	1.43		
	נפל	2	4	1.43		
	אמר	3	7	1.23		
	ברך	2	5	1.15		
	יהוה	21	58	1.04		
16 and 19	ארח	2	3	4.21	31.41	0.52
	שמח	3	5	3.79		
	לילה	3	5	3.79		
	אמר	4	7	3.61		
	ידע	2	4	3.16		
	שמר	2	6	2.10		
	נצח	2	6	2.10		
	לבב	3	10	1.89		
	ארץ	2	8	1.58		
	נפש	2	8	1.58		
	כבד	2	10	1.26		
	יהוה	11	58	1.20		
	דוד	2	11	1.15		
16 and 20	יעץ	2	2	8.63	43.42	0.72
	שם	4	7	4.93		
	ימין	3	6	4.31		
	קדש	3	6	4.31		
	ידע	2	4	4.31		
	נפל	2	4	4.31		
	נצח	2	6	2.88		
	כל	4	19	1.82		
	נתן	2	10	1.73		
	לבב	2	10	1.73		
	דוד	2	11	1.57		
	אל	4	22	1.57		
	יהוה	9	58	1.34		
16 and 21	גיל	2	2	7.34	57.90	0.97
	שמח	4	5	5.87		
	טוב	2	3	4.89		
	שוה	2	3	4.89		
	ברך	3	5	4.40		
	מוט	2	4	3.67		

Psalms	Lexeme	$n_{e\,(ps\,pr)}$	$n_{e\,(15\text{-}24)}$	p	Total	Adjusted
16 and 21	ימין	3	6	3.67		
	שפה	2	5	2.94		
	נצח	2	6	2.45		
	בטח	2	6	2.45		
	נתן	3	10	2.20		
	חסד	2	7	2.10		
	חיה	2	7	2.10		
	פנה	4	16	1.83		
	ארץ	2	8	1.83		
	לבב	2	10	1.47		
	כבד	2	10	1.47		
	דוד	2	11	1.33		
	יהוה	8	58	1.01		
16 and 22	אדון	2	2	4.14	45.22	0.75
	עזב	2	2	4.14		
	גורל	2	2	4.14		
	בטח	5	6	3.45		
	ראה	3	4	3.10		
	חפץ	2	3	2.76		
	חלק	2	3	2.76		
	כל	10	19	2.18		
	שבע	2	4	2.07		
	נפל	2	4	2.07		
	חיה	3	7	1.77		
	לילה	2	5	1.66		
	שפה	2	5	1.66		
	ארץ	3	8	1.55		
	נפש	3	8	1.55		
	קדש	2	6	1.38		
	נצח	2	6	1.38		
	לבב	3	10	1.24		
	שם	2	7	1.18		
	פנה	4	16	1.03		
16 and 23	כוס	2	2	10.00	30.04	0.50
	טוב	2	3	6.67		
	שם	2	7	2.86		
	חיה	2	7	2.86		
	נפש	2	8	2.50		
	דוד	2	11	1.82		
	פנה	2	16	1.25		
	כל	2	19	1.05		
	יהוה	6	58	1.03		
16 and 24	נשא	7	8	7.06	27.34	0.46
	כבד	6	10	4.84		
	ברך	2	5	3.23		
	קדש	2	6	2.69		
	ארץ	2	8	2.02		
	נפש	2	8	2.02		
	לבב	2	10	1.61		
	דוד	2	11	1.47		
	יהוה	10	58	1.39		
	פנה	2	16	1.01		
17 and 18	אזן	4	4	2.58	53.33	0.89

Psalms	Lexeme	$n_{e\,(ps\,pr)}$	$n_{e\,(15\text{-}24)}$	p	Total	Adjusted
17 and 18	רשע	3	3	2.58		
	עבר	2	2	2.58		
	כנף	2	2	2.58		
	צרף	2	2	2.58		
	סגר	2	2	2.58		
	איב	7	8	2.26		
	בן	3	4	1.93		
	קדם	3	4	1.93		
	נטה	3	4	1.93		
	חסה	3	4	1.93		
	עין	5	7	1.84		
	שמע	5	7	1.84		
	פלט	4	6	1.72		
	שמר	4	6	1.72		
	שפט	2	3	1.72		
	קום	5	8	1.61		
	דבר	5	8	1.61		
	קרא	3	5	1.55		
	סבב	3	5	1.55		
	חסד	4	7	1.47		
	יד	5	9	1.43		
	אל	12	22	1.41		
	פה	3	6	1.29		
	סתר	3	6	1.29		
	כרע	2	4	1.29		
	ישע	8	17	1.21		
	צדק	4	9	1.15		
	אמר	3	7	1.11		
	יצא	2	5	1.03		
17 and 19	פקד	2	2	5.07	51.38	0.86
	ישר	2	2	5.07		
	יצא	4	5	4.05		
	סתר	4	6	3.38		
	שפט	2	3	3.38		
	ארח	2	3	3.38		
	לילה	3	5	3.04		
	עין	4	7	2.90		
	אמר	4	7	2.90		
	פה	3	6	2.53		
	שמר	3	6	2.53		
	שמע	3	7	2.17		
	דבר	3	8	1.90		
	נפש	3	8	1.90		
	צדק	3	9	1.69		
	פנה	5	16	1.58		
	לבב	3	10	1.52		
	ארץ	2	8	1.27		
	יד	2	9	1.13		
17 and 20	רנן	2	2	6.46	29.38	0.49
	מלא	3	4	4.84		
	כרע	2	4	3.23		
	קרא	2	5	2.58		
	קום	3	8	2.42		

Psalms	Lexeme	$n_{e\,(ps\,pr)}$	$n_{e\,(15\text{-}24)}$	p	Total	Adjusted
17 and 20	ענה	4	12	2.15		
	ימין	2	6	2.15		
	ישע	5	17	1.90		
	לבב	2	10	1.29		
	אל	4	22	1.17		
	דוד	2	11	1.17		
17 and 21	מצא	3	3	5.71	55.91	0.93
	זמם	2	2	5.71		
	יתר	2	2	5.71		
	שית	5	6	4.76		
	נטה	3	4	4.28		
	אדם	2	3	3.80		
	שפה	3	5	3.42		
	קדם	2	4	2.85		
	מוט	2	4	2.85		
	בן	2	4	2.85		
	פנה	7	16	2.50		
	ימין	2	6	1.90		
	חסד	2	7	1.63		
	חיה	2	7	1.63		
	ארץ	2	8	1.43		
	איב	2	8	1.43		
	יד	2	9	1.27		
	לבב	2	10	1.14		
	דוד	2	11	1.04		
	ישע	3	17	1.01		
	ארי	4	4	3.56	59.99	1.00
17 and 22	נקף	2	2	3.56		
	טרף	2	2	3.56		
	חרב	2	2	3.56		
	שדד	2	2	3.56		
	סבב	3	4	2.67		
	בטן	3	4	2.67		
	שבע	3	4	2.67		
	פה	4	6	2.38		
	ישב	2	3	2.38		
	אדם	2	3	2.38		
	חלק	2	3	2.38		
	שפה	3	5	2.14		
	נפש	4	8	1.78		
	כרע	2	4	1.78		
	ענה	6	12	1.78		
	פלט	3	6	1.78		
	סתר	3	6	1.78		
	פנה	7	16	1.56		
	שמע	3	7	1.53		
	חיה	3	7	1.53		
	קרא	2	5	1.43		
	לילה	2	5	1.43		
	ארץ	3	8	1.34		
	דבר	3	8	1.34		
	יד	3	9	1.19		
	צדק	3	9	1.19		

Psalms	Lexeme	$n_{e\,(ps\,pr)}$	$n_{e\,(15\text{-}24)}$	p	Total	Adjusted
17 and 22	לבב	3	10	1.07		
17 and 23	נוח	2	2	7.20	26.70	0.45
	צל	2	2	7.20		
	נפש	3	8	2.70		
	צדק	3	9	2.40		
	חסד	2	7	2.06		
	חיה	2	7	2.06		
	פנה	5	16	1.78		
	דוד	2	11	1.31		
17 and 24	רמה	2	2	6.14	26.53	0.44
	ישב	2	3	4.09		
	קום	4	8	3.07		
	מלא	2	4	3.07		
	נפש	3	8	2.30		
	צדק	3	9	2.05		
	פנה	5	16	1.92		
	ארץ	2	8	1.54		
	לבב	2	10	1.23		
	דוד	2	11	1.12		
18 and 19	צור	4	4	2.59	48.83	0.81
	קול	3	3	2.59		
	רוץ	2	2	2.59		
	שים	2	2	2.59		
	אור	2	2	2.59		
	תמם	7	8	2.26		
	ברר	5	6	2.15		
	שמים	4	5	2.07		
	יצא	4	5	2.07		
	עבד	4	5	2.07		
	היה	3	4	1.94		
	רבב	5	7	1.85		
	אמר	5	7	1.85		
	שפט	2	3	1.72		
	תבל	2	3	1.72		
	שמע	4	7	1.48		
	שוב	4	7	1.48		
	יד	5	9	1.44		
	אל	12	22	1.41		
	דבר	4	8	1.29		
	שמר	3	6	1.29		
	סתר	3	6	1.29		
	ידע	2	4	1.29		
	יום	4	9	1.15		
	עין	3	7	1.11		
	יהוה	24	58	1.07		
	עשה	2	5	1.03		
18 and 20	שלח	3	3	2.90	38.19	0.64
	שגב	2	2	2.90		
	רכב	2	2	2.90		
	סעד	2	2	2.90		
	משיח	2	2	2.90		
	שאל	2	3	1.94		
	ישע	11	17	1.88		

Psalms	Lexeme	$n_{e\,(ps\,pr)}$	$n_{e\,(15\text{-}24)}$	p	Total	Adjusted
18 and 20	אל	14	22	1.85		
	נתן	6	10	1.74		
	שמים	3	5	1.74		
	קרא	3	5	1.74		
	שם	4	7	1.66		
	ענה	6	12	1.45		
	קום	4	8	1.45		
	ידע	2	4	1.45		
	כרע	2	4	1.45		
	נפל	2	4	1.45		
	צרר	2	4	1.45		
	יום	4	9	1.29		
	יהוה	22	58	1.10		
18 and 21	אף	3	3	2.74	49.50	0.83
	שׂנא	3	3	2.74		
	רום	5	5	2.74		
	אש	5	5	2.74		
	גדל	2	2	2.74		
	יכל	2	2	2.74		
	שיר	2	2	2.74		
	עליון	2	2	2.74		
	איב	7	8	2.40		
	שית	5	6	2.29		
	בן	3	4	2.06		
	קדם	3	4	2.06		
	עזז	3	4	2.06		
	נתן	7	10	1.92		
	שוה	2	3	1.83		
	שאל	2	3	1.83		
	ברך	3	5	1.65		
	חסד	4	7	1.57		
	יד	5	9	1.52		
	ישע	9	17	1.45		
	אכל	2	4	1.37		
	נטה	2	4	1.37		
	זרע	2	5	1.10		
	עולם	2	5	1.10		
18 and 22	הלל	6	6	2.13	50.84	0.85
	נצל	5	5	2.13		
	גוי	4	4	2.13		
	עפר	3	3	2.13		
	מות	3	3	2.13		
	קרן	2	2	2.13		
	רחם	2	2	2.13		
	ירד	2	2	2.13		
	אילה	2	2	2.13		
	איש	2	2	2.13		
	זרע	5	6	1.77		
	פלט	4	5	1.70		
	מים	4	5	1.70		
	רגל	4	5	1.70		
	ראה	3	4	1.60		
	היה	3	4	1.60		

Psalms	Lexeme	n_e (ps pr)	n_e (15-24)	p	Total	Adjusted
18 and 22	אל	15	22	1.45		
	ענה	8	12	1.42		
	יד	6	9	1.42		
	חפץ	2	3	1.42		
	כל	12	19	1.34		
	סבב	3	5	1.28		
	שמע	4	7	1.22		
	רכב	4	7	1.22		
	שוב	4	7	1.22		
	ישע	9	17	1.13		
	פה	3	6	1.06		
	דבר	4	8	1.06		
	כרע	2	4	1.06		
	בוא	2	4	1.06		
	נפל	2	4	1.06		
	צרר	2	4	1.06		
18 and 23	שען	2	2	3.05	14.31	0.24
	מים	4	5	2.44		
	שוב	5	7	2.18		
	חסד	4	7	1.74		
	צרר	2	4	1.52		
	יום	4	9	1.35		
	צדק	3	9	1.02		
	ראש	2	6	1.02		
18 and 24	זה	4	4	2.84	32.15	0.54
	כף	2	2	2.84		
	לחם	3	3	2.84		
	ברר	5	6	2.37		
	ברא	3	4	2.13		
	יסד	2	3	1.89		
	תבל	2	3	1.89		
	הר	2	3	1.89		
	קום	5	8	1.77		
	מלך	6	10	1.70		
	עולם	3	5	1.70		
	אל	12	22	1.55		
	עזז	2	4	1.42		
	גבר	3	6	1.42		
	ראש	3	6	1.42		
	ישע	8	17	1.34		
	ברך	2	5	1.14		
	יהוה	23	58	1.13		
19 and 20	עוד	2	2	6.49	26.07	0.43
	שמים	3	5	3.90		
	ידע	2	4	3.25		
	עקב	2	4	3.25		
	יום	4	9	2.89		
	גבר	2	6	2.16		
	נצח	2	6	2.16		
	לבב	3	10	1.95		
	זמר	2	9	1.44		
	כל	4	19	1.37		
	יהוה	12	58	1.34		

Psalms	Lexeme	$n_{e\,(ps\,pr)}$	$n_{e\,(15\text{-}24)}$	p	Total	Adjusted
19 and 20	אל	4	22	1.18		
	דוד	2	11	1.18		
19 and 21	פז	2	2	5.74	33.71	0.56
	עד	3	4	4.30		
	שׂמח	3	5	3.44		
	עבד	3	5	3.44		
	יום	3	9	1.91		
	זמר	3	9	1.91		
	גבר	2	6	1.91		
	נצח	2	6	1.91		
	לבב	3	10	1.72		
	פנה	4	16	1.43		
	ארץ	2	8	1.43		
	יד	2	9	1.27		
	כבד	2	10	1.15		
	יהוה	11	58	1.09		
	דוד	2	11	1.04		
19 and 22	ספר	4	4	3.58	43.13	0.72
	חוה	3	3	3.58		
	נגד	2	2	3.58		
	משׁל	2	2	3.58		
	רבב	5	7	2.55		
	ירא	3	5	2.15		
	לילה	3	5	2.15		
	כל	10	19	1.88		
	פה	3	6	1.79		
	סתר	3	6	1.79		
	עקב	2	4	1.79		
	עד	2	4	1.79		
	היה	2	4	1.79		
	לבב	4	10	1.43		
	עשׂה	2	5	1.43		
	ארץ	3	8	1.34		
	נפשׁ	3	8	1.34		
	יום	3	9	1.19		
	יד	3	9	1.19		
	נצח	2	6	1.19		
	שׁמע	2	7	1.02		
	שׁוב	2	7	1.02		
19 and 23	יום	4	9	3.22	16.69	0.28
	שׁוב	3	7	3.10		
	ירא	2	5	2.90		
	נפשׁ	2	8	1.81		
	צדק	2	9	1.61		
	זמר	2	9	1.61		
	דוד	2	11	1.32		
	יהוה	9	58	1.12		
19 and 24	נקה	3	4	4.63	30.88	0.51
	תבל	2	3	4.12		
	כבד	6	10	3.70		
	גבר	3	6	3.09		
	עקב	2	4	3.09		
	ברר	2	6	2.06		

Psalms	Lexeme	$n_{e\,(ps\,pr)}$	$n_{e\,(15-24)}$	p	Total	Adjusted
19 and 24	לבב	3	10	1.85		
	ארץ	2	8	1.54		
	נפש	2	8	1.54		
	יהוה	13	58	1.38		
	צדק	2	9	1.37		
	זמר	2	9	1.37		
	דוד	2	11	1.12		
20 and 21	שאל	2	3	5.06	33.84	0.56
	עוד	3	7	3.25		
	ישע	6	17	2.68		
	יום	3	9	2.53		
	זמר	3	9	2.53		
	ימין	2	6	2.53		
	גבר	2	6	2.53		
	נצח	2	6	2.53		
	נתן	3	10	2.28		
	מלך	3	10	2.28		
	כל	4	19	1.60		
	לבב	2	10	1.52		
	דוד	2	11	1.38		
	יהוה	9	58	1.18		
20 and 22	זכר	3	3	4.22	36.15	0.60
	עזר	3	3	4.22		
	ענה	8	12	2.81		
	דשן	2	3	2.81		
	כל	12	19	2.66		
	שם	4	7	2.41		
	כרע	2	4	2.11		
	עקב	2	4	2.11		
	צרר	2	4	2.11		
	קדש	3	6	2.11		
	קרע	2	5	1.69		
	ישע	6	17	1.49		
	נצח	2	6	1.41		
	יום	3	9	1.41		
	אל	7	22	1.34		
	לבב	3	10	1.26		
20 and 23	דשן	2	3	6.98	30.53	0.51
	שם	4	7	5.98		
	צרר	2	4	5.23		
	יום	4	9	4.65		
	זמר	2	9	2.33		
	כל	4	19	2.20		
	דוד	2	11	1.90		
	יהוה	7	58	1.26		
20 and 24	מלא	3	4	6.28	37.62	0.63
	מלך	6	10	5.02		
	גבר	3	6	4.19		
	קדש	3	6	4.19		
	עקב	2	4	4.19		
	קום	3	8	3.14		
	ישע	5	17	2.46		
	זמר	2	9	1.86		

Psalms	Lexeme	n_e (ps pr)	n_e (15-24)	p	Total	Adjusted
20 and 24	לבב	2	10	1.67		
	יהוה	11	58	1.59		
	אל	4	22	1.52		
	דוד	2	11	1.52		
21 and 22	בטח	5	6	3.24	29.08	0.48
	זרע	4	5	3.11		
	עד	3	4	2.91		
	אדם	2	3	2.59		
	כל	10	19	2.04		
	חיה	3	7	1.66		
	רעע	2	5	1.55		
	שׂפה	2	5	1.55		
	פנה	6	16	1.46		
	ארץ	3	8	1.46		
	יד	3	9	1.29		
	זמר	3	9	1.29		
	ראשׁ	2	6	1.29		
	נצח	2	6	1.29		
	מלך	3	10	1.16		
	לבב	3	10	1.16		
21 and 23	ארך	2	2	8.63	35.11	0.59
	טוב	2	3	5.75		
	רעע	2	5	3.45		
	יום	3	9	2.88		
	זמר	3	9	2.88		
	ראשׁ	2	6	2.88		
	חסד	2	7	2.46		
	חיה	2	7	2.46		
	פנה	4	16	2.16		
	דוד	2	11	1.57		
21 and 24	כון	2	2	7.15	40.87	0.68
	עזז	3	4	5.36		
	מלך	7	10	5.01		
	עולם	3	5	4.29		
	ברך	3	5	4.29		
	ראשׁ	3	6	3.58		
	זמר	3	9	2.38		
	פנה	4	16	1.79		
	ארץ	2	8	1.79		
	לבב	2	10	1.43		
	דוד	2	11	1.30		
	ישׁע	3	17	1.26		
	יהוה	10	58	1.23		
22 and 23	דשׁן	2	3	3.01	27.62	0.46
	כל	11	19	2.62		
	שׁם	4	7	2.58		
	צרר	2	4	2.26		
	שׁוב	3	7	1.94		
	חיה	3	7	1.94		
	רעע	2	5	1.81		
	מים	2	5	1.81		
	ירא	2	5	1.81		
	נפשׁ	3	8	1.70		

Psalms	Lexeme	n_e (ps pr)	n_e (15-24)	p	Total	Adjusted
22 and 23	יום	3	9	1.51		
	ראש	2	6	1.51		
	פנה	4	16	1.13		
	צדק	2	9	1.00		
	זמר	2	9	1.00		
22 and 24	דרש	3	3	4.08	27.13	0.45
	דוד	2	2	4.08		
	בוא	3	4	3.06		
	ישב	2	3	2.72		
	מלך	6	10	2.45		
	ראש	3	6	2.04		
	עקב	2	4	2.04		
	ארץ	3	8	1.53		
	נפש	3	8	1.53		
	קדש	2	6	1.36		
	לבב	3	10	1.22		
	פנה	4	16	1.02		
23 and 24	ראש	3	6	4.83	17.04	0.28
	נפש	3	8	3.62		
	צדק	2	9	2.15		
	זמר	2	9	2.15		
	דוד	2	11	1.76		
	יהוה	8	58	1.33		
	פנה	2	16	1.21		

TABLE B. DISTINCTIVE MORPHOLOGIES
AND STRENGTHS OF COHESION

In table B on distinctive morphologies, the morphological forms are abbreviated as follows in column 3:

ampa	masculine plural absolute adjective
ampc	masculine plural construct adjective
amsa	masculine singular absolute adjective
amsc	masculine singular construct adjective
nbda	both (genders) dual absolute noun
nbdc	both (genders) dual construct noun
nbpc	both (genders) plural construct noun
nbsa	both (genders) singular absolute noun
nbsc	both (genders) singular construct noun
nfdc	feminine dual construct noun
nfpc	feminine plural construct noun
nfsa	feminine singular absolute noun
nfsc	feminine singular construct noun
nmpa	masculine plural absolute noun
nmpc	masculine plural construct noun

nmsa	masculine singular absolute noun
nmsc	masculine singular construct noun
np	proper noun
vhi3ms	*Hiphil* imperfect third-person masculine singular verb
vhvms	*Hiphil* imperative masculine singular verb
vni3ms	*Niphal* imperfect third-person masculine singular verb
vnp3ms	*Niphal* perfect third-person masculine singular verb
vpi1cs	*Piel* imperfect first-person common singular verb
vpPmsa	*Piel* participle masculine singular absolute verb
vqi1cs	*Qal* imperfect first-person common singular verb
vqi2ms	*Qal* imperfect second-person masculine singular verb
vqi3fs	*Qal* imperfect third-person feminine singular verb
vqi3mp	*Qal* imperfect third-person masculine plural verb
vqi3ms	*Qal* imperfect third-person masculine singular verb
vqp1cs	*Qal* perfect first-person common singular verb
vqp2ms	*Qal* perfect second-person masculine singular verb
vqp3cp	*Qal* perfect third-person common plural verb
vqp3ms	*Qal* perfect third-person masculine singular verb
vqPmpa	*Qal* participle masculine plural absolute verb
vqPmpc	*Qal* participle masculine plural construct verb
vqPmsa	*Qal* participle masculine singular absolute verb
vqvms	*Qal* imperative masculine singular verb

TABLE B

Psalms	Lexeme	Morphology	$n_{e\,(ps\,pr)}$	$n_{lex\,(ps\,pr)}$	$n_{e\,(15\text{-}24)}$	$n_{lex\,(15\text{-}24)}$	p	Total	Adjusted
15 and 17	צדק	ncmsa	3	3	4	9	2.25	3.56	0.22
	עין	ncbdc	3	4	4	7	1.31		
15 and 18	תמם	amsa of תמים	5	6	5	8	1.33	2.50	0.16
	עין	ncbdc	2	3	4	7	1.17		
15 and 19	זמר	ncmsa of מזמור	2	2	7	9	1.29	1.29	0.08
15 and 20	לבב	ncmsc	2	2	3	10	3.33	5.95	0.37
	קדש	ncmsc	2	3	3	6	1.33		
	זמר	ncmsa of מזמור	2	2	7	9	1.29		
15 and 21	מוט	vni3ms	2	2	2	4	2.00	3.67	0.23
	רעע	ncfsa of רעה	2	3	2	5	1.67		
15 and 22	לבב	ncmsc	2	3	3	10	2.22	6.84	0.43
	ירא	ampc	3	3	3	5	1.67		
	עשה	vqp3ms	2	3	2	5	1.67		

Psalms	Lexeme	Morphology	$n_{e\,(ps\,pr)}$	$n_{lex\,(ps\,pr)}$	$n_{e\,(15\text{-}24)}$	$n_{lex\,(15\text{-}24)}$	p	Total	Adjusted
15 and 22	זמר	ncmsa of מזמור	2	2	7	9	1.29		
15 and 23	צדק	ncmsa	2	2	4	9	2.25	3.54	**0.22**
	זמר	ncmsa of מזמור	2	2	7	9	1.29		
15 and 24	קדש	ncmsc	2	2	3	6	2.00	5.93	**0.37**
	הר	ncmsc	2	2	2	3	1.50		
	זמר	ncmsa of מזמור	2	2	7	9	1.29		
	נשא	vqp3ms	2	7	2	8	1.14		
16 and 17	חיה	ncmpa of חי	2	2	2	7	4.50	13.92	**0.87**
	אל	ncmsa	2	2	6	22	3.67		
	לבב	ncmsc of לב	2	2	5	10	2.00		
	שמר	vqvms	2	3	2	6	2.00		
	חלק	ncmsc	2	2	2	3	1.50		
	שפה	ncfdc	3	3	4	5	1.25		
16 and 18	אל	ncmsa	4	12	6	22	1.22	1.22	**0.08**
16 and 19	אל	ncmsa	2	2	6	22	3.67	8.33	**0.52**
	כבד	ncmsc of כבוד	2	2	3	10	3.33		
	לבב	ncmsc of לב	2	3	5	10	1.33		
16 and 20	נפל	vqp3cp	2	2	2	4	2.00	2.00	**0.13**
16 and 21	כבד	ncmsc of כבוד	2	2	3	10	3.33	6.58	**0.41**
	לבב	ncmsc of לב	2	2	5	10	2.00		
	שפה	ncfdc	2	2	4	5	1.25		
16 and 22	לבב	ncmsc of לב	2	3	5	10	1.33	2.67	**0.17**
	נפש	ncbsc	3	3	6	8	1.33		
16 and 23	נפש	ncbsc	2	2	6	8	1.33	1.33	**0.08**
16 and 24	נפש	ncbsc	2	2	6	8	1.33	1.33	**0.08**
17 and 18	אמר	ncfpc of אמרה	2	3	2	7	2.33	10.71	**0.67**
	ישע	ncmsa of מושיע	2	8	2	17	2.13		
	שמר	vqp1cs	2	4	2	6	1.50		
	חסה	vqPmpa	2	3	2	4	1.33		
	אל	ncmsa	4	12	6	22	1.22		
	איב	ncmpc	7	7	7	8	1.14		
	עין	ncbdc	3	5	4	7	1.05		
17 and 19	אל	ncmsa	2	2	6	22	3.67	8.92	**0.56**
	נפש	ncbsa	2	3	2	8	2.67		

Psalms	Lexeme	Morphology	$n_{e\,(ps\,pr)}$	$n_{lex\,(ps\,pr)}$	$n_{e\,(15\text{-}24)}$	$n_{lex\,(15\text{-}24)}$	p	Total	Adjusted
17 and 19	לבב	ncmsc of לב	2	3	5	10	1.33		
	לילה	ncmsa	3	3	4	5	1.25		
17 and 21	יד	ncfsc	2	2	4	9	2.25	6.64	**0.42**
	לבב	ncmsc of לב	2	2	5	10	2.00		
	שפה	ncfdc	3	3	4	5	1.25		
	איב	ncmpc	2	2	7	8	1.14		
17 and 22	ענה	vqi2ms	2	6	2	12	2.00	7.42	**0.46**
	יד	ncfsc	2	3	4	9	1.50		
	לבב	ncmsc of לב	2	3	5	10	1.33		
	שבע	vqi3mp	2	3	2	4	1.33		
	לילה	ncmsa	2	2	4	5	1.25		
17 and 23	צדק	ncmsa	3	3	4	9	2.25	2.25	**0.14**
18 and 19	עין	ncbda	2	3	2	7	2.33	14.22	**0.89**
	יום	ncmsa	3	4	3	9	2.25		
	צור	ncmsc	4	3	3	4	1.78		
	שפט	ncmpc of משפט	2	2	2	3	1.50		
	יד	ncfdc	4	5	5	9	1.44		
	שמים	ncmpa	4	4	4	5	1.25		
	עבד	ncmsc	3	4	3	5	1.25		
	אל	ncmsa	4	12	6	22	1.22		
	נצח	vpPmsa	2	2	5	6	1.20		
18 and 20	ידע	vqp1cs	2	2	2	4	2.00	10.24	**0.64**
	יום	ncmsc	3	4	4	9	1.69		
	נתן	vqi3ms	2	6	2	10	1.67		
	אל	ncmpc of אלהים	9	14	11	22	1.29		
	ישע	ncmsc	4	11	5	17	1.24		
	נצח	vpPmsa	2	2	5	6	1.20		
	שם	ncmsc	4	4	6	7	1.17		
18 and 21	זמר	vpi1cs	2	3	2	9	3.00	10.21	**0.64**
	ראש	ncmsc	2	2	3	6	2.00		
	נתן	vqp2ms	3	7	3	10	1.43		
	בן	ncmpc	3	3	3	4	1.33		
	זרע	ncmsc	2	2	4	5	1.25		

Psalms	Lexeme	Morphology	$n_{e\,(ps\,pr)}$	$n_{lex\,(ps\,pr)}$	$n_{e\,(15\text{-}24)}$	$n_{lex\,(15\text{-}24)}$	p	Total	Adjusted
18 and 21	נצח	vpPmsa	2	2	5	6	1.20		
18 and 22	דבר	ncmpc	2	4	2	8	2.00	15.95	1.00
	רבב	ampa of רב	2	4	2	7	1.75		
	קרא	vqi1cs	3	3	3	5	1.67		
	ענה	amsa of עני	2	8	2	12	1.50		
	חפץ	vqp3ms	2	2	2	3	1.50		
	אל	ncmsc	4	15	4	22	1.47		
	רגל	ncfdc	4	4	4	5	1.25		
	מים	ncmpa	4	4	4	5	1.25		
	יד	ncfdc	4	6	5	9	1.20		
	נצח	vpPmsa	2	2	5	6	1.20		
	שם	ncmsc	2	2	6	7	1.17		
18 and 23	ראש	ncmsc	2	2	3	6	2.00	4.92	0.31
	חסד	ncmsa	2	4	2	7	1.75		
	שם	ncmsc	2	2	6	7	1.17		
18 and 24	מלך	ncmsc	6	6	5	10	2.00	4.87	0.31
	ישע	ncmsc	4	8	5	17	1.70		
	אל	ncmpc of אלהים	7	12	11	22	1.17		
19 and 20	זמר	ncmsa of מזמור	2	2	7	9	1.29	2.49	0.16
	נצח	vpPmsa	2	2	5	6	1.20		
19 and 21	כבד	ncmsc of כבוד	2	2	3	10	3.33	5.87	0.37
	לבב	ncmsc of לב	2	3	5	10	1.33		
	נצח	vpPmsa	2	2	5	6	1.20		
19 and 22	רבב	amsa of רב	4	5	4	7	1.40	6.34	0.40
	זמר	ncmsa of מזמור	2	2	7	9	1.29		
	לילה	ncmsa	3	3	4	5	1.25		
	יד	ncfdc	2	3	5	9	1.20		
	נצח	vpPmsa	2	2	5	6	1.20		
19 and 23	זמר	ncmsa of מזמור	2	2	7	9	1.29	1.29	0.08
19 and 24	גבר	amsa of גבור	2	3	2	6	2.00	3.29	0.21
	זמר	ncmsa of מזמור	2	2	7	9	1.29		
20 and 21	מלך	ncmsa	3	3	3	10	3.33	6.66	0.42
	ישע	ncfsc of ישועה	3	6	4	17	2.13		

Psalms	Lexeme	Morphology	$n_{e\,(ps\,pr)}$	$n_{lex\,(ps\,pr)}$	$n_{e\,(15\text{-}24)}$	$n_{lex\,(15\text{-}24)}$	p	Total	Adjusted
20 and 21	נצח	vpPmsa	2	2	5	6	1.20		
20 and 22	ישע	vhvms	2	6	2	17	2.83	15.55	**0.98**
	לבב	ncmsc	2	3	3	10	2.22		
	אל	ncmsa	4	7	6	22	2.10		
	צרר	ncfsa of צרה	2	2	2	4	2.00		
	ישע	ncfsc of ישועה	2	6	4	17	1.42		
	עקב	np of יעקוב	2	2	3	4	1.33		
	זמר	ncmsa of מזמור	2	2	7	9	1.29		
	נצח	vpPmsa	2	2	5	6	1.20		
	שם	ncmsc	4	4	6	7	1.17		
20 and 23	זמר	ncmsa of מזמור	2	2	7	9	1.29	2.45	**0.15**
	שם	ncmsc	4	4	6	7	1.17		
20 and 24	אל	ncmsa	4	4	6	22	3.67	8.98	**0.56**
	ישע	ncmsc	2	5	5	17	1.36		
	קדש	ncmsc	2	3	3	6	1.33		
	עקב	np of יעקוב	2	2	3	4	1.33		
	זמר	ncmsa of מזמור	2	2	7	9	1.29		
21 and 22	ישע	ncfsc of ישועה	3	4	4	17	3.19	7.22	**0.45**
	יד	ncfsc	2	3	4	9	1.50		
	לבב	ncmsc of לב	2	3	5	10	1.33		
	נצח	vpPmsa	2	2	5	6	1.20		
21 and 23	יום	ncmpa	2	3	2	9	3.00	6.50	**0.41**
	ראש	ncmsc	2	2	3	6	2.00		
	טוב	ncmsa	2	2	2	3	1.50		
22 and 23	נפש	ncbsc	3	3	6	8	1.33	3.79	**0.24**
	זמר	ncmsa of מזמור	2	2	7	9	1.29		
	שם	ncmsc	2	2	6	7	1.17		
22 and 24	נפש	ncbsc	3	3	6	8	1.33	5.42	**0.34**
	אל	ncmsa	2	5	6	22	1.47		
	עקב	np of יעקוב	2	2	3	4	1.33		
	זמר	ncmsa of מזמור	2	2	7	9	1.29		
23 and 24	נפש	ncbsc	2	2	6	8	1.33	2.62	**0.16**
	זמר	ncmsa of מזמור	2	2	7	9	1.29		

TABLE C. DISTINCTIVE PHRASES
AND STRENGTHS OF COHESION

A phrasal link involves the repetition of at least two corresponding lexemes used within the same clause. Unlike lexical links, phrasal links may include the following, if it seems that they are used to construct recognizable corresponding phrases: conjunctions, prepositions, particles, negative adverbs, and pronouns.

TABLE C

Psalms	Phrase	n_e (ps pr)	n_e (15-24)	p	Total	Adjusted
15 and 16	בל/לא מוט	2	4	5.14	15.41	0.52
	לא־נתן	2	2	10.27		
15 and 17	בל/לא מוט	2	4	3.67	3.67	0.12
15 and 21	בל/לא מוט	2	4	4.41	4.41	0.15
15 and 22	יראי יהוה	2	2	4.57	4.57	0.15
15 and 24	מי...קדש	2	2	9.91	*29.74	*1.00
	מי...הר	2	2	9.91		
	לא־נשא	2	2	9.91		
16 and 17	בל/לא מוט	2	4	3.14	3.14	0.11
16 and 19	שמח לב	2	2	6.31	6.31	0.21
16 and 21	בל/לא מוט	2	4	3.67	3.67	0.12
17 and 21	בל/לא מוט	2	4	2.85	2.85	0.10
17 and 22	חרב נפשי	2	2	3.56	10.69	0.36
	אריה...טרף	2	2	3.56		
	אל קרא ענה	2	2	3.56		
18 and 20	ישע מלך	2	2	2.90	8.71	0.29
	יהוה אלהי(נו)	2	2	2.90		
	ישע...משיח	2	2	2.90		
18 and 21	כל איב	2	2	2.74	8.23	0.28
	אכל אש	2	2	2.74		
	עד עולם	2	2	2.74		
18 and 22	כי חפץ ב	2	2	2.13	2.13	0.07
18 and 24	אלהים ישע	2	2	2.84	2.84	0.10
19 and 23	שוב נפש	2	2	7.24	7.24	0.24
20 and 21	לב(ב) נתן	2	2	7.58	7.58	0.26
21 and 23	ארך ימים	2	2	8.63	8.63	0.29

TABLE D. DISTINCTIVE THEMES
AND STRENGTHS OF COHESION

Table D provides the data for each shared theme per psalm pair. The themes in the collection and the psalms in which they are found are as follows:

Theme	Psalms
Affliction/Distress/Enemies	17, 18, 20, 21, 22
Community	20, 21, 22, 24
Covenant Love/Promise	18, 21, 23
Creation Imagery	18, 19, 24
Deliverance	17, 18, 20, 21, 22
Enemies as Predatorial Animals	17, 22
Entering Yhwh's Dwelling Place	15, 24
Fire/Anger	18, 21
Forever/Finality	15, 16, 21, 22, 23, 24
God Fulfills King's Plans/Requests	20, 21
Human King	18, 20, 21
Human Warrior	18, 20
Joy	20, 21
Life/Delight/Goodness	16, 21, 23
Provision/Inheritance	16, 23
Righteousness	15, 16, 17, 18, 19, 20, 23, 24
Safety/Protection/Comfort/Refuge	16, 18, 23
Satisfaction/Feast	17, 22, 23
Speech	15, 19, 24
Torah/Instruction	18, 19
Trust in Yhwh	16, 17, 20, 21, 22, 23
Yhwh as King	22, 24
Yhwh as Mighty Warrior	18, 19, 20, 21, 24
Yhwh Gives Support and Strength in Battle	18, 20, 21
Yhwh Guides/Leads	16, 23
Yhwh's Presence	15, 19, 22, 23, 24

TABLE D

Psalms	Theme	$n_{e\,(15\text{-}24)}$	p	Total	Adjusted
15 and 16	Righteousness	8	2.57	5.99	**0.14**
	Forever/Finality	6	3.42		
15 and 17	Righteousness	8	1.83	1.83	**0.04**
15 and 18	Righteousness	8	0.77	0.00	**0.00**
15 and 19	Yhwh's Presence	5	2.95	9.72	**0.23**
	Righteousness	8	1.85		
	Speech	3	4.92		
15 and 20	Righteousness	8	2.69	2.69	**0.06**
15 and 21	Forever/Finality	6	2.94	2.94	**0.07**
15 and 22	Yhwh's Presence	5	1.83	3.35	**0.08**
	Forever/Finality	6	1.52		
15 and 23	Yhwh's Presence	5	5.20	12.77	**0.30**
	Righteousness	8	3.25		
	Forever/Finality	6	4.33		
15 and 24	Yhwh's Presence	5	3.96	26.27	**0.62**
	Entering Yhwh's Dwelling Place	2	9.91		
	Righteousness	8	2.48		
	Speech	3	6.61		
	Forever/Finality	6	3.30		
16 and 17	Righteousness	8	1.57	3.66	**0.09**
	Trust in Yhwh	6	2.09		
16 and 18	Righteousness	8	0.72	1.91	**0.04**
	Safety/Protection/Comfort/Refuge	3	1.91		
16 and 19	Righteousness	8	1.58	1.58	**0.04**
16 and 20	Righteousness	8	2.16	5.03	**0.12**
	Trust in Yhwh	6	2.88		
16 and 21	Forever/Finality	6	2.45	9.78	**0.23**
	Trust in Yhwh	6	2.45		
	Life/Delight/Goodness	3	4.89		
16 and 22	Forever/Finality	6	1.38	2.76	**0.06**
	Trust in Yhwh	6	1.38		
16 and 23	Righteousness	8	2.50	*42.50	*1.00
	Trust in Yhwh	6	3.33		
	Safety/Protection/Comfort/Refuge	3	6.67		
	Yhwh Guides/Leads	2	10.00		
	Forever/Finality	6	3.33		
	Provision/Inheritance	2	10.00		
	Life/Delight/Goodness	3	6.67		
16 and 24	Righteousness	8	2.02	4.71	**0.11**
	Forever/Finality	6	2.69		
17 and 18	Righteousness	8	0.64	2.06	**0.05**
	Affliction/Distress/Enemies	5	1.03		
	Deliverance	5	1.03		
17 and 19	Righteousness	8	1.27	1.27	**0.03**
17 and 20	Righteousness	8	1.61	8.93	**0.21**

17 and 20	Trust in Yhwh	6	2.15		
	Affliction/Distress/Enemies	5	2.58		
	Deliverance	5	2.58		
17 and 21	Affliction/Distress/Enemies	5	2.28	6.47	0.15
	Trust in Yhwh	6	1.90		
	Deliverance	5	2.28		
17 and 22	Affliction/Distress/Enemies	5	1.43	9.98	0.23
	Trust in Yhwh	6	1.19		
	Enemies as Predatorial Animals	2	3.56		
	Deliverance	5	1.43		
	Satisfaction/Feast	3	2.38		
17 and 23	Satisfaction/Feast	3	4.80	9.00	0.21
	Trust in Yhwh	6	2.40		
	Righteousness	8	1.80		
17 and 24	Righteousness	8	1.54	1.54	0.04
18 and 19	Righteousness	8	0.65	5.34	0.13
	Torah/Instruction	2	2.59		
	Yhwh as Mighty Warrior	5	1.03		
	Creation Imagery	3	1.72		
18 and 20	Righteousness	8	0.73	10.26	0.24
	Affliction/Distress/Enemies	5	1.16		
	Deliverance	5	1.16		
	Yhwh as Mighty Warrior	5	1.16		
	Human King	3	1.94		
	Human Warrior	2	2.90		
	Yhwh Gives Support and Strength in Battle	3	1.94		
18 and 21	Affliction/Distress/Enemies	5	1.10	11.52	0.27
	Deliverance	5	1.10		
	Yhwh as Mighty Warrior	5	1.10		
	Fire/Anger	2	2.74		
	Human King	3	1.83		
	Yhwh Gives Support and Strength in Battle	3	1.83		
	Covenant Love/Promise	3	1.83		
18 and 22	Affliction/Distress/Enemies	5	0.85	0.00	0.00
	Deliverance	5	0.85		
18 and 23	Righteousness	8	0.76	4.06	0.10
	Safety/Protection/Comfort/Refuge	3	2.03		
	Covenant Love/Promise	3	2.03		
18 and 24	Righteousness	8	0.71	3.03	0.07
	Yhwh as Mighty Warrior	5	1.14		
	Creation Imagery	3	1.89		
19 and 20	Righteousness	8	1.62	4.22	0.10
	Yhwh as Mighty Warrior	5	2.60		
19 and 21	Yhwh as Mighty Warrior	5	2.29	2.29	0.05
19 and 22	Yhwh's Presence	5	1.43	1.43	0.03
19 and 23	Yhwh's Presence	5	2.90	4.71	0.11
	Righteousness	8	1.81		

19 and 24	Yhwh's Presence	5	2.47	14.72	**0.35**
	Righteousness	8	1.54		
	Speech	3	4.12		
	Yhwh as Mighty Warrior	5	2.47		
	Creation Imagery	3	4.12		
20 and 21	Affliction/Distress/Enemies	5	3.03	40.70	**0.96**
	Trust in Yhwh	6	2.53		
	Deliverance	5	3.03		
	Community	4	3.79		
	Yhwh as Mighty Warrior	5	3.03		
	Human King	3	5.06		
	Yhwh Gives Support and Strength in Battle	3	5.06		
	God Fulfills King's Plans/Requests	2	7.58		
	Joy	2	7.58		
20 and 22	Affliction/Distress/Enemies	5	1.69	6.89	**0.16**
	Trust in Yhwh	6	1.41		
	Deliverance	5	1.69		
	Community	4	2.11		
20 and 23	Righteousness	8	2.62	6.10	**0.14**
	Trust in Yhwh	6	3.49		
20 and 24	Righteousness	8	2.09	9.63	**0.23**
	Community	4	4.19		
	Yhwh as Mighty Warrior	5	3.35		
21 and 22	Affliction/Distress/Enemies	5	1.55	7.64	**0.18**
	Trust in Yhwh	6	1.29		
	Deliverance	5	1.55		
	Community	4	1.94		
	Forever/Finality	6	1.29		
21 and 23	Forever/Finality	6	2.88	17.25	**0.41**
	Trust in Yhwh	6	2.88		
	Life/Delight/Goodness	3	5.75		
	Covenant Love/Promise	3	5.75		
21 and 24	Community	4	3.58	8.82	**0.21**
	Yhwh as Mighty Warrior	5	2.86		
	Forever/Finality	6	2.38		
22 and 23	Yhwh's Presence	5	1.81	7.83	**0.18**
	Trust in Yhwh	6	1.51		
	Forever/Finality	6	1.51		
	Satisfaction/Feast	3	3.01		
22 and 24	Yhwh's Presence	5	1.63	9.11	**0.21**
	Community	4	2.04		
	Yhwh as King	2	4.08		
	Forever/Finality	6	1.36		
23 and 24	Yhwh's Presence	5	3.86	9.50	**0.22**
	Righteousness	8	2.41		
	Forever/Finality	6	3.22		

TABLE E. DISTINCTIVE STRUCTURES AND STRENGTHS OF COHESION

Table E provides the data for each distinctive corresponding structure.

Psalm Pair	Structure	n_e (Pss 15-24)	p	Total	Adjusted
Psalms 15 and 19	Structural Similarities among Frame	3	3.33	3.33	0.67
Psalms 15 and 24	Structural Similarities among Frame	3	3.33	3.33	0.67
Psalms 16 and 23	Thematic Ordering	2	5.00	*5.00	*1.00
Psalms 17 and 22	Lament Structure	2	5.00	*5.00	*1.00
Psalms 19 and 24	Structural Similarities among Frame	3	3.33	3.33	0.67

TABLE F. DISTINCTIVE SUPERSCRIPTS AND STRENGTHS OF COHESION

Table F provides the data for each shared superscript per psalm pair. Elements of a superscript include author designation, designation of psalm type, or other non-incidental lexemes. The elements of a superscript (e.g., rwmzm, dwdl, and xcnml) and the exact superscript (e.g., dwdl rwmzm) are both listed, so that two psalms that share the same elements and also have the exact same superscript (e.g., Pss 15 and 23) show a higher strength of cohesion than psalms that share the same elements but do not have the exact same superscript (e.g., Pss 15 and 22).

TABLE F

Psalms	Superscript	n_e (Pss 15-24)	p	Total	Adjusted
15 and 19	מזמור	7	1.43	1.43	0.21
15 and 20	מזמור	7	1.43	1.43	0.21
15 and 21	מזמור	7	1.43	1.43	0.21
15 and 22	מזמור	7	1.43	1.43	0.21
15 and 23	מזמור לדוד	3	3.33	4.76	0.70
	מזמור	7	1.43		
15 and 24	מזמור לדוד	3	3.33	4.76	0.70
	מזמור	7	1.43		
18 and 19	למנצח	5	2	2	0.30
18 and 20	למנצח	5	2	2	0.30
18 and 21	למנצח	5	2	2	0.30
18 and 22	למנצח	5	2	2	0.30
19 and 20	למנצח מזמור לדוד	3	3.33	6.76*	1.00*
	מזמור	7	1.43		
	למנצח	5	2		
19 and 21	למנצח מזמור לדוד	3	3.33	6.76*	1.00*
	מזמור	7	1.43		
	למנצח	5	2		
19 and 22	מזמור	7	1.43	3.43	0.51

Psalms	Superscript	$n_{e\ (Pss\ 15\text{-}24)}$	p	Total	Adjusted
	למנצח	5	2		
19 and 23	מזמור	7	1.43	1.43	0.21
19 and 24	מזמור	7	1.43	1.43	0.21
20 and 21	למנצח מזמור לדוד	3	3.33	6.76*	1.00*
	מזמור	7	1.43		
	למנצח	5	2		
20 and 22	מזמור	7	1.43	3.43	0.51
	למנצח	5	2		
20 and 23	מזמור	7	1.43	1.43	0.21
20 and 24	מזמור	7	1.43	1.43	0.21
21 and 22	מזמור	7	1.43	3.43	0.51
	למנצח	5	2		
21 and 23	מזמור	7	1.43	1.43	0.21
21 and 24	מזמור	7	1.43	1.43	0.21
22 and 23	מזמור	7	1.43	1.43	0.21
22 and 24	מזמור	7	1.43	1.43	0.21
23 and 24	מזמור לדוד	3	3.33	4.76	0.70
	מזמור	7	1.43		

Appendix 3

List of Lexemes in Psalms 15–24

In appendix 3, I list of all of the non-incidental lexemes in Psalms 15–24. Incidental lexemes include those words that are common to a majority of psalms: conjunctions, prepositions, particles, negative adverbs, and pronouns. Incidental lexemes are neither included below, nor used in analysis of lexical cohesion between psalms. The number of non-incidental lexemes (per psalm and in the collection) are as follows:

Psalms	n_l
15	42
16	68
17	112
18	326
19	111
20	63
21	86
22	205
23	45
24	72
Psalms 15–24	1130
Book I	4232

The root of each lexeme found in Psalms 15–24 is listed below, followed by each of the variations of that root that exist in the collection, and the number of occurrences in the collection ($n_{e\ (Pss\ 15-24)}$).

List of Lexemes in Psalms 15–24

Lexeme	Variations	n_e (Pss 15-24)	Lexeme	Variations	n_e (Pss 15-24)
בן		4	מלך	מלוכה	10
ברך	ברכה	5	מלא		4
ברר	בר	6	משיח		2
בטח		6	משל		2
בטן		3	מצא		3
בוא		4	מות		3
בזה		3	מוט		4
דבר		8	מים		5
דרש		3	נגד		2
דשן		3	נחל	נחלה	2
דוד		11	נפל		4
דור		2	נפש		8
גבר	גבור, גבורה	6	נקה	נקי	4
גדל	גדול	2	נקף		2
גור		2	נצח		6
גורל		2	נצל		5
גוי		4	נשא		8
גיל		2	נטה		4
חבל		3	נתן		10
הלך		2	נוח	מנוחה	2
הלל	תהלה	6	פה		6
חלק		3	פלט		6
חפץ		3	פנה		16
הר		3	פקד		2
חרב		2	פז		2
חרפה		2	פעל	פעלה	2
חסד	חסיד	7	קדם		4
חסה		4	קדש	קדוש	6
חוה		3	קרב	קרוב	2
היה		4	קרן		2
חיה	חי	7	קרא		5
חזה		2	קול		3
כבד	כבוד	10	קום	מקום	8
כל		19	רבב	רב	7
כנף		2	רבה		2
כף		2	רגל		5
כרע		4	רחם		2
כסף		2	רכב		2
כון	מכון	2	רמה	מרמה	2
כוס		2	רנן	רנה	2
לבב	לב	10	רשע		3
לחם	מלחמה	3	רום	מרום	5
לקח		2	רוץ		2
לשון		2	ראה		4
לילה		5	ראש		6

Lexeme	Variations	n_e (Pss 15-24)
רעע	רע, רעה	5
סבב		5
שבע		2
שבע		4
שדד	שד	2
צדק	צדקה	9
שגב	משגב	2
סגר	מסגרת	2
שכן		2
סלה		4
שלח		3
צל	צלמות	2
שם		7
שמח	שמחה	5
שמר		6
שמים		5
שמע		7
שנא		3
שפה		5
ספר		4
שפט	משפט	3
צרף		2
צרר	צרה	4
סתר	מסתר	6
שוב		7
שוה		3
צור		4
שים		2
שיר	שירה	2
שית		6
שאל (Saul)	שאול, משאלה	3
שאול (Sheol)		2
סעד		2
שען	משענת, משען	2
תבל		3
תמך		2
תמם	תמים	8
טרף		2
טוב	טובה	3
יד		9
ידע	דעת	4
יהוה		58
יכל		2
ימין		6
ירד		2
ירא	יראה	5

Lexeme	Variations	n_e (Pss 15-24)
ישב		3
יסד	מוסד, מוסדה	3
ישר	מישרים	2
יצא	מוצא	5
ישע	ישועה, מושיע	17
יתר	מיתר	2
יום		9
יעץ	עצה	2
זה		4
זכר		3
זמם	מזמה	2
זמר	מזמור	9
זרע		5
אדם		3
אדון		2
אהל		2
אכל		4
אל	אלוה, אלהים	22
אמן	אמת	3
אמר	אמרה	7
אף		3
ארי	אריה	4
ארח		3
ארך		2
ארץ		8
אש		5
אור		2
איב		8
אילה		2
איש		2
אזן		4
עבד		5
עבר		2
עד		4
ענה	ענות, עני, ענו, ענוה	12
עפר		3
עקב	יעקב	4
עשה	מעשה	5
עוד	עדות	2
עולם		5
עין		7
עוב		2
עזר	עזרה	3
עזז	עזוז, עז	4
עליון		2

Bibliography

Ahn, S. K. "I Salmi 146-150 come conclusione del Salterio." PhD diss., Pontifical Biblical Institute, 2008.

Alden, R. L. "Chiastic Psalms: A Study in the Mechanics of Semitic Poetry in Psalms 1-50." *Journal of the Evangelical Theological Society* 17 (1974): 11-28.

———. "Chiastic Psalms (II): A Study in the Mechanics of Semitic Poetry in Psalms 51-100." *Journal of the Evangelical Theological Society* 19 (1976): 191-200.

———. "Chiastic Psalms (III): A Study in the Mechanics of Semitic Poetry in Psalms 101-150." *Journal of the Evangelical Theological Society* 21 (1978): 199-210.

Alexander, J. A. *The Psalms Translated and Explained.* 6th ed. New York: Charles Scribner, 1865.

———. *The Psalms.* 3 vols. New York: Baker & Scribner, 1850.

Allen, L. C. "David as Exemplar of Spirituality: The Redactional Function of Psalm 19." *Biblica* 67 (1986): 544-46.

Alonso-Schökel, L. *Estudios de Poetica Hebrea.* Barcelona: Juan Flores, 1963.

Alter, R. "Psalms." *The Art of Biblical Narrative.* 2nd ed. New York: Basic Books, 2011.

———. *The Art of Biblical Poetry.* 2nd ed. New York: Basic Books, 2011.

———. Pages 244-62 in *The Literary Guide to the Bible.* Edited by R. Alter and F. Kermode. Cambridge, MA: Harvard University Press, 1987.

Anderson, A. A. "Psalm Study between 1955 and 1969." *Baptist Quarterly* 23 (1969): 155-64.

———. *Psalms: 1-72.* NCBC. Grand Rapids: Eerdmans, 1972.

Anderson, J. "The Ancestral Covenant in Psalms 105 and 106: Their Function as the Conclusion to Book Four of the Psalter." Paper Presentation, Society of Biblical Literature. November 23, 2008.

Ap-Thomas, D. R. "All the King's Horses." Pages 135-51 in *Proclamation and Presence: Old Testament Essays in Honour of G. H. Davies.* Edited by J. I. Durham and J. R. Porter. Richmond, VA: John Knox Press, 1970.

Arens, A. "Hat der Psalter Seinen 'Sitz im Leben' in der Synagogalen Leseordnung des Pentateuch?" Pages 107-31 in *Le Psautier; ses origines, ses problèmes littéraires, son influence. Études présentées aux XIIe journées bibliques.* Edited by R. de Langhe. Orientalie at Biblica Lovaniensia. Vol. 4. Louvian: Publications Universitaires, 1962.

Assis, E. "Chiasmus in Biblical Narrative: Rhetoric of Characterization." *Prooftexts* 22 (2002): 273-304.

Athanasius. *Epistula ad Marcellinum de Interpretation Psalmorum.* Patrology. Edited
by Quasten J. and A. di Berardino. Vol. 3. Westminster, MD: Christian
Classics, 1950–86.

Auffret, P. "C'est un peuple humilié que tu sauves: Étude structurelle du Psaume 18."
Science et Esprit 46, no. 3 (1994): 273–91.

———. "C'est un peuple humilié que tu sauves: Étude structurelle du Psaume 18
(2éme partie)." *Science et Esprit* 47, no. 1 (1995): 81–101.

———. "Complements sur la structure littéraire du Ps 2 et son rapport au Ps 1."
Biblische Notizen 35 (1986): 7–13.

———. "'Dans ta force se réjouit le rio': Étude structurelle du Psaume XXI." *Vetus
Testamentum* 40, no. 4 (1990): 385–410.

———. "En memoire eternelle sera le juste: Étude structurelle du Psaume cxii." *Vetus
Testamentum* 48 (1998): 2–14.

———. "Essai sur la structure littéraire de Psaume XV." *Vetus Testamentum* 31, no. 4
(1981): 385–99.

———. "Les Psaulmes 15 à 24." Pages 407–38 in *La sagesse a bâti sa maison: Études de
structures littéraires dans l'Ancien Testament et spécialment dans les psaumes.*
OBO 49. Göttingen: Vandenhoeck & Ruprecht, 1982.

———. "Short Notes: Note sur la structure littéraire du Psaume XXI." *Vetus
Testamentum* 30, no. 1 (1980): 91–93.

———. "Yhwh, qui sejournera en ta tente? Étude strructurelle du Psaume XV." *Vetus
Testamentum* 50, no. 2 (2000): 143–51.

Augustine. *Enarrationes in Psalmos I–L.* Edited by E. Dekkers and J. Fraipont. CCSL
38. Steenbrugge: Brepols, 1990.

Auwers, J.-M. *La composition littéraire du Psautier: un état de la question.* CahRB 46.
Paris: Gabalda, 2000.

———. "Le Psautier comme livre biblique: Édition, redaction, function." Pages 67–89
in *The Composition of the Book of Psalms.* Edited by E. Zenger. Bibliotheca ephermeridum theologicarum lovaniensium 238. Louvain: Peeters, 2010.

Baethgen, D. F. *Die Psalmen.* Handbuch zum Alten Testament 2.2. Göttingen:
Vandenhoeck & Ruprecht, 1897.

Barbiero, G. *Das erste Psalmenbuch als Einheit: Eine synchrone Analyse von Psalm 1–41.*
Österreichische Biblische Studien 16. Frankfurt: Peter Lang, 1999.

Barré, M. L., and J. S. Kselman. "New Exodus, Covenant, and Restoration in Psalm
23." Pages 97–127 in *The Word of the Lord Shall Go Forth.* Edited by C. L.
Meyers and M. O'Connor. Winona Lake, IN: Eisenbrauns, 1983.

Barth, C. "Concatenatio im ersten Buch des Psalters." Pages 30–40 in *Wort and
Wirklichkeit: Studien zur Afrikanistik und Orientalistik.* Edited by B. Benzing,
O. Böcher and G. Mayer. Meisenheim am Glan: Hain, 1976.

Bartholomew, C. G., and R. P. O'Dowd. *Old Testament Wisdom Literature: A
Theological Introduction.* Downers Grove, IL: InterVarsity, 2011.

Barton, J. *Oracles of God.* London: Darton, Longman & Todd, 1986.

Bazak, J. "The Set of the Six Chapters of the 'Hallel': Numerological Ornamentation
and Formal Structure." *Beth Mikra* 36 (1991): 91–93.

———. "The Six Chapters of the 'Hallel': Numerological Ornamentation and Formal
Structure (Psalms 113–118)." *Beth Mikra* 34 (1990): 182–91.

Beaucamp, E. "L'unité du recueil des montées, Psaumes 120-134." *Liber Annuus Studii Biblici Franciscani* 29 (1979): 73-90.

Beckwith, R. "The Early History of the Psalter." *Tyndale Bulletin* 46 (1995): 1-26.

Beekman, J., J. Callow, and M. Kopesec. *The Semantic Structure of Written Communication.* Rev. ed. Dallas: Summer Institute of Linguistics, 1981.

Berlin, A. *The Dynamics of Biblical Parallelism.* Rev. ed. Grand Rapids: Eerdmans, 2008.

———. *Poetics and Interpretation of Biblical Narrative.* Bible and Literature Series 9. Sheffield: The Almond Press, 1983.

Black, J. A. "Some Structural Features of Sumerian Narrative Poetry." Pages 71-101 in *Mesopotamian Epic Literature: Oral or Aural?.* Edited by Marianna E. Vogelzang and H. L. J. Vanstiphout. Lampeter, Wales: Edwin Mellen, 1992.

Botha, P. J. "Answers Disguised as Questions: Rhetoric and Reasoning in Psalm 24." *Old Testament Essays* 22, no.3 (2009): 535-53.

Bott, T. "Willful Sin or Arrogant Men? The Ethics of Psalm 19:14 in Context." Paper Presentation, Society of Biblical Literature. November 22, 2010.

Boulet, A. "The Prayer of Manasseh: A Window Into the Shape and Shaping of the Hebrew Psalter." Paper Presentation, Society of Biblical Literature. November 23, 2009.

Bratcher, R. G., and W. D. Reyburn. *A Handbook on Psalms.* New York: United Bible Societies, 1991.

Braude, W. G., trans. *The Midrash on Psalms.* 2 vols. Yale Judaica Series 13. New Haven, CT: Yale University Press, 1954-9.

Breck, J. "Biblical Chiasmus: Exploring Structure for Meaning." *Biblical Theology Bulletin* 17 (1987): 70-74.

Brennan, J. P. "Psalms 1-8: Some Hidden Harmonies." *Biblical Theology Bulletin* 10 (1980): 25-29.

———. "Some Hidden Harmonies in the Fifth Book of Psalms." Pages 126-58 in *Essays in Honor of Joseph P. Brennan.* Edited by R. F. McNamara. Rochester, NY: St Bernard's Seminary, 1976.

Brewer-Boydston, G. "The Commanding, Saving, Protecting Power of the Voice of God: The Function of Yahweh's *kôl* in the Psalter." Paper Presentation, Society of Biblical Literature. November 17, 2012.

Briggs, C. A., and E. G. Briggs, *A Critical and Exegetical Commentary on the Book of Psalms.* Vol. 1. Edinburgh: T&T Clark, 1906.

Brower, K. F. "The Multiple Readings of Psalm 60: Through the Lenses of Prophet, Poet, and Exegete." Paper Presentation, Society of Biblical Literature. November 17, 2012.

Brown, W. P. "'Here Comes the Sun!': The Metaphorical Theology of Psalms 15-24." Pages 259-77 in *The Composition of the Book of Psalms.* Edited by E. Zenger. BELT 238. Leuven: Peeters, 2010.

———. "Psalms as Collections and Clusters." Pages 85-107 in *Psalms.* Interpreting Biblical Texts. Nashville: Abingdon, 2010.

Broyles, C. *Psalms.* New International Biblical Commentary. Peabody: Hendrickson Publishers, 1999.

Brueggemann, W. "Bounded by Obedience and Praise: The Psalms as Canon."
    JSOTournal for the Study of the Old Testament 50 (1991): 63–92.
——. *The Message of the Psalms: A Theological Commentary*. Augsburg Old Testament
    Studies. Minneapolis: Fortress, 1984.
Bullock, C. H. *Encountering the Book of Psalms: A Literary and Theological Introduction*.
    Grand Rapids: Baker, 2001.
Buttenwieser, M. *The Psalms: Chronologically Treated with a New Translation*.
    Chicago: University of Chicago, 1938.
Cabaniss, A. "The Harrowing of Hell, Psalm 24, and Pliny the Younger: A Note."
    Vigilae Christianae 7, no. 2 (1953): 65–74.
Calès, J. *Le livre des Psaumes*. 5th ed. 2 vols. Paris: Gabriel Beauchesne, 1936.
Calvin, J. *Commentary on the Book of Psalms*. Translated by J. Anderson. Vol. 1. Repr.,
    Grand Rapids: Eerdmans, 1949. 5 vols. Edinburgh: Calvin Translation
    Society, 1557.
Casanowics, I. "Paranomasia in the Old Testament." *Journal of Biblical Literature* 12
    (1983): 105–67.
Cassuto, P. and G. Dorival. "Le Textes rabbiniques sur le Psaume 21 (22 TM)." Pages
    165–224 in *Recherches sur le Psaume 21 (22 TM)*. Paris: Peeters, 2002.
Cassuto, U. "The Sequence and Arrangement of the Biblical Sections." Pages 1–6 in
    his *Biblical and Oriental Studies*. Vol. 1. Jerusalem: Magnes, 1973.
Ceresko, A. R. "The Sage in the Psalms." Pages 217–30 in *The Sage in Israel and the
    Ancient Near East*. Edited by J. G. Gammie and L. G. Purdue. Winona Lake,
    IN: Eisenbrauns, 1990.
Charney, D. "Persuading God to Take Sides: The Rhetoric of Denunciation in the
    Individual Psalms." Paper Presentation, Society of Biblical Literature.
    November 22, 2011.
——. "Praise as Currency in the Divine Realm." Paper Presentation, Society of
    Biblical Literature. November 17, 2012.
Cheyne, T. K. *The Book of Psalms or The Praises of Israel: A New Translation, with
    Commentary*. London: Kegan Paul, Trench, 1888.
Childs, B. S. *Introduction to the Old Testament as Scripture*. Philadelphia:
    Fortress, 1979.
——. *Old Testament in a Canonical Context*. Philadelphia: Fortress, 1985.
Clements, R. "Worship and Ethics: A Re-Examination of Psalm 15." Pages 78–94 in
    Worship and the Hebrew Bible: Essays in Honour of John T. Willis. Edited by M.
    Graham, R. Marrs, and S. McKenzie. Sheffield: Sheffield Academic, 1999.
Clendenen, R. E. "Discourse Strategies in Jeremiah 10:1–16." *Journal of Biblical
    Literature* 106 no. 3 (1987): 401–8.
Clifford, R. J. *Psalms 1–72*. Abingdon Old Testament Commentaries. Nashville:
    Abingdon, 2002.
Clines, D. J. A. "A World Established on Water (Psalm 24): Reader-Response,
    Deconstruction and Bespoke Interpretation." Pages 79–90 in *The New
    Literary Criticism of the Hebrew Bible*, Edited by J. Cheryl Exum and David J. A.
    Clines. Sheffield: JSOT, 1994.
Cohen, A. *The Psalms*. London: Soncino, 1969.
Cole, R. L. "An Integrated Reading of Psalms 1 and 2." *JSOT* 98 (2002): 75–88.

——. *Psalms 1-2: Gateway to the Psalter.* Sheffield: Sheffield Phoenix, 2012.

——. *The Shape and Message of Book III: Psalms 73-89.* JSOTSup 307. Sheffield: Sheffield Academic, 2000.

Collins, T. "Decoding the Psalms: A Structural Approach to the Psalter." *JSOT* 37 (1987): 41-60.

Corwin, C. M. "Poetic Analysis, Context, Spirituality: Theology of the Psalter?" Paper Presentation, Society of Biblical Literature. November 23, 2008.

——. "Psalms 23-29: A Sequence?" Paper Presentation, Society of Biblical Literature. November 23, 2009.

Craigie, P. C. *Psalms 1-50.* 2nd ed. WBC 19. Nashville: Thomas Nelson, 2004.

Creach, J. F. D. *Yahweh as Refuge and the Editing of the Hebrew Psalter.* JSOTSup 217. Sheffield: Sheffield Academic, 1996.

Crenshaw, J. L. "Wisdom Psalms?" *Currents in Research: Biblical Studies* 8 (2000): 9-17.

Crim, K. R. *The Royal Psalms.* Richmond, VA: John Knox, 1962.

Croatto, J. S. "Psalm 23:1-6." Pages 57-62 in *Return to Babel.* Edited by. J. R. Levison and R. Pope-Levison. Louisville: Westminster John Knox, 1999.

Cruse, D. A. *Lexical Semantics.* Cambridge Textbooks in Linguistics. Cambridge: University Press, 1986.

Dahood, M. "Chiasmus in Job: A Text-Critical and Philological Criterion." Pages 119-30 in *A Light unto My Path: Old Testament Studies in Honor of Jacob M. Myers.* Edited by H. N. Bream, R. D. Heim, and C. A. Moore. Philadelphia: Temple University Press, 1974.

——. *Psalms.* Anchor Bible. Vols. 16-17A. Garden City, NY: Doubleday, 1965-70.

Dahse, J. *Das Rätsel des Psalters gelöst.* Essen: Lichtweg-Verlag, 1927.

Davis, B. C. "A Contextual Analysis of Psalms 107-118." PhD diss., Trinity Evangelical Divinity School, 1996.

Davis, E. F. "Exploding the Limits: Form and Function in Psalm 22." *JSOT* 53 (1992): 97-103.

de Beaugrand, R.-A., and W. U. Dressler. *Introduction to Text Linguistics.* London: Longman, 1981.

de Lagarde, P. A. *Analecta Syriaca.* Leipzig: Teubner, 1858.

——. *Hippolytus Romanus.* Leipzig: Teubner, 1858.

——. *Orientalia.* Osnabrück: Otto Zeller Verlag, 1879-80.

deClaissé-Walford, N. L. "The Canonical Approach to Scripture and the Editing of the Hebrew Psalter." Pages 1-11 in *The Shape and Shaping of the Book of Psalms: The Current State of Scholarship.* Edited by N. L. deClaissé-Walford. AIL 20. Atlanta: SBL Press, 2014.

——. "Finding the Feminine in Psalms 90, 91, and 92." Paper Presentation, Society of Biblical Literature. November 25, 2013.

——. "An Intertextual Reading of Psalms 22, 23, and 24." Pages 139-52 in *The Book of Psalms: Composition and Reception.* Edited by P. W. Flint, P. D. Miller, A. Brunell, and R. Roberts. Leiden; Boston: Brill, 2005.

——. "The Meta-Narrative of the Psalter." Pages 363-75 in *Oxford Handbook of the Psalms.* Edited by W. P Brown. Oxford: Oxford University Press, 2000.

——. "Psalm 44: O God, Why Do You Hide Your Face?" Paper Presentation, Society of Biblical Literature. November 21, 2006.

——. "Reading Backwards from the Beginning: My Life with the Psalter." *Verbum et Ecclessia* 27 (2006): 455–76.

——. *Reading from the Beginning: The Shaping of the Hebrew Psalter*. Macon: Mercer University Press, 1997.

deClaissé-Walford, N. L., R. A. Jacobson, and B. L. Tanner. *The Book of Psalms*. NICOT. Grand Rapids: Eerdmans, 2014.

de Wette, W. M. L. *Commentar über die Psalmen*. Edited by G. Baur. Heidelberg: Mohr, 1856.

Delamarter, S. "Scribal Practices in Ethiopian Psalters as Expressions of Identification and Differentiation: An Illustrated Lecture." Paper Presentation, Society of Biblical Literature. November 21, 2006.

Delitzsch, F. *Biblical Commentary on the Psalms*. 3 vols. Translated by F. Bolten. Grand Rapids: Eerdmans, 1881.

——. *Messianiche Weissagungen in Geschichtlicher Folge*. Leipzig: Faber, 1890.

——. *The Psalms*. Translated by F. Bolton. Commentary on the Old Testament. Vol. 1. Repr., Grand Rapids: Eerdmans, 1982.

——. *Symbolae ad Psalmos Illustrandos Isagogicœ*. Leipzig: Faber, 1846.

Dorsey, D. A. *The Literary Structure of the Old Testament: A Commentary on Genesis-Malachi*. Grand Rapids: Baker Books, 1999.

Driver, D. R. "'He Led His People Out with Gladness': Psalm 105 and the Return from Exile." Paper Presentation, Society of Biblical Literature. November 17, 2007.

Driver, S. R. *Studies in the Psalms*. Edited by C. F. Burney. London: Hodder & Stoughton, 1915.

Duhm, B. *Psalmen*. Leipzig and Tübingen: Mohr, 1899.

Eaton, J. H. *Kingship and the Psalms*. 2nd ed. The Biblical Seminar. Vol. 3. Sheffield: JSOT, 1986.

——. *Psalms*. London: SCM Press, 1967.

Estes, D. J. *Handbook on the Wisdom Books and Psalms*. Grand Rapids: Baker Academic, 2005.

Ewald, G. H. A. *Psalmen*. Leipzig and Tübingen: Mohr, 1899.

Fensham, F. C. "Psalm 2: A Covenant-Song?" *Zeitschrift für die alttestamentliche Wissenschaft* 77 (1965): 193–202.

Firth, D., and P. S. Johnston. *Interpreting the Psalms: Issues and Approaches*. Grand Rapids: IVP Academic, 2005.

Fischer, J. A. "Everyone a King: A Study of the Psalms." *Bible Today* 97 (1978): 1683–1689.

Flint, P. W. *The Dead Sea Psalms Scrolls and the Book of Psalms*. Studies on the Texts of the Desert of Judah 17. Leiden: Brill, 1997.

——. "The Dead Sea Psalms Scrolls: Psalms Manuscripts, Editions, and the *Oxford Hebrew Bible*." Pages 11–33 in *Jewish and Christian Approaches to the Psalms: Conflict and Convergence*. Edited by S. E. Gillingham. Oxford: University Press, 2013.

——. "The Psalms Scrolls from the Judaean Desert: Relationships and Textual Affiliations." Pages 31–52 in *New Qumran Texts and Studies: Proceedings of the*

First Meeting of the International Organization for Qumran Studies, Paris 1992. Edited by G. J. Brooke. Leiden: Brill, 1994.

Flint, P. W., and P. D. Miller Jr., eds. *The Book of Psalms: Composition and Reception*. Vetus Testamentum Supplements 99. Leiden: Brill, 2005.

Fohrer G., and E. Sellin. *Introduction to the Old Testament*. Nashville: Abingdon, 1968.

Fokkelman, J. P. *Major Poems of the Hebrew Bible: At the Interface of Prosody and Structural Analysis*. Vol. 3. SSN 43. Assen: Royal Van Gorcum, 2003.

Forbes, J. *Studies on the Book of Psalms*. Edinburgh: T&T Clark, 1888.

Freedman, D. N. "The Twenty-Third Psalm." Pages 139–66 in *Michigan Oriental Studies in Honor of George G. Cameron*. Edited by L. L. Orlin. Ann Arbor: University of Michigan Press, 1976.

Füglister, N. "Die Verwendung des Psalters zur Zeit Jesu: Der Psalter als Lehr- und Lebensbuch." *BK* 47 (1992): 200–8.

Futato, M. D. *The Book of Psalms*. Cornerstone Biblical Commentary. Carol Stream, IL: Tyndale House, 2005.

———. *Interpreting the Psalms: An Exegetical Handbook*. Handbooks for Old Testament Exegesis. Grand Rapids: Kregel, 2007.

Gaertner, J. "The Tora in Psalm 106 and Psalm 136." Paper Presentation, Society of Biblical Literature. November 17, 2007.

García Martínez, F. *The Dead Sea Scrolls Translated: The Qumran Texts in English*. Translated by W. G. E. Watson. Leiden, Brill; Grand Rapids: Eerdmans, 1996.

Garsiel, M. "Puns upon Names: Subtle Colophons in the Bible." *Jewish Bible Quarterly* 23 (1995): 182–7.

Garton, R. "The Death of a Psalmist: A Structural Analysis and Literary Reading of Psalm 88." Paper Presentation, Society of Biblical Literature. November 23, 2009.

Geerard, M., and F. Glorie, eds. *Clavis Patrum Graecorum*. Corpus Christianorum Series Graeca, 5 vols. Turnhout: Brepols, 1974–87.

Gerstenberger, E. S. "Der Psalter als Buch and als Sammlung." Pages 3–13 in *Neue Wege der Psalmenforschung*. Edited by K. Seybold and E. Zenger. Herders biblische Studien 1. Freiburg: Herder, 1994.

———. *Psalms: Part 1*. FOTL. Grand Rapids: Eerdmans, 1988.

Gillingham, S. E. *The Image, the Depths and the Surface: Multivalent Approaches to Biblical Study*. JSOTSup 354. Sheffield: Sheffield Academic, 2002.

———. *One Bible, Many Voices: Different Approaches to Biblical Studies*. Trowbridge, Wilts: Redwood, 1998.

Ginsburg, C. D. *Introduction to the Massoretico-Critical Edition of the Hebrew Bible*. New York: Ktav, 1966.

Girard, M. *Les Psaumes Redécouverts: De la structure au sens*. Vol. 3. Montreal: Bellarmin, 1994.

Glück, J. J. "Paranomasia in Biblical Literature." *Semitics* 1. Golani, S. J. "Three Oppressors and Four Saviors—The Three-Four Pattern and the List of Saviors in 1 Sam 12,9–11." *ZAW* 127, no. 2 (2015): 294–303.

Goldingay, J. "The Dynamic Cycle of Praise and Prayer in the Psalms." *JSOT* 20 (1981): 85–90.

———. *Psalms*. Vol. 1. Baker Commentary on the Old Testament: Wisdom and Psalms. Grand Rapids: Baker Academic, 2006.

———. "Repetition and Variation in the Psalms." *Jewish Quarterly Review* 68 (1978): 146–51.

Goulder, M. "David and Yahweh in Psalms 23 and 24." *JSOT* 30, no. 3 (2006): 463–73.

———. "The Fourth Book of the Psalter." *Journal of Theological Studies* 26 (1975): 269–89.

———. *The Prayers of David: Psalms 51–72*. Sheffield: Sheffield Academic, 1990.

———. *The Psalms of the Sons of Korah*. JSOTSup 20. Sheffield: JSOT, 1982.

Graetz, H. *Kritischer Commentar zu den Psalmen*, 2 vols. Breslau: Schottlaender, 1882.

Grant, J. A. "Editorial Criticism." Pages 149–56 in *Dictionary of the Old Testament: Wisdom, Poetry & Writings*. Edited by T. Longman III and P. Enns. Downers Grove, IL: IVP Academic, 2008.

———. *The King as Exemplar: The Function of Deuteronomy's Kingship Law in the Shaping of the Book of Psalms*. Atlanta: Society of Biblical Literature, 2004.

———. "The Psalms and the King." Pages 101–18 in *Interpreting the Psalms: Issues and Approaches*. Edited by D. Firth and P. S. Johnston. Downers Grove, IL: IVP Academic, 2005.

Gregory of Nyssa. *Inscriptiones Psalmorum*. Edited by J. McDonough and P. Alexander. Gregorii Nysseni Opera 5. Leiden: Brill, 1962.

Greswell, J. J. *Grammatical Analysis of the Hebrew Psalter*. Oxford: J. Parker, 1873.

Grossberg, D. *Centripetal and Centrifugal Structures in Biblical Poetry*. Society of Biblical Literature Manuscript Series 39. Atlanta: Scholars Press, 1989.

———. "The Disparate Elements of the Inclusio in Psalms." *Hebrew Annual Review* 6 (1982): 97–104.

Grossfeld, B. "The Translation of the Biblical Hebrew dqp in the Targum, Peshitta, Vulgate and Septuagint." *ZAW* 96 (1984): 83–101.

Gruber, M. I. *Rashi's Commentary on Psalms*. Philadelphia, PA: Jewish Publication Society, 2008.

Gualandi, D. "Salmo 17 (16), 13–14." *Biblica* 37 (1956): 199–208.

Guilding, A. "Some Obscured Rubrics and Lectionary Allusions in the Psalter." *Journal of Theological Studies* 3 (1952): 41–55.

Gunkel, H. *Die Psalmen*. 4th ed. Göttingen: Vandenhoeck & Ruprecht, 1926.

———. *Introduction to the Psalms: The Genres of the Religious Lyric of Israel*. Translated by J. D. Nogalski. Macon: Mercer University Press, 1998.

———. "Psalm 24: An Interpretation." *The Biblical World* 21, no. 5 (1903): 366–70.

———. *The Psalms: A Form-critical Introduction*. Translated by T. M. Horner. Philadelphia: Fortress, 1967.

Gunkel, H., and J. Begrich. *Einleitung in Die Psalmen: die Gattungen der religiösen Lyrik Israels*. Göttinger Handkommentar zum Alten Testament. Göttingen: Vandenhoeck & Ruprecht, 1933.

Hamilton, J. M., Jr. *Psalms*. 2 vols. EBTC. Edited by T. Desmond Alexander, Thomas R. Schreiner, and Andreas J. Köstenberger. Bellingham, WA: Lexham, 2021.

Haney, R. G. *Text and Concept Analysis in Royal Psalms*. Studies in Biblical Literature 30. New York: Peter Lang, 2002.

Haran, M. "11QPs^a and the Canonical Book of Psalms." Pages 193-201 in *Minhah le-Nahum*. Edited by M. Brettler and M. Fishbane, JSOTSup 154. Sheffield: JSOT, 1993.

———. "11QPs^a and the Composition of the Book of Psalms." Pages 123-28 in *"Sha'arei Talmon": Studies in the Bible, Qumran, and the Ancient Near East Presented to Shemaryahu Talmon*. Edited by M. Fishbane, E. Tov, and W. W. Fields. Winona Lake, IN: Eisenbrauns, 1992.

Hartenstein, F., and B. Janowski. *Psalmen*. Biblischer Kommentar Alten Testamentum 15, vol. 1. Neukirchen-Vluyn: Neukirchener, 2012.

Hengstenberg, E. W. *Commentary on the Psalms*. Translated by P. Fairbairn and J. Thompson. Edinburgh: T&T Clark, 1845-48.

Hirsch, D. H. "Translatable Structure, Untranslatable Poem: Psalm 24." *Modern Language Studies* 12, no. 4 (1982): 21-34.

Hirsch, S. R. *The Psalms*. 2 vols. New York: Feldheim, 1960.

Hitzig, F. *Die Psalmen*. Leipzig and Heidelberg, 1863-65.

Ho, P. C. W. *The Design of the Psalter: A Macrostructural Analysis*. Eugene, OR: Pickwick, 2019.

Hobbs, G. "Martin Bucer and the Englishing of the Psalms." Pages 161-78 in *Martin Bucer: Reforming Church and Community*. Edited by D. Wright. Cambridge: Cambridge University Press, 1994.

Holmes, M. W., ed. and trans. *The Apostolic Fathers: Greek Texts and English Translations*. Grand Rapids: Baker, 2007.

Hossfeld, F.-L., and E. Zenger. *Die Psalmen I: Psalmen 1-50*. Die Neue Echter Bibel 29. Würzburg: Echter, 1993.

———. *Psalms 2: A Commentary on Psalms 51-100*. Translated by L. M. Maloney. Hermeneia. Minneapolis: Fortress, 2005.

———. *Psalms 3: A Commentary on Psalms 101-150*. Translated by L. M. Maloney. Hermeneia. Minneapolis: Fortress, 2011.

———. "'Wer darf hinaufziehn zum Berg JHWHs?' Zur Redaktionsgeschichte und Theologie der Psalmengruppe 15-24." Pages 166-82 in *Biblische Theologie und gesellschaftlicher Wandel: für Norbert Lohfink*. Edited by G. Braulik, W. Gross, and S. McEvenue. Freiburg: Herder, 1993.

Howard, D. M., Jr. "Divine and Human Kingship as Organizing Motifs in the Psalter." Pages 197-207 in *The Psalms: Language for All Seasons of the Soul*. Edited by A. J. Schmutzer and D. M. Howard Jr. Chicago: Moody Publishers, 2013.

———. "Editorial Activity in the Psalter: A State-of-the-Field Survey." *Word & World* 9, no. 3 (1989): 274-85.

———. "Editorial Activity in the Psalter: A State-of-the-Field Survey." Pages 52-70 in *The Shape and Shaping of the Psalter*. Edited by J. C. McCann Jr. JSOTSup 159. Sheffield: JSOT, 1993.

———. "The Proto-MT Psalter, the King, and Psalms 1 and 2: A Response to Klaus Seybold." Pages 182-89 in *Jewish and Christian Approaches to the Psalms: Conflict and Convergence*. Edited by S. E. Gillingham. Oxford: University Press, 2013.

———. "Psalm 88 and the Rhetoric of Lament." Pages 132–46 in *My Words are Lovely: Studies in the Rhetoric of the Psalms*. Edited by R. L. Foster and Howard. LHB/OTS 467. New York: T&T Clark, 2008.

———. *The Structure of Psalms 93–100*. UCSD Biblical and Judaic Studies 5. Winona Lake, IN: Eisenbrauns, 1997.

Hunter, A. G. "Psalms at Sukkot: The Use of Psalms in the Jerusalem Cultus of the Late Tanakh Period." Paper Presentation, Society of Biblical Literature. November 23, 2008.

———. "'The Righteous Generation': The Use of DOR in Psalms 14 and 24." Pages 187–205 in *Reflection and Refraction: Studies in Biblical Historiography in Honour of A. Graeme Auld*. Edited by Robert Rezetko, Timothy H. Lim, and Brian W. Auker. Leiden: Brill, 2006.

Hunter, J. H. "The Literary Composition of Theophany Passages in the Hebrew Psalms." *Journal of Northwest Semitic Languages* 15 (1989): 97–107.

Hupfeld. H. *Die Psalmen*. Gotha: Perthes, 1855.

Jacobson, K. N. *"Perhaps Yahweh is Sleeping": Awake ('ûrâ) and Contend (rîb) in the Book of Psalms*. Paper Presentation, Society of Biblical Literature. November 22, 2011.

Jerome. *Commentarioli in Psalmos*. Edited by G. Morin. Corpus Christianorum Series Latina 72. Turnhout: Brepols, 1959.

Johnson, A. R. *The Cultic Prophet and Israel's Psalmody*. Cardiff: University of Wales Press, 1979.

Justin Martyr. "Dialogue of Justin, Philosopher and Martyr, with Trypho, a Jew." Pages 263–384 in *The Apostolic Fathers with Justin Martyr and Irenaeus*. Edited by P. Schaff. CCEL vol. 1, 1819–93.

Kautzsch, E., ed. *Gesenius' Hebrew Grammar*. Revised by A. E. Cowley. 2nd English ed. Oxford: Clarendon, 1910.

Keel-Leu, O. "Nochmals Psalm 22,28–32." *Biblica* 51 (1970): 405–13.

Keil, C. F., and F. Delitzsch. *Commentary on the Old Testament*. 10 vols. Peabody, MA: Hendrickson Publishers, 2006.

Kermode, R., and R. Alter, eds. *The Literary Guide to the Bible*. Cambridge, MA: Harvard University Press, 1987.

Kidner, D. *Psalms 1–72: An Introduction and Commentary on Books I–II of the Psalms*. Tyndale Old Testament Commentaries. London: InterVarsity, 1973.

———. *Psalms 73–150: A Commentary on Books III–V of the Psalms*. Tyndale Old Testament Commentaries. London: InterVarsity, 1975.

Kim, J. "Strategic Arrangement of Royal Psalms in the Last Two Books of the Psalter." Paper Presentation, Society of Biblical Literature. November 17, 2007.

Kimḥi, D. *The First Book of Psalms according to the Text of the Cambridge MS Bible with the Longer Commentary of R. David Qimch*. Edited by S. M. Schiller-Szinessy. Cambridge: Deighton, Bell, 1883.

Kimmitt, F. X. "The Shape of Psalms 42–49." PhD diss., New Orleans Baptist Theological Seminary, 2000.

King, E. G. *The Psalms*. 3 vols. Cambridge: Deighton, Bell, 1889–1905.

Kirkpatrick, A. F. *The Book of Psalms: With Introduction and Notes.* Cambridge: Cambridge University Press, 1902.

Kissane, M. E. J. *The Book of Psalms.* Dublin: Brown & Nolan, 1953–54.

Klouda, S. L. "The Dialectical Interplay of Seeing and Hearing in Psalm 19 and Its Connection to Wisdom." *BBR* 10, no. 2 (2000): 181–95.

Koch, K. "Der Psalter und seine Redaktionsgeschichte." Pages 243–77 in *Neue Wege der Psalmenforschung.* Edited by K. Seybold and E. Zenger. Herders biblische Studien 1. Freiburg: Herder, 1994.

Koehler, L., and W. Baumgartner. *The Hebrew and Aramaic Lexicon of the Old Testament.* 2 vols. Translated and edited by M. E. J. Richardson. Leiden: Brill, 2001.

Krahmalkov, C. "Psalm 22,28–32." *Biblica* 50 (1969): 389–92.

Kraus, H.-J. *Psalmen.* 5th ed. 2 vols. Neukirchen: Neukirchener, 1978.

———. *Psalms.* Translated by H. C. Oswald. Vol. 1. Minneapolis: Augsburg, 1988.

Krispenz, J. "Inside and Outside: The Psalm's View on the Temple." Paper Presentation, Society of Biblical Literature. November 21, 2006.

Kugel, J. K. *The Idea of Biblical Poetry: Parallelism and Its History.* New Haven, CT: Yale University Press, 1981.

Kuntz, J. K. "King Triumphant: A Rhetorical Study of Psalms 20–21." *HAR* 10 (1986): 157–76.

Kynes, W. "Doxology in Disputation: The Use of Psalms 8 and 107 in the Book of Job." Paper Presentation, Society of Biblical Literature. November 23, 2009.

Lam, J. "Psalm 2 and the Disinheritance of Earthly Rulers." Paper Presentation, Society of Biblical Literature. November 17, 2012.

Lane, N. C. "Yhwh's Gracious and Compassionate Reign: Exodus 34:6–7 and the Psalter." Paper Presentation, Society of Biblical Literature. November 22, 2010.

LeFebvre, M. "Torah-Meditation and the Psalms: The Invitation of Psalm 1." Pages 159–74 in *Interpreting the Psalms: Issues and Approaches.* Edited by D. Firth and P. S. Johnston. Downers Grove, IL: IVP Academic, 2005.

LeMon, J. M. "The Ethics of the Psalms and the Problem of Violence." Paper Presentation, Society of Biblical Literature. November 23, 2009.

Leonard, J. M. "'He Led His People Out with Gladness': Psalm 105 and the Return from Exile." Paper Presentation, Society of Biblical Literature. November 23, 2008.

Leslie, E. A. *The Psalms: Translated and Interpreted in the Light of Hebrew Life and Worship.* New York: Abingdon, 1949.

Leuenberger, M. *Konzeptionen des Königtums Gottes im Psalter: Untersuchungen zu Komposition und Redaktion der theokratischen Bücher IV-V im Psalter.* ATANT 83. Zürich: Theologischer Verlag, 2004.

Leupold, H. C. *Exposition of the Psalms.* Grand Rapids: Baker, 1959.

Linville, J. "Psalm 22:17B: A New Guess." *JBL* 124 (2005): 733–44.

Lipiński, É. "L'hymne à Yahwé Roi en Psaume 22,28–32." *Biblica* 50 (1969): 153–68.

Lohfink, N. "Der Psalter und die Christliche Meditation: Die Bedeutung der Endredaktion für das Verständnis des Psalters." *BK* 47 (1992): 195–200.

———. "Psalmengebet und Psalterredaktion." *Archiv für Literaturewissenschaft* 34 (1992): 1–22.

Longacre, R. E. *Joseph: A Story of Divine Providence: A Text Theoretical and Textlinguistic Analysis of Genesis 37 and 39–48*. Winona Lake, IN: Eisenbrauns, 1989.

Longman, T., III. "Lament." Pages 197–216 in *Cracking Old Testament Codes: A Guide to Interpreting the Literary Genres of the Old Testament*. Edited by D. B. Sandy and R. L. Giese. Nashville: Broadman & Holman, 1995.

Longman, T., III, and P. Enns, eds. *Dictionary of the Old Testament: Wisdom, Poetry & Writings*. Downers Grove, IL: IVP Academic, 2008.

Louth, A. *Discerning the Mystery: An Essay on the Nature of Theology*. Clarendon Paperbacks. New York: Oxford University Press USA, 1990.

Luther, M. *Luthers Werke*. 63 vols. Weimar: Böhlau, 1883–1987.

Lyu, S. M. "The Righteous Petitioner in the Psalter." Paper Presentation, Society of Biblical Literature. November 21, 2006.

Mandolfl, C. "Not for Women Only: Feminist Interpretation of the Psalms." Paper Presentation, Society of Biblical Literature. November 22, 2011.

Mannati, M. "Les Psaumes Graduels Constituent-ils un Genre Littéraire Distinct à L'interieur du Psautier Biblique?" *Semeia* 29 (1979): 85–100.

Maxwell, N. "The Psalmist in the Psalm: A Persona-Critical Analysis of Psalm 101." Paper Presentation, Society of Biblical Literature. November 22, 2010.

Mays, J. L. "'In a Vision': The Portrayal of the Messiah in the Psalms." *Ex Auditu* 7 (1991): 1–8.

———. "The Place of the Torah-Psalms in the Psalter." *JBL* 106 (1987): 3–12.

———. "Prayer and Christology: Psalm 22 as a Perspective on the Passion." *Theology Today* 42 (1985): 322–33.

———. *Psalms*. Interpretation. Louisville: John Knox, 1994.

———. "The Question of Context in Psalm Interpretation." Pages 14–20 in *The Shape and Shaping of the Psalter*. Edited by J. C. McCann Jr. JSOTSup 159. Sheffield: JSOT, 1993.

Mazor, Y. "Psalm 24." *Scandinavian Journal of the Old Testament* 7 (1993): 303–16.

McCann, J. C., Jr. *A Theological Introduction to the Book of Psalms*. Nashville: Abingdon, 1993.

———. "Books I–III and the Editorial Purpose of the Hebrew Psalter." Pages 93–107 in *The Shape and Shaping of the Psalter*. Edited by J. C. McCann Jr. JSOTSup 159. Sheffield: JSOT, 1993.

"The Book of Psalms: Introduction, Commentary, and Reflections." Pages 639–1280 in *The New Interpreter's Bible*. Vol. 4. Nashville: Abingdon, 1996.

———, ed. *The Shape and Shaping of the Psalter*. JSOTSup 159. Sheffield: JSOT, 1993.

McConville, J. G. *The Midrash on Psalms*. Translated by W. G. Braude. Vol. 1. Yale Judaica Series 13. New Haven, CT: Yale University Press, 1954.

———. "The Psalmist as Persona: The Concept of Human Flourishing in the Psalms." Paper Presentation, Society of Biblical Literature. November 22, 2011.

Mihaila, C. "The Theological and Canonical Place of Psalm 73." *Faith and Mission* 18, no. 3 (2001): 52–57.

Millard, M. *Die Komposition des Psalters: Ein formgeschichtlicher Ansatz*. FAT 9. Tübingen: J. C. B. Mohr, 1994.

Miller, P. D., Jr. "The Beginning of the Psalter." Pages 83–92 in *The Shape and Shaping of the Psalter*. Edited by J. C. McCann Jr. JSOTSup 159. Sheffield: JSOT, 1993.

———. "Current Issues in Psalms Studies." *Word & World* 5 (1985): 132–43.

———. *Interpreting the Psalms*. Philadelphia: Fortress, 1986.

———. "Kingship, Torah Obedience, and Prayer: The Theology of Psalms 15–24." Pages 127–42 in *Neue Wege der Psalmenforschung*. Edited by K. Seybold and E. Zenger. HBS 1. Freiburg: Herder, 1994.

———. "The Psalms as Praise and Poetry." *The Hymn* 40 (1989): 12–16.

———. "Synonymous-Sequential Parallelism in the Psalms." *Biblica* 61 (1980): 256–60.

Milne, P. "Psalm 23: Echoes of the Exodus." *Studies in Religion/Sciences Religieuses* 4 (1974–75): 237–47.

Mitchell, D. C. "'God will Redeem my Soul from Sheol': The Psalms of the Sons of Korah." *JSOT* 30, no. 3 (2006): 365–84.

———. "Lord, Remember David: G. H. Wilson and the Message of the Psalter." *VT* 56 (2006): 526–48.

———. *The Message of the Psalter: An Eschatological Programme in the Book of Psalms*. JSOTSup 252. Sheffield: JSOT, 1997.

Morgan, G. "The Heavenly Horses." *History Today* (February 1973): 77–83.

Mosis, R. "Die Mauern Jerusalems: Beobachtungen zu Psalm 51,20f." Pages 201–15 in *Alttestamentliche Glaube und Biblische Theologie: Festschrift für Horst Dietrich Preuß zum 65. Geburtstag*. Edited by J. Hausann and J.-J. Zobel. Stuttgart: Kohlhammer, 1992.

Mowinckel, S. *Psalmenstudien: Das Thronbesteigungsfest Jahwäs and der Ursprung der Eschatologie*. Kristiania, Dybwad, 1922.

———. *Psalmenstudien I-VI*. Kristiania: Skrifter utgitt av Det Norske Videnskaps-Akademi i Oslo, 1921–24.

———. *The Psalms in Israel's Worship*. 2 vols. New York: Abingdon, 1962.

Muilenburg, J. "Form Criticism and Beyond." *JBL* 88 (1969): 1–18.

Murphy, R. E. "Reflections on Contextual Interpretation of the Psalms." Pages 21–28 in *The Shape and Shaping of the Psalter*. Edited by J. C. McCann Jr. JSOTSup 159. Sheffield: JSOT, 1993.

Myers, E. A. "Literary Dependence between 1 Peter and Hebrews: A Probability Analysis of Intertextual Parallels." Paper Presentation, Society of Biblical Literature. November 24, 2013.

Nasuti, H. P. "The Interpretive Significance of Sequence and Selection in the Book of Psalms." Pages 311–39 in *The Book of Psalms: Composition and Reception*. Edited by P. W. Flint and P. D. Miller. Vetus Testamentum Supplements 99. Leiden: Brill, 2005.

———. *Tradition History and the Psalms of Asaph*. Society of Biblical Literature Dissertation Series, 88. Atlanta: Scholars Press, 1988.

Noble, P. L. *The Canonical Approach: A Critical Reconstruction of the Hermeneutics of Brevard S. Childs*. New York: Brill, 1995.

Nötscher, F. *Die Psalmen*. Wurzburg: Echter, 1952.

Oesterley, W. O. E. *A Fresh Approach to the Psalms*. New York: Charles Scribner's
    Sons, 1937.
———. *The Psalms: Translated with Text-Critical and Exegetical Notes*. London: Society
    for Promoting Christian Knowledge, 1939.
Olbricht, T. H. "Apostolic Fathers." Pages 81–85 in *Dictionary of New Testament
    Background: A Compendium of Contemporary Biblical Scholarship*. Edited by C.
    A. Evans and S. E. Porter. Downers Grove, IL: InterVarsity, 2000.
Olshausen, J. *Die Psalmen*. Leipzig: Hirzel, 1853.
Origen. *Originis Opera Omnia*. Edited by C. H. E. Lommatzsch. Berlin: Haude et
    Spener, 1831–38.
Overland, P. "Chiasm." Pages 54–57 in *Dictionary of the Old Testament: Wisdom, Poetry
    & Writings*. Downers Grove, IL: IVP Academic, 2008.
Parrish, V. S. *A Story of the Psalms: Conversation, Canon, and Congregation*.
    Collegeville: Liturgical Press, 2003.
Parunak, H. V. D. "Oral Typesetting: Some Uses of Biblical Structure." *Biblica* 62
    (1981): 153–68.
———. "Transitional Techniques in the Bible." *Journal of Biblical Literature* 102
    (1983): 525–48.
Paul, S. M. *A Commentary on the Book of Amos*. Hermeneia. Minneapolis:
    Fortress, 1991.
Pemberton, G. "After Lament: Changing the Paradigm of Lament to Thanksgiving."
    Paper Presentation, Society of Biblical Literature. November 25, 2013.
———. "When God is the Problem: Reconciliation in Psalms of Lament." Paper
    Presentation, Society of Biblical Literature. November 17, 2012.
Perowne, J. J. S. *The Book of Psalms: A New Translation with Introductions and Notes
    Explanatory and Critical*. 2 vols. Andover, MA: W. F. Draper, 1882.
Peshiṭta Institute. *The Old Testament in Syriac: According to the Peshiṭta Version*.
    Edited on behalf of the International Organization for the Study of the Old
    Testament by the Peshiṭta Institute. Leiden: Brill, 1972.
Peters, J. P. *The Psalms as Liturgies*. The Paddock Lectures for 1920. London: Hodder
    & Stoughton, 1922.
Petrany, C. "Instruction, Performance, and Prayer: The Didactic Function of
    Psalmic Wisdom." Paper Presentation, Society of Biblical Literature.
    November 22, 2011.
Pfenniger, J. "A Foreign Noblewoman Praises a King: A Lexical Comparison of
    'Daughter of a King' in Psalm 45:14 and 'Daughter of a Noble' in the Song of
    Songs 7:2." Paper Presentation, Society of Biblical Literature. November
    25, 2013.
Pitra, J. B. *Analecta*. Sacra. 4 vols. Paris: Jouby et Roger, 1876–84.
Podella, T. "Transformationen kultischer darstellungen: Toraliturgien in Ps 15 und
    24." *SJOT* 13, no. 1 (1999): 95–130.
Power, E. "The Shepherd's Two Rods in Modern Palestine and in Some Passages of
    the Old Testament." *Biblica* 9 (1928): 434–42.
Pritchard, J. B., ed. *Ancient Near Eastern Texts Relating to the Old Testament*. 3rd ed.
    Princeton, NJ: Princeton University Press, 1969.

Quasten, J., and A. di Berardino. *Patrology*. 4 vols. Westminster, MD: Christian Classics, 1950-86.

Quinn, C. "A Methodology for the Cohesion of Psalms: Psalms 15, 19, and 24 as a Test Case." In *Holistic Readings on the Psalms and the Twelve*. Edited by M. Ayars and P. C. W. Ho. Forthcoming.

Rabinowitz, L. "Does Midrash Reflect the Triennial Cycle of Psalms?" *Jewish Quarterly Review* 26 (1936): 349-68.

Rad, G. von. *Wisdom in Israel*. London: Bloomsbury T&T Clark, 1972.

Rata, C. G. "The Finite Verb in Biblical Hebrew Poetry." Paper Presentation, Society of Biblical Literature. November 25, 2013.

Rendsburg, G. A. "Word Play in Biblical Hebrew: An Eclectic Collection." Pages 137-62 in *Puns and Pundits: Word Play in the Hebrew Bible and Ancient Near Eastern Literature*. Edited by S. B. Noegel. Bethesda, MD: The University Press of Maryland, 2000.

Reifsnyder, R. W. "Psalm 24." *Interpretation* 51, no. 3 (1997): 284-88.

Reindl, J. "Weisheitliche Beitung von Psalmen: Ein Beitrag zum Verständnis der Sammlung des Psalter." Pages 333-56 in *Congress Volume, Vienna 1980*. Vetus Testamentum Supplements 32. Edited by J. A. Emerton. Leiden: Brill, 1981.

Reynolds, K. A. "Unique Uses of Traditional Religious Language in Psalm 119." Paper Presentation, Society of Biblical Literature. November 23, 2008.

Ridderbos, N. H. *Die Psalmen*. Stilistische Verfahren und Aufbau mit besondere Berücksichtigung von Psa. 1-41. Beihefte zur Zeitschrift für die alttestamentliche Wissenschaft 117. Berlin: de Gruyter 1973.

Ringgren, H. *The Faith of the Psalmists*. Philadelphia: Fortress, 1963.

Rix, C. "Note the Silence: Reading Psalm 137 through Messiaen and Bak." Paper Presentation, Society of Biblical Literature. November 17, 2007.

Robertson, O. P. *The Flow of the Psalms: Discovering Their Structure and Theology*. Phillipsburg, NJ: P&R, 2015.

Rösel, C. *Die messianische Redaktion des Psalters: Studien zu Entstehung und Theologie der Sammlung Psalm 2-89*. Stuttgart: Calwer, 1999.

Ross, A. P. *A Commentary on the Psalms*. Vol. 1. Kregel Exegetical Library. Grand Rapids: Kregel, 2011.

Roth, M. T. *Law Collections from Mesopotamia and Asia Minor*. 2nd ed. SBLWAW 6. Atlanta: Scholars Press, 1997.

Sanders, J. A. *The Dead Sea Psalms Scroll*. Ithaca, NY: Cornell University Press, 1967.

———. "The Qumran Psalms Scroll (11QPs^a) Reviewed." In *On Language, Culture, and Religion: In Honor of Eugene A. Nida*. The Hague: Mouton, 1974.

———. "Variorum in the Psalms Scroll (11QPs^a)." *Catholic Biblical Quarterly* 27 (1966): 11-14.

Sasson, J. M. "Wordplay in the OT." *Interpreter's Dictionary of the Bible Supplement* (1976): 968-70.

Schaefer, K. *Psalms*. Berit Olam. Edited by D. W. Cotter. Collegeville, MN: Liturgical Press, 2001.

Schaff, P. *The Apostolic Fathers with Justin Martyr and Irenaeus*. Christian Classics Ethereal Library Vol. 1. New York: Christian Literature Publishing, 1819-93.

Schimmelpenninck, M. A. *Psalms: According to the Authorized Version.* London: J. & A. Arch, 1825.

Schmidt, H. *Die Psalmen.* Tübingen: J. C. B. Mohr, 1934.

Schmutzer, A. J., and D. M. Howard Jr., eds. *The Psalms: Language for All Seasons of the Soul.* Chicago, IL: Moody Publishers, 2013.

Scott, R. B. Y. *The Way of Wisdom in the Old Testament.* New York: MacMillan, 1971.

Seybold, K. *Die Psalmen.* HAT I. Vol. 15. Tübingen: J. C. B. Mohr, 1996.

———. *Die Wallfahrtpsalmen: Studien zur Entstehungsgeschichte van Psalmen.* Neukirchen: Neukirchener, 1978.

———. *Introducing the Psalms.* Translated by R. Graeme Dunphy. Edinburgh: T&T Clark, 1990.

———. "The Psalter as a Book." Pages 168–80 in *Jewish and Christian Approaches to the Psalms: Conflict and Convergence.* Edited by S. E. Gillingham. Oxford: Oxford University Press, 2013.

Sheppard, G. T. "Theology and the Book of Psalms." *Interpretation* 46 (1992): 143–55.

———. *Wisdom as a Hermeneutical Construct: A Study in the Sapientializing of the Old Testament.* New York: De Gruyter, 1980.

Skehan, P. W. "Qumran and Old Testament Criticism." Pages 163–82 in *Qumrân: sa piété, sa théologie et son milieu.* Edited by M. Delcor. Bibliotheca ephermeridum theologicarum lovaniensium 46. Paris: Leuven, 1978.

Smart, J. D. "The Eschatological Interpretation of Psalm 24." *Journal of Biblical Literature* 53 (1933): 175–80.

Smith, J. L. *Psalms of the Northern Levites: Asaph, Ethan, and the Sons of Korah.* Anchorage, AK: White Stone, 2003.

Snearly, M. K. "The Return of the King: Book V as a Witness to Messianic Hope in the Psalter." Pages 209–17 in *The Psalms: Language for All Seasons of the Soul.* Edited by A. J. Schmutzer and D. M. Howard Jr. Chicago, IL: Moody Publishers, 2013.

———. "The Return of the King: An Editorial-Critical Analysis of Psalms 107–150." PhD diss., Golden Gate Baptist Theological Seminary, 2012.

———. *The Return of the King: Messianic Expectation in Book V of the Psalter.* LHB/OTS 624. London: Bloomsbury T&T Clark, 2015.

Spiegel, S. *A Prophetic Attestation of the Decalogue: Hosea 6:5, with Some Observations on Psalms 15 and 24.* Cambridge, MA: Harvard University Press, 1934.

Stec, D. M., trans. *The Targum of Psalms: Translated, with a Critical Introduction, Apparatus, and Notes.* London: T&T Clark, 2004.

Sternberg, M. "How Narrativity Makes a Difference." *Narrative* 9 (2001): 115–22.

Steussy, M. J. *Psalms.* St. Louis: Chalice, 2004.

Suderman, W. D. "Deaf Communities: Considering the Ethical Cost of Losing Lament." Paper Presentation, Society of Biblical Literature. November 22, 2010.

Sumpter, P. E. "The Coherence of Psalms 15–24." *Biblica* 94 (2013): 186–209.

———. "The Substance of Psalm 24: An Attempt to Read the Bible after Brevard Childs." PhD diss., University of Gloucestershire, 2011.

Talmon, S. "The Topped Triad in the Hebrew Bible and the Ascending Numerical Pattern." Pages 77–124 in *Literary Motifs and Patterns in the Hebrew Bible: Collected Studies*. University Park: Penn State University Press, 2013.

Tanner, B. "King Yahweh as the Good Shepherd." Pages 267–84 in *David and Zion: Biblical Studies in Honor of J. J. M. Roberts*. Edited by B. F. Batto and K. L. Roberts. Winona Lake, IN: Eisenbrauns, 2004.

Tappy, R. E. "Psalm 23: Symbolism and Structure." *CBQ* 57, no. 2 (1995): 266–68.

Tate, M. E. *Psalms 51–100*. WBC 20. Waco, TX: Word, 1990.

Tertullianus, Quintus Septimus Florens. "An Answer to the Jews." Pages 206–41 in *Latin Christianity: Its Founder, Tertullian*. Edited by P. Schaff. Christian Classics Ethereal Library Vol. 3. New York: Christian Literature Publishing, 1819–93.

Thirtle, J. *The Titles of the Psalms: Their Nature and Meaning Explained*. London: Henry Frowde, 1904.

Thiselton, A. C. *Hermeneutics: An Introduction*. Grand Rapids: Eerdmans, 2009.

Tov, E. *Textual Criticism of the Hebrew Bible*. 2nd rev. ed. Minneapolis: Fortress, 2001.

Tromp, N. J. "Jacob in Psalm 24: Apposition, Aphaeresis or Apostrophe?" Pages 271–82 in *Von Kanaan bis Kerala, Festschrift J. P. M. Van der Ploeg*. Edited by W. C. Delsman, J. R. T. M. Peters, and J. T. Nelis. Kevelaer: Butzon & Bercker, 1982.

Tucker, W. D. "Hortatory Discourse in the Psalter: An Initial Inquiry." Paper Presentation, Society of Biblical Literature. November 21, 2006.

Ulrich, E. "The Bible in the Making: The Scriptures found at Qumran." Pages 51–66 in *The Bible at Qumran: Text, Shape, and Interpretation*. Edited by P. W. Flint. Grand Rapids: Eerdmans, 2001.

Urquiola, V. Y., and C. Codoñer, eds. *De viris illustribus*. Corpus Christianorum Series Latina 114A. Turnhout: Brepols Publishers, 2007.

Vall, G. "Psalm 22:17b: 'The Old Guess.'" *JBL* 116 (1997): 45–56.

Van der Lugt, P. *Cantos and Strophes in Biblical Hebrew Poetry: With Special Reference to the First Book of the Psalter*. Leiden: Brill, 2006.

Van der Ploeg, J. P. M. "Fragments d'un manuscrit de Psaumes de Qumran (11QPs^b)." *Revue biblique* 74 (1967): 408–12.

———. "Un petit rouleau des psaumes apocryphes (11QPsAp^a)." Pages 128–39 in *Tradition und Glaube: Das frühe Christentum in seiner Umwelt: Festbage für Karl Georg Kuhn zum 65. Geburtstag*. Edited by G. Jeremias et al. Göttingen: Vanderhoeck & Ruprecht, 1971.

Vangemeren, W. A. "Entering the Textual World of the Psalms: Literary Analysis." Pages 29–48 in *The Psalms: Language for All Seasons of the Soul*. Edited by A. J. Schmutzer and D. M. Howard Jr.. Chicago: Moody Publishers, 2013.

———. *Psalms*. Vol. 5. *The Expositor's Bible Commentary*. Rev. ed. Edited by T. Longman III and D. E. Garland. Grand Rapids: Zondervan, 2008.

Vermès, G. *The Complete Dead Sea Scrolls in English*. London: Allen Lane; New York: Penguin Press, 1997.

Vermeylen, J. "Une prière pour le renouveau du jérusalem. Le Psaume 51." *ETL* 68 (1992): 257–83.

Vesco, J.-L. *Le Psautier de David traduit et commenté*. 2 vols. Paris: Cerf, 2006.

Von Ewald, G. H. A. *Commentary on the Psalms*. 2nd ed. Translated by E. Johnson. 2 vols. London: Williams & Norgate, 1880–81.

Von Rad, G. "The Royal Ritual in Judah." Pages 222–31 in *The Problem of the Hexateuch and Other Essays*. New York: McGraw-Hill, 1966.

———. *Wisdom in Israel*. London: Bloomsbury T&T Clark, 1972.

Vosté, J.-M. "Sur les titres des Psaumes dans la Pešitta." *Biblica* 25 (1944): 210–35.

Wagner, J. R. "From the Heavens to the Heart: The Dynamics of Psalm 19 as Prayer." *CBQ* 61, no. 2 (1999): 245–61.

Wahl, H.-M. "Psalm 67. Erwägungen zu Aufbau, Gattung und Datierung." *Biblica* 73 (1992): 240–47.

Wallace, R. E. "Back to the Beginning: Yahweh as King, Moses as Mediator and Psalms 104–106." Paper Presentation, Society of Biblical Literature. November 17, 2007.

Waltke, B. K, and J. M Houston. *The Psalms as Christian Worship: A Historical Commentary*. Grand Rapids: Eerdmans, 2010.

Waltke, B. K. "A Canonical Process Approach to the Psalms." Pages 3–18 in *Tradition and Testament*. Edited by J. Feinberg. Chicago: Moody Press, 1982.

———. "Biblical Theology of the Psalms Today: A Personal Perspective." Pages 19–28 in *The Psalms: Language for All Seasons of the Soul*. Edited by A. J. Schmutzer and D. M. Howard Jr. Chicago: Moody Publishers, 2013.

———. "Superscripts, Postscripts, or Both." *Journal of Biblical Literature* 110 (1991): 583–96.

———. "Theology of the Psalms." Edited by W. A. VanGemeren. *NIDOTTE* 4 (1997): 1101–2.

Walton, J. H. *The Lost World of Genesis 1: Ancient Cosmology and the Origins Debate*. Downers Grove, IL: InterVarsity, 2009.

———. "Psalms: A Cantata about the Davidic Covenant." *JETS* 34 (1991): 21–31.

Watson, W. G. E. "Chiastic Patterns in Biblical Hebrew Poetry." Pages 118–68 in *Chiasmus in Antiquity: Structures, Analyses, Exegesis*. Edited by J. W. Welch. Hildesheim: Gerstenberg, 1981.

———. *Classical Hebrew Poetry: A Guide to its Techniques*. 2nd ed. Sheffield: JSOT, 1986.

Weber, B. *Werkbuch Psalmen I: Die Psalmen 1–72*. Stuttgart: Kohlhammer, 2001.

Weiser, A. *The Psalms*. Philadelphia: Westminster, 1959–62.

Wellhausen, J. *The Book of Psalms: A New English Translation with Explanatory Notes and an Appendix on the Music of the Ancient Hebrews*. Translated by H. H. Furness, J. Taylor, and J. A. Paterson. New York: Dodd, Mead, 1898.

———. *The Book of Psalms: Critical Edition of the Hebrew Text Printed in Colors*. The Sacred Books of the Old Testament 14. Edited by J. D. Prince. Leipzig: Hinrichs, 1895.

Wenham, G. *Psalms as Torah: Reading Biblical Song Ethically*. Studies in Theological Interpretation. Grand Rapids: Baker Academic, 2012.

———. "Towards a Canonical Reading of the Psalms." Pages 333–49 in *Canon and Biblical Interpretation*. Edited by C. G. Bartholomew, S. Hahn, R. Parry, C. Seitz, and A. Wolters. Grand Rapids: Zondervan, 2006.

Westermann, C. "The Formation of the Psalter." Pages 250–58 in *Praise and Lament in the Psalms.* Translated by K. R. Crim and R. N. Soulen. Atlanta: John Knox, 1981.

———. *The Living Psalms.* Grand Rapids: Eerdmans, 1989.

———. *The Psalms: Structure, Content and Message.* 7th ed. Minneapolis: Augsburg Fortress, 1980.

———. "The Role of the Lament in the Theology of the Old Testament." *Interpretation* 28 (1974): 20–38.

———. "Zur Sammlung des Psalters." Pages 336–43 in *Forschung am Alten Testament.* Edited by Rainer Albertz and Eberhard Ruprecht. München: Kaiser, 1964.

Whybray, N. *Reading the Psalms as a Book.* JSOTSup 222. Sheffield: Sheffield Academic, 1999.

Wiemar, P. "Psalm 22, Beobachtungen zur Komposition und Entstehungsgeschichte." Pages 471–94 in *Freude an der Weisung des Herrn, Beiträge zur Theologie der Psalmen, Festgabe H. Gross.* Edited by E. Haag and F.-L. Hossfeld. Stuttgart: Verlag Katholisches Bibelwerk, 1986.

Willis, J. T. "The Diversity of Sacrifices in Psalmic Texts." Paper Presentation, Society of Biblical Literature. November 25, 2013.

Wilson, G. H. *The Editing of the Hebrew Psalter.* Society of Biblical Literature Dissertation Series 76. Chico, CA: Scholars Press, 1985.

———. "Evidence of Editorial Divisions in the Hebrew Psalter." *Vetus Testamentum* 34 (1984): 337–52.

———. "King, Messiah, and the Reign of God: Revisiting the Royal Psalms and the Shape of the Psalter." Pages 391–406 in *The Book of Psalms: Composition and Reception.* Edited by P. W. Flint and P. D. Miller Jr. Vetus Testamentum Supplements 99. Leiden: Brill, 2005.

———. *Psalms.* Vol. 1. New International Version Application Commentary. Grand Rapids: Zondervan, 2002.

———. "The Shape of the Book of Psalms." *Interpretation* 46 (1992): 129–42.

———. "Shaping the Psalter: A Consideration of Editorial Linkage in the Book of Psalms." Pages 72–82 in *The Shape and Shaping of the Psalter.* Edited by J. C. McCann Jr. JSOTSup 159. Sheffield: JSOT, 1993.

———. "The Structure of the Psalter." Pages 229–46 in *Interpreting the Psalms: Issues and Approaches.* Edited by P. Johnston and D. Firth. Downers Grove, IL: InterVarsity, 2005.

———. "Understanding the Purposeful Arrangement of Psalms in the Psalter: Pitfalls and Promise." Pages 42–51 in *The Shape and Shaping of the Psalter.* Edited by J. C. McCann Jr. JSOTSup 159. Sheffield: JSOT, 1993.

———. "The Use of Royal Psalms at the 'Seams' of the Hebrew Psalter." *JSOT* 35 (1986): 85–94.

———. "The Use of 'Untitled' Psalms in the Hebrew Psalter." *ZAW* 97, no. 3 (1985): 404–13.

Wray Beal, L. "Psalms 3: History of Interpretation." Pages 606–13 in *Dictionary of the Old Testament: Wisdom, Poetry & Writings.* Edited by T. Longman III and P. Enns. Downers Grove, IL: IVP Academic, 2008.

Zakovitch, Y. "For Three…and for Four": The Pattern of the Numerical Sequence Three-Four in the Bible. 2 vols. Jerusalem: Makor, 1979.

Zenger, E. "The Composition and Theology of the Fifth Book of Psalms." JSOT 23 (September 1998): 77–102.

———, ed. The Composition of the Book of Psalms. Bibliotheca ephermeridum theologicarum lovaniensium 238. Leuven: Uitgeverij Peeters, 2010.

———. "'Daß alles Fleisch den Namen seiner Heiligung segne' (Ps 145,21): Die Komposition Ps 145–150 als Anstoß zu einer christlich-jüdischen Psalmenhermeneutik." Biblische Zeitschrift 41 (1997): 1–27.

———. "Der Psalter als Buch: Beobachtungen zu seiner Entstehung, Komposition und Funktion." Pages 1–57 in Der Psalter in Judentum und Christentum. Edited by E. Zenger. Herders biblische Studien 18. Freiburg: Herder, 1998.

———. "New Approaches to the Study of the Psalter." Proceedings of the Irish Biblical Association 17 (1994): 37–54.

———. "Psalmenexegese und Psalterexegese: Eine Forschungsskizze." Pages 17–65 in The Composition of the Book of Psalms. Edited by E. Zenger. BETL 238. Leuven: Peeters, 2010.

———. "Psalmenforschung nach Hermann Gunkel und Sigmund Mowinckel." Pages 399–435 in Congress Volume Oslo. Edited by A. Lemaire and M. Sæbø. Vetus Testamentum Supplements 80. Leiden: Brill, 2000.

Zimmerli, W. "Zwillingspsalmen." Pages 105–13 in Wort, Lied, und Gottesspruch: Beiträge zu Psalmen und Propheten. Edited by J. Schreiner. Würzburg: Echter, 1972.

Subject & Author Index

Scripture Index

Old Testament

Genesis

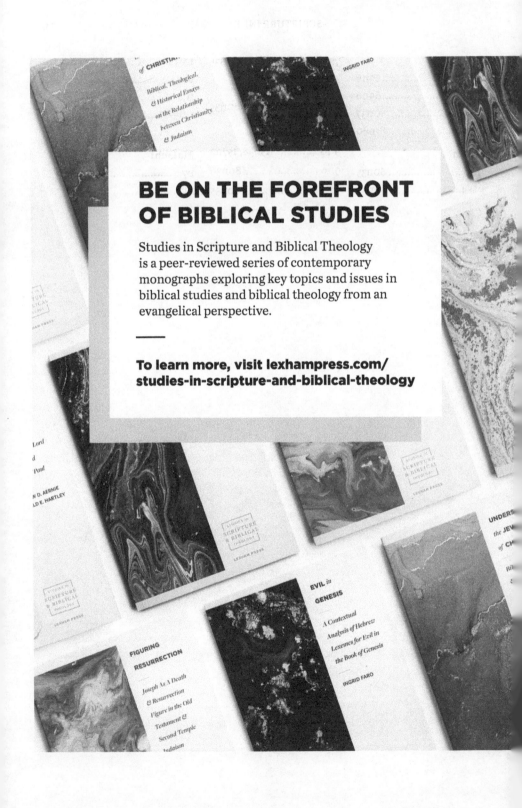